IMITATION:
A Developmental Perspective

IMITATION:
A Developmental Perspective

REGINA YANDO
Harvard University

VICTORIA SEITZ
Yale University

EDWARD ZIGLER
Yale University

 LAWRENCE ERLBAUM ASSOCIATES, PUBLISHERS
1978 HILLSDALE, NEW JERSEY

DISTRIBUTED BY THE HALSTED PRESS DIVISION OF

JOHN WILEY & SONS
New York   Toronto   London   Sydney

Lawrence Erlbaum Associates, Inc., Publishers
62 Maria Drive
Hillsdale, New Jersey 07642

Distributed solely by Halsted Press Division
John Wiley & Sons, Inc., New York

Library of Congress Cataloging in Publication Data

Yando, Regina.
  Imitation.

  Includes bibliographical references and indexes.
  1. Imitation in children. I. Seitz, Victoria,
joint author. II. Zigler, Edward Frank, 1930–
joint author. III. Title.
BF723.I53Y36.   155.4'13   78-6049
ISBN 0-470-26358-X

Printed in the United States of America

Contents

Preface

The phenomenon of imitation in young children is a striking one. In our own research we have become increasingly impressed with the accuracy and extent of imitation shown by even very young children, and we have become increasingly interested in exploring the possible meaning of this phenomenon for human development.

Our major aim in writing this book has been to develop an integrated position with respect to knowledge about imitation. We have attempted to document the need for a synthesis of existing viewpoints and, in our first and final chapters, we have offered our own developmental, two-factor theory. Finally, since we are suggesting new lines of research, we have taken the first step in testing the usefulness of our theory by conducting and reporting the results of an exploratory study.

A guide to the organization of the book might be helpful. The first chapter provides a general overview of issues which we believe must be addressed in imitation research. In Chapters 2–4 we have reviewed theoretical and empirical literature. In Chapters 5–7 we present the method, results, and discussion of an exploratory study which we have conducted to examine developmental changes in children's imitation. In the final chapter, we re-examine the issues raised at the beginning of the book in the light of the information in the intervening chapters, and we elaborate on our two-factor theory. In this theory, we have argued that imitation serves two major functions – that of enhancing intellectual competence in the species and that of serving as a mechanism for affecting the strength of attachment bonds among human beings. It is our hope that future research on imitation will be enriched by espousing the developmental, two-factor approach we are advocating and that as a result of our arguments there will be an increasing degree of productive cross-fertilization of ideas among researchers.

The first author wishes to make one final comment. The authors are not in complete agreement regarding the contents of this book. Therefore, it is necessary to point out that the first author (RY) is primarily responsible for the conduct of the empirical study and substantial portions of Chapters 4 and 5. Her contribution to the remaining material has been minimal. The second and third authors (VS and EZ) are primarily responsible for the interpretive and theoretical viewpoints presented.

REGINA YANDO
VICTORIA SEITZ
EDWARD ZIGLER

Acknowledgments

Numerous persons have helped to make the present book possible. We wish to thank Nancy Beloungie and Susan Rubin who ably served as experimenters for the empirical study upon which this book is based. Nancy Beloungie also contributed substantially in typing and editorial work, as did Sammy Carr, Linda Hughes, Cheryl LaRossa, and Lisa Rosenberg. We also thank Phyllis LaFarge for her excellent editorial suggestions.

Many school systems and school personnel contributed to the present effort. We would especially like to thank C. Louis Cedrone of the Westwood Public School System, Westwood, Massachusetts for his extensive assistance. We thank the many teachers, principals. and guidance personnel within the Westwood Schools who were helpful in making this study possible: Joseph Atchue, Marian Burke, Julie Davis, Marie Lyddy, Noreen O'Leary, Teresa Pacitto, Mary Ryan, and Patricia Stauffer of Deerfield School; Betty Baas, Susan Bray, Carol Brown, Elinor Devlin, Esther Dooley, Jack Fitzpatrick, Ruth Gallup, Patricia Lane, Deidre Patrick, Margaret Semple, and Mary White of Downey School; Marjorie Hall, Joseph Hanley, Ruth Hart, and James Russell of Edmond W. Thurston Junior High School; Dorie Ballantine, Anita Bradley, William Doub, Margaret Holdsworth, Lily Mooncai, Marcia Nichols, Stephanie Nicholas, Joyce Preston, Irene Quinn, Lynne Robinson, Susan Schindler, and Jane Wright of Pond Plain School.

The following nursery school directors and teachers graciously gave of their time and provided facilities to make this study possible: Mary Barron and Phyllis Regan of the Carousel Nursery School, Waltham, Massachusetts; Nikki Sibley of the First Church Nursery School, Belmont, Massachusetts; Hannah Samuelson and Marain Schoppett of Hancock United Church of Christ Nursery

School, Lexington, Massachusetts; Ann Roesner of the Lincoln Nursery School, Lincoln, Massachusetts; Elizabeth Jellis of the Neighborhood Cooperative Nursery School, Winchester, Massachusetts; Dale Salm, Evelyn Sundquist, and Joan Wefald of St. John's Nursery School, Westwood, Massachusetts; Priscilla Burke, Mildred Forbes, and Libby Nash of the Second Church of Newton Nursery School, Newton, Massachusetts.

The research was supported by Research Grant HD-03008 from the United States Public Health Service.

A special thanks is due Willard W. Hartup who critically read an early draft of the manuscript. The manuscript has benefited greatly from his scholarly remarks.

Finally, we wish to thank the many parents and children who donated their time for the pilot study as well as those who participated in the final study. The enthusiastic participation and helpful comments of the children made conducting the study a great pleasure.

IMITATION:
A Developmental Perspective

1
Introduction

Imitation is a common yet fascinating aspect of human behavior. The two-year-old child hesitantly repeating his mother's phrases, the four-year-old solemnly "reading" her book of nursery rhymes, and the preschool child parroting the actions and slogans of a television commercial are familiar examples. Imitation is also evident among school-aged children, especially in their play activities. Many games are learned by younger children, largely through imitation of older children. "London Bridge" and chants such as "It's raining, it's pouring, the old man is snoring. . ." form part of an unwritten heritage of childhood in many societies; the fact that many such games and sayings persist essentially unchanged for generations attests to the effectiveness of imitative learning. (For an interesting review of such activities from a cross-cultural and historical perspective, see Opie and Opie, 1959.) Among adolescents imitation is also frequently observed in the context of conformity in clothing, speech, and mannerisms to the models established or valued by a peer group.

Upon casual consideration imitation appears to be less common among adults than children. This observation could lead one to conclude that the developmental pattern of imitation is essentially a decreasing one. Such an impression, however, might be misleading. Since children often repeat only the most distinctive features of modeled behavior, their imitations may have a quality of caricature that makes them particularly amusing and noticeable to adults. It is not clear, then, whether adults imitate less than children do, or whether adult imitation is so subtle that it is harder to detect. Surprisingly, although psychologists have been studying imitation for more than half a century, a clear picture of the nature of developmental changes in imitation has not yet emerged. The major purpose of the present book is to address the issue of imitation within a developmental framework.

In the present chapter we will consider some reasons for the current lack of knowledge about age changes in imitation, and we will suggest several hypotheses

1

about how children's changing abilities and motives might influence the kind of imitation they show at different ages. In later chapters we will more extensively review empirical studies of age changes in imitation and will present a developmental study of our own. We will also discuss theories of imitation, and we will conclude the book by proposing a theory of our own.

SOME REASONS FOR THE CURRENT LACK OF DEVELOP-MENTAL INFORMATION CONCERNING IMITATION

Imitation has been a popular subject for psychological inquiry, and, as a concept, it has been assigned significant explanatory power in theories of both socialization and personality development. It is therefore somewhat surprising that there exists no consistent body of information regarding age-related changes in imitation. A major reason for this lack of information is simply the scarcity of relevant empirical studies. While there have been numerous studies of other aspects of imitation, few have been designed in a manner that permits the examination of developmental trends. In a thorough review of the literature less than a decade ago, Hartup and Coates (1970) reported finding only eight studies or dissertations that had examined some aspect of imitative behavior for children of more than one age-level. In the present book we have undertaken a similar literature review (presented in Chapter 4), which reveals that, although there are now many more studies that can be added to the list begun by Hartup and Coates, the empirical basis for describing developmental differences in imitation is not much stronger now than it was at the time of the earlier review.

One major reason for the scarcity of developmental data is that for many years learning theories have been the dominant force in American research on imitation. Perhaps the most influential has been the social learning theory advanced by Bandura (Bandura, 1969c; 1971a; 1977), a theory that has stimulated an impressive number of studies on many different aspects of imitation. Other learning theories that have also influenced much research have been those that stress the role of external rewards and punishments in determining imitation (e.g. Baer, Peterson, & Sherman, 1967; Gewirtz, 1971a; Gewirtz & Stingle, 1968).

While positions based on learning theory have provided many valuable contributions to our understanding of imitation, they have consistently been nondevelopmental in approach. As Zigler and Child (1973) pointed out, the significance of adopting a nondevelopmental rather than a developmental approach is reflected in the nature of the explanatory principles that are sought and the kinds of experiments that are performed. In particular:

> Learning theorists tend to view behavior as a function of forces applied to the child, whereas developmentalists tend to focus on sequential changes in the psychological structure of the child himself. The changes developmentalists find in formal structure convince them that behavior is mediated by very different processes at different ages,

whereas learning theorists view the same underlying processes as operative throughout the life cycle. . . . To learning theorists growth may require at most only changing the value of one element in an equation, whereas to the developmentalists growth has to be treated as the central content of the theory [p. 27]. (© 1973. Reprinted by permission of Addison-Wesley Publishing Co., Reading, Mass., and by permission of the authors.)

Because they assume it is possible to find explanatory principles applicable to all ages, learning theorists typically employ subjects at only one developmental level. Investigators in such studies usually interpret their findings as being descriptive of human imitation in general.

In contrast, other theorists have laid great emphasis upon developmental changes in imitation. Two clear-cut examples are seen in psychoanalytic (Freud, 1905/1953, 1921/1955, 1917/1957a, 1914/1957b, 1924/1961a, 1923/1961b, 1933/1964) and cognitive-developmental (Piaget, 1962a, b) views. As will be described in later chapters, both Freud and Piaget have provided extensive descriptions of changes in the child's motives for imitating during the first few years of life. However, despite the potential theoretical significance of these developmental positions, they have thus far generated relatively little empirical research on imitation. Perhaps one reason is a stylistic one. Neither the psychoanalytic nor the cognitive-developmental position is to be found stated concisely with propositions formulated in simple, testable terms (Lindzey, 1968; Sarnoff, 1971). Researchers have therefore often been uncertain as to how such theories might be examined empirically. Another contributing factor is that even when specific aspects of these theories can be made testable, the necessary studies tend to be more difficult than those that can be designed to examine the propositions of learning theories. The most adequate tests of both Freudian and Piagetian propositions require longitudinal studies of very young children, and such studies are understandably scarce. As Sarnoff (1971, p. 4) has noted, experimental psychologists have often demonstrated a "sheer reluctance to face the labor" required for adequate methodological tests of Freudian concepts.

Developmental and nondevelopmental approaches might be bridged in the interests of gaining a fuller perspective on the nature and functions of imitation. Symptomatic of the relative isolation among theories has been the considerable difference in methodology and subject matter. As will be discussed at greater length in chapter 2, each of the major theories has addressed only certain aspects of imitation, and even the developmental theories have examined children across only relatively limited age spans. The present status of the empirical and theoretical literature on imitation, therefore, leaves the developmental psychologist with the tantalizing problem of piecing together a coherent picture of how imitation changes over the life span. One aim in the present book is to attempt the beginnings of such a synthesis in the interests of determining how existing theories might be modified in order to create a single, more comprehensive theory of human imitation.

DEFINING IMITATION

One necessary step in creating a developmental theory of imitation is establishing a suitably broad definition of the term. The origins of imitative acts may be quite diverse, reflecting very different underlying information-processing abilities and motives. In response to this fact, imitation has been defined in a multitude of ways, and one can find important imitation research under such diverse labels as *identification, social facilitation, modeling, observational learning, matching behavior,* and *choice-matching dispositions.* All of these terms inevitably have some excess meaning, since each derives from a particular theory developed to explain certain kinds of imitative behavior in certain kinds of organisms. The excess meaning and necessary commitment to only one theory is troublesome when the goal is to gain a larger overview of how these different manifestations of imitation might be related.

The position of the present authors is that the use of a single term, *imitation,* defined by observable referents, would bridge theories and permit a fresh look at what these many theories have in common. In the present book imitation is defined as the motoric or verbal performance of specific acts or sounds that are like those previously performed by a model. This behavioristic definition has the advantage of leaving open the nature of the constructs that will be invoked to explain imitative behavior at different points in development. Many of the distinctions presently in existence can be reintroduced within the context of the larger, unified framework we propose.

Several issues related to our definition require comment. First, the imitation of modeled acts need not be immediate; delayed imitation is a common event. Second, fidelity of imitation may vary since reproduction of a modeled act can occur across a wide range of accuracy, and since individuals often imitate only portions of what has been modeled. Employing a behavioristic definition need raise no serious problems in dealing with such instances. Imitations that are of poor quality or incomplete can and should be considered legitimate forms of imitation. (Later we will propose that accuracy of imitation is a measurable aspect that changes developmentally.) Finally, the imitation of events that are not directly observable is more problematic. Such phenomena as the incorporation of broad attitudinal, moral, or religious-belief systems are important and may represent to some readers the aspects of imitation most worthy of study. While our definition need not exclude such broad classes of events, our definition does require that there be some overt and measurable manifestation of underlying attitudes before imitation can be said to exist.

While it is not part of our definition, we take the position that imitation might profitably be regarded as a capacity that is built into the human species much as language appears to be built in. (In our discussion later in this chapter of the possible evolutionary significance of imitation, we present the basis for this argument.) If the parallel between language and imitation is accurate, there are several important implications. Both language and imitation seem to be adaptive mechanisms for the species. As is true for language, imitation can be employed in order to communicate with others, and it can be employed to enhance learning. Moreover, while a child must be taught a specific language, he apparently does not have to be taught the more basic skill of how to learn a language (Lenneberg, 1967). Similarly, we propose that while a child may be taught specific imitative acts, he does not have to be taught the more basic skill of how to imitate. On this point we disagree fundamentally with theorists who have regarded imitation as a process that can be fully explained by principles of operant conditioning (e.g., Baer, Peterson, & Sherman, 1967; Gewirtz, 1971a, b; Gewirtz & Stingle, 1968; Staats, 1968; Steinman, 1970a, b). Rather, we are in closer agreement with theorists who have stressed the intrinsic motives that guide the development of human competence (Bruner, 1972, 1973; Piaget, 1962b; White, 1960).

In the remainder of this chapter we will explore some of the issues that are raised by taking a developmental approach to imitation. Our presentation is somewhat in the nature of a preview, since we will return to these issues in later chapters after we have examined the theoretical and empirical literature on imitation. Because our position depends to a considerable extent upon insights gained from the literature on animal imitation, we begin with an examination of implications that infrahuman imitation provides for understanding human imitativeness.

IMPLICATIONS OF INFRAHUMAN IMITATION FOR A DEVELOPMENTAL PSYCHOLOGY OF IMITATION

Comparative psychology and developmental psychology have many points of common interest, and the study of what is known about imitation in infrahumans is a rich source for hypotheses about the nature of developmental changes in human imitation (see Kessen, 1968). Two hypotheses that may be derived from the literature on animal imitativeness and that have particular interest for a developmental theory are (a) that there is a predictable relationship between the level of complexity of an observer's cognitive abilities and the kind of imitativeness that the observer can show, and (b) that human imitation has had survival value, has been selected for in evolution, and thus has a probable genetic basis. These two issues will be discussed in turn.

The Relationship Between Cognitive Complexity and Imitation

Studies of imitation in a variety of animals suggest that the ability to show delayed imitation indicates the existence of a relatively high cognitive ability. Immediate imitation is a much simpler matter. A number of lower organisms can imitate what they observe if they are allowed to do so immediately and if they are reinforced for doing so. Many animals can also be taught, when given a signal from the trainer, to repeat an imitative act that they have previously performed. However, the ability to delay any overt imitative response until some time long after the initial observation implies the ability to form some kind of internal representation for maintaining memory across time and to employ such a representation rather than the modeled act itself for guiding behavior. Such delayed imitation following passive observation has often been called "observational learning."

As might be expected, evidence indicates that observational learning is to be found among organisms with relatively highly evolved brains rather than among simpler organisms. In a careful review Aronfreed (1969) concludes that "there does not appear to be a clear demonstration of true observational learning among rats [p. 237]," that the phenomenon possibly exists among cats (e.g., Adler, 1955; Herbert & Harsh, 1944; John, Chesler, Bartlett, & Victor, 1968), but that there is no doubt of its existence in the higher primates. Numerous and detailed accounts document observational learning by monkeys and chimpanzees (Baldwin & Baldwin, 1974; DeVore, 1965; Dolhinow & Bishop, 1970; Goodall, 1965; Hall, 1963, 1968; Hamburg, 1968; Harlow, 1959; Hayes & Hayes, 1952; Köhler, 1925; Reynolds, 1965; Rumbaugh, 1970; Stephenson, 1967; Van Lawick-Goodall, 1968; Wechkin, 1970; Yerkes, 1927, 1934; Yerkes & Yerkes, 1929). Interestingly, there is also evidence of observational learning by dolphins (Tayler & Saayman, 1973).

Turning to the question of human development, there is some evidence to suggest that ontogeny is indeed recapitulating phylogeny in the development of imitative skills. The human brain appears to require maturation before the infant can demonstrate delayed imitation. It is interesting that in comparison to the imitative abilities of adult chimpanzees the imitative abilities of human infants are decidedly inferior. It appears to be the case that human infants during the first few months of life lack the cognitive abilities necessary to permit true observational learning, although they can show other, more immediate forms of imitation (Baldwin, 1906; Guillaume, 1926, 1971; Parton, 1976; Piaget, 1962b; Valentine, 1930). On the basis of what is known about infant imitation, it seems likely that the first significant change in human imitation involves the translation from being able to engage in only simple, immediate forms of imitation to the capacity for delayed imitation, a transition that is probably completed early in the second year of life. Subsequent developmental changes in the nature of human imitation can also be predicted.

A study of the animal imitation literature suggests that there will always be a regularity of correspondence between the level of complexity of the imitativeness that an organism can exhibit and the level of its intellectual capacities. An important corollary of this principle is that an increase in cognitive abilities not only results in an increase in the amount of behavior that can be imitated or in the accuracy of imitation but also may lead to changes in the ways that imitation is controlled. In seeking a guide to the kinds of cognitive changes that might be directly related to changes in imitation, we have been influenced by the description of cognitive growth given by Bruner and his colleagues (Bruner, 1964; Bruner, Olver, & Greenfield, 1966). These investigators have noted that children can, from a very early age, employ physical activity to represent or code external events and that this primitive form of motoric memory continues to be useful even to adults. An adult can drink a cup of coffee with his eyes closed because familiar cues of weight in the hand and feedback from receptors in the mouth carry most of the information needed for such a task. At a much more sophisticated level, pianists and typists often employ their fingers to execute complex sequences with immense rapidity, suggesting that motoric codes can become very complex indeed, even though they are a primitive form of representation. Much of the cognitive behavior of rats and other subprimate mammals, Bruner suggests, may well consist of motoric coding or muscle memory.

In the course of development, humans (and many animals) become capable of an additional form of coding, based upon visual imagery. This development adds a major new dimension to the observer's skills in representing outside events. The nature of visual imagery undoubtedly needs less comment than that of motoric coding, since it is so familiar. As we have already suggested, however, it appears that the acquisition of the ability to employ visual imagery in addition to motoric coding underlies the important transition into the capacity to show observational learning.

If one takes Bruner's classification as a guide, the final form of representational coding that humans eventually achieve is symbolic coding, usually in the form of language. Since language acquisition brings with it so many major changes in cognition, we have every reason to expect that the nature of human imitation might again change radically when language is available for mediation. The most important years of life for investigating presymbolic imitation may be the ages of 1 through 5 years, a time period that has not yet received the full attention it merits. This long period is characterized by increasing language abilities along with a rather uncertain relationship between linguistic and nonlinguistic thinking. Researchers have long been impressed by the fact that the preschool child, even after acquiring substantial language skills, often does not employ them (Flavell, 1970; Kendler & Kendler, 1961). This is surprising because when the 4- or 5-year-old child is reminded to do so, he often uses linguistic mediation to improve substantially his success with problem solving (Coates & Hartup, 1969; Weir, 1964). It appears that the linguistic representation system exists in competition with the preschool child's other and preferred ways of dealing with the outside world. It is not until the child is older, at some time between 5 and 7 years of age, that the linguistic system seems to be used reliably and in preference to other representational modes. Important corroborating evidence can be found in Luria's ingenious studies (1957, 1961) of the way in which language comes to be employed by the child as a means of controlling his own behavior. Luria's findings suggest an early stage of independence between motoric and verbal systems and later stages of conflict between them, which are superseded finally by a substantial control of motor behavior by language.

Several investigators have pinpointed the period of approximately 5 to 7 years of age as a time of many significant developmental transitions, including the development of deliberate linguistic control over problem-solving activities. (White, 1965, provides a systematic review and discussion of this literature.) One might, therefore, expect a major difference in imitation to be seen when comparing the performance of children 5 and younger with that of children 7 and older if one employed sufficiently demanding imitation tasks. (We will provide such a comparison ourselves in an empirical study described in chapters 5 - 7.) Many studies comparing children younger than 5 with those older than 7 have been designed to test whether a developmental transition into the stage of concrete operations, as suggested by Piaget (1970), underlies significant changes in the kinds of acts the child can imitate. Still further changes might also be associated with the attainment of the Piagetian stage of formal operations around the age of 11 years. As we shall see in Chapter 3, the evidence concerning the relationship between Piagetian cognitive stages and imitative abilities is equivocal, and the issue must remain open as to whether there are important changes in the cognitive bases for imitative acts beyond the age at which the child becomes linguistically competent.

On the Evolutionary Significance of Imitative Behavior

Another important conclusion from the infrahuman literature with implications for developmental theory is that imitation in humans appears to have had survival value and to have been selected for. In a thoughtful examination of this issue, Bruner (1972) has suggested that imitation among the higher primates serves the major function of enhancing tool-using competency and educability in general. According to this view, high imitativeness is part of a constellation of characteristics that have been part of primate evolution, characteristics including a prolonged period of immaturity, increased interactions with parents, increased flexibility in interacting with the environment, playfulness, and high curiosity. As Bruner (1972) notes, in the development of higher primates as compared with lesser forms, "The maternal buffering and protection of the young not only lengthens materially but undergoes qualitative changes. . . . The most important, I believe, is the appearance of a pattern involving an enormous amount of observation of adult behavior by the young, with incorporation of what has been learned into a pattern of play [p. 690] ." This partially imitative "serious play," Bruner is convinced, is the essential means by which the highly adaptive problem-solving skills of humans and other primates are practiced and perfected. That there is an evolutionary advantage of imitation and playfulness follows from his argument, since the imitative, playful individual is also likely to have the most sophisticated and effective skills when they are needed at times of danger.

There is something undeniably appealing about the notion that basic competencies are built through play (a position also advanced by Piaget, 1962b). The implications of this position for theories of imitation will be discussed more fully in a later chapter. For the present, it is worth exploring the possibility that imitativeness has a genetic basis. This possibility has not yet been explored to any great extent, but it follows reasonably from the argument that imitation has an evolutionary advantage.

We propose that a polygenic model, similar to the models that have been proposed for the inheritance of metric characteristics such as height and intelligence (Burt, 1971; Falconer, 1960; Gottesman, 1963; Jensen, 1967), might be appropriate for describing imitativeness. Since early imitation appears to be based upon a number of sensorimotor abilities, it is certainly plausible that a polygenic model might be appropriate, at least for early imitation. This polygenic model might be built upon a number of lesser components that enter into imitation, such as attention, motoric ability, and representational capacity. Whether later imitation has much similarity to the imitation shown by infants and young children is, of course, an open question, and occurrence of imitativeness in older children might well be found to be less adequately accounted for by a genetic model in comparison to early imitativeness.

Unlike the early instinct theories of imitation, which deservedly fell into disrepute for being unsuited to empirical tests of their validity, a polygenic model implies the existence of considerable biological variability. One would expect to find some children who rarely imitate, some who are highly imitative, and most falling somewhere in between. Given a prevailing interest in environmental rather than biological explanations, most studies of imitation have not examined variability in imitation but instead have considered it to be a nuisance variable that obscures more important findings. Two recent studies of very young children, however, confirm the existence of substantial variability in imitativeness both for verbal imitation (Bloom, Hood, & Lightbown, 1974) and for gestural imitation (Waxler & Yarrow, 1975).

The usual kinds of evidence for a genetic basis for a trait might also be sought for imitativeness, as in comparisons of identical versus fraternal twin pairs. While little evidence of this kind currently exists, one recent study (Matheny, 1975) has reported that 1-year-old identical twins are more concordant in imitativeness than are 1-year-old same-sex fraternal twins. The study is impressive for its methodology, since each member of a twin pair was tested by a different examiner and the examiners were unaware of the zygosity of the twins. The number of tests for imitation was very limited, however, and similar studies employing a wider range of tests of imitativeness would constitute a valuable follow-up to these data. For example, a more sensitive test could be made through longitudinal study of identical and fraternal twin pairs to ascertain whether the ages for emergence of delayed imitation, imitation of novel events, and linguistic imitation are more concordant for identical twins than for fraternal twins. In summary, the possible genetic basis for imitation is a valuable hypothesis that we believe deserves more extensive examination. We do not make such a test ourselves in the study to be reported later in this book, but we have raised the issue here because we believe it must be recognized early in any discussion of what is presently known and not known about imitation.

CRITICAL ASPECTS OF DEVELOPMENTAL CHANGES IN IMITATION

As we have just noted, the literature on infrahuman imitation leads us to propose that the cognitive-developmental level of the observer is a factor of major significance for imitation. (Such a conclusion can also be reached independently from an examination of human imitativeness, as we will discuss in chapters 2 and 3.) Critical though this factor may be, much of our own earlier work has led us to be cautious of any theoretical or explanatory system that does not also provide a role for motivation (Yando & Zigler, 1971; Zigler, 1969, 1971; Zigler & Yando, 1972). In deriving a series of predictions about how imitation changes with age, we would therefore propose that both cognitive-developmental level and motivational factors should be examined. The first factor alone should be predictive of the amount and kind of imitative skill that an observer can display if fully motivated to do so. The second factor should be predictive of the kind of imitation that is actually likely to occur within the limits made possible by the observer's capabilities. In the remainder of this chapter we offer speculations as to how both imitative skill and motivation might change developmentally.

Imitative Skill

It is a commonplace observation that skill in imitation generally improves during childhood. Nevertheless, it is necessary to recognize that such improvement has both qualitative and quantitative aspects. Children become better at producing more accurate imitations, but they also become capable of imitating an increased number of kinds of acts. We will loosely speak of imitative skill, therefore, as encompassing some combination of both accuracy and breadth in what can be imitated.

Because we hypothesize that physical and cognitive growth underlie developmental changes in imitative skills, a general representation of the function relating age and imitative skill might be as diagrammed in Figure 1. The impression that Figure 1 is meant to convey is not a strictly quantitative one, but is rather that of a generally positive slope with points of inflection in the curve. Since both cognitive growth and physical growth occur not in a simple, straight-line incremental fashion but in spurts and plateaus, we might expect the same to be true of growth in children's ability to imitate skillfully. Also, as we have just argued, there should be periods of especially rapid improvement in imitative skills corresponding to the times when a child gains new modes of representational abilities.

The nature of some of the probable change points can be described as follows. Points A through D are based upon Piaget's (1962b) observations of changes in the nature of imitation during infancy. (These observations will be discussed more fully in chapter 2.) Initially, Piaget argues, the infant is incapable of imitating at all. Point A designates the emergence of the ability to imitate a limited number of acts, an ability that appears to be controlled by external reward. The next two points refer to the emergence of internally motivated, spontaneous imitation: Point B of acts that are already familiar; and Point C of acts that are new and unfamiliar. Point D reflects the emergence of imitation based upon visual imagery approximately at the time of 12-15 months, an accomplishment discussed earlier in this chapter. This point is widely recognized as the beginning of a period of major increases in the frequency of imitation (Guillaume, 1926/ 1971; Piaget, 1962b; Valentine, 1930) and is so designated in Figure 1. The period from the end of the first year through 4 or 5 years of age has received relatively little study to date. Future investigations may locate several points of change during this period; due to the present lack of evidence, no such points are indicated in Figure 1. The final point, E, designates the emergence of linguistic coding as a preferred form of mediation. As previously noted, such a change

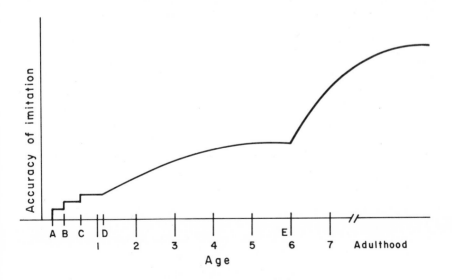

FIG.1   Developmental changes in accuracy of imitation

appears to occur somewhere during the 5-7 age period. (In Figure 1, the midpoint of this time period, age 6, is arbitrarily taken as the point of transition.)

As Figure 1 illustrates, transition points imply a relatively sudden change in slope. We postulate, for example, that children just past transition Point E show a greater rate of increase in skill with age than do children who have not yet mastered linguistic mediation. The rationale for such an argument, which applies equally to the postulated increase in rate of growth depicted after age 12-15 months, is this: the greater the number of intellectual tools children have at their disposal, the greater the rate of change they can show. Clearly such increases in rate cannot continue indefinitely; thus, a gradual decrease in rate of change is shown, leveling off just before the acquisition of a new ability (in the case of the preschool children) or at adulthood (for the school-aged children and for adolescents). Whether further points of change occur and whether the general slopes are as depicted are open questions for empirical research.

Motivation for Imitation

If people habitually imitated all that they were capable of imitating, then one would expect to see increasing imitativeness with age. In fact, however, imitation appears to occur considerably less often than it might on the basis of capacity alone, and the amount of spontaneous overt imitation very likely decreases rather than increases with age. One must therefore assume that motivational factors are of great significance for imitation.

A survey of the extensive literature on motivation for imitation leads to the conclusion that imitation among older children and adults is often controlled by external reinforcement in the form of tangible rewards and also in the form of affection or nurturance from the model. A large number of studies have shown that if children are directly rewarded for imitating or if they observe that the model received a reward, they are more likely to imitate the model's behavior (examples and discussions of such studies may be found in Allen & Liebert, 1969; Bandura, 1965, 1971a, b; Flanders, 1968; Gewirtz, 1971a, b; Gewirtz & Stingle, 1968; Liebert & Fernandez, 1970; Liebert & Poulos, 1973; McDavid, 1959; Masters, Gordon, & Clark, 1976; Miller & Dollard, 1941; Sears, 1957). Bandura (1971a) has also argued that model characteristics such as prestige, competence, or dominance can signal to the child that imitation of such models is likely to result in reinforcement (examples of such studies are Bandura, Ross, & Ross, 1963a; Grusec & Mischel, 1966; Hetherington, 1965; Miller & Dollard, 1941; see also Flanders, 1968, for a review of such studies). Qualities of the model relating directly to affect, such as nurturance, have often been shown to increase imitation (Bandura, Grusec, & Menlove, 1967; Bandura & Huston, 1961; Hetherington & Frankie, 1967; Sears, Rau, & Alpert, 1965). Some evidence also exists that concern on the observer's part that he is behaving as the model expects increases imitation (Aronfreed, 1969; Flanders, 1968; Kohlberg, 1969; Thelen & Rennie, 1972; Walters, 1968; Waxler & Yarrow, 1970).

We find the concept of external reinforcement to be incomplete, however, when dealing with developmental questions. The role of intrinsic reinforcement also needs to be considered. Moreover, the age-relatedness of motives must be an issue. A major difficulty in interpreting existing studies from the viewpoint of determining developmental changes is that the nature of what is reinforcing itself varies developmentally. A smile, a few cooing sounds, and light taps on the stomach are procedures that have been found to serve as effective reinforcers for babies (Brackbill, 1958; Rheingold, Gewirtz, & Ross, 1959), whereas such procedures would not elicit much enthusiasm from 7-year-olds. The literature on social reinforcement shows that nods of approval or saying "good" to a child vary in effectiveness with age, and there also appear to be developmental differences in preferences for tangible rewards rather than abstract indicators of correctness (Havighurst, 1970; P. S. Siegel, 1968; Zigler & Kanzer, 1962). The existing studies often do not examine in sufficient detail the exact nature of the underlying motives for imitation. Some studies that have reported that reinforcement increases imitation have employed tangible prizes; other studies have given reinforcement in the form of social approval from the model. It would be quite difficult at the present time to assemble from these various studies any satisfying picture of how motives for imitation change developmentally. We will therefore pursue the question of motivation from a slightly different, deliberately developmental, perspective.

A developmental approach to motivation.   It appears that just as a child's ability to imitate changes developmentally, so also do his motives for imitating. It seems certain that a 2-year-old does not generally imitate for the same reasons that a 7-year-old does, and that adults may imitate for still different reasons. We would suggest that motives for imitating are relatively few when the child is immature, but that imitation in the older child can reflect a larger number of underlying motives. We would also suggest that a basic distinction should be made between intrinsic and extrinsic reinforcement.

One early motive for human imitation is to gain external reinforcement in the form of physically or emotionally positive events, a motive that humans share with many infrahumans. Piaget has observed such imitation very early, although he designates it "imitation by training" to distinguish it from the more spontaneous behavior shown by the older infant. The procedure for producing such imitation consists of selectively rewarding the infant for behavior that resembles the desired imitative behavior, such as smiling or cooing. The reward consists of an external consequence such as hugging the child or vocalizing. In a variation of this procedure, often employed with nonverbal subjects such as animals and autistic children, the model may actually physically guide the subject's body through the desired motions, providing reinforcement afterwards. Once the subject has learned the desired behavior, he can be taught to perform it only after a model has first demonstrated the behavior, thus producing instances of imitation. (See, for example, Baer et al., 1967; Metz, 1965; and Mowrer, 1960, Chapter 7, who describes the procedure in teaching a dog to "shake hands.")

The above procedures establish imitative behavior through operant conditioning and appear to require no more than a motoric mediational capacity of the organism. For a number of cognitively deficient or impaired organisms, this kind of imitation may be essentially the only kind of which they are capable. Although imitation controlled by some form of external reward appears to be a legitimate early form of human imitation, some caution is needed in any attempt to compare normal children with impaired organisms or with infrahumans. Even though very young infants appear to be capable of learning to behave imitatively in this manner in the laboratory (e.g., Brackbill, 1958), it is unclear how much imitative behavior of this sort they actually show in natural settings. What we are arguing here is that extrinsic rewards seem to be most important in situations where the child is taking a passive role, as in the laboratory. Laboratory studies make clear that external rewards can be a very important factor in controlling imitation; however; under natural circumstances, where the child is taking an active role, it is much more likely that intrinsic motivation would be the important factor.

In examining intrinsic motives, a reassuring degree of order and simplicity is introduced by noting that intrinsically motivated imitation appears to serve only two major classes of needs, those related to effective problem solving and those involving the quality of emotional relationships with other human beings. We will discuss these two classes of motives as the *competence* and the *attachment* motives, respectively. An important fact about these motives is that initially they appear to be so closely related that they might also be considered a fused competence-attachment motive for imitation. During development, however, these two kinds of motives become distinguishable to the point where they can in some cases be in conflict with each other.

In suggesting that motives for imitation become increasingly differentiated with age we have been guided by a more general differentiation principle, which has been advanced in several forms by a number of developmental theorists. Perhaps the clearest statement of this principle is provided by Werner (1940, 1946), who has asserted that all development is characterized by a progression from an initial state of globality and lack of differentiation to an increasingly differentiated, articulated, and hierarchically integrated condition.

Because the differentiation principle is central to our argument concerning developmental changes in imitation, we provide several examples of the utility of this principle in other theoretical endeavors. One example of differentiation is provided by the classic study of Bridges (1932). Bridges traced the development of human emotion from its initial condition, which, she argued, is limited to the expression of general excitement by the neonate, through progressive developments such as fear, anger, and disgust, and finally into highly articulated emotions such as jealousy, joy, and elation. The commonly described egocentrism of the young child seems also to fit the differentiation principle. As Looft (1972) has noted, various theorists have described the young child's egocentrism in such terms as an inability to distinguish self from environment (A. Freud, 1965), an inability to differentiate one's own point of view from that of others (Langer, 1969), or a failure to differentiate the subject from the object in evaluating subject-object relationships (Inhelder & Piaget, 1958; Piaget, 1950). In psychometric assessments of intellectual development, Anastasi (1948) has commented on "the increasing differentiation of ability and clearer emergence of specialized traits with age [p. 134] " (see, for example, Balinsky, 1941; Garrett, 1938, 1946; Jones, 1949, 1954), and Gibson and Gibson have provided much evidence that perceptual learning consists of a progressive differentiation of detail during observation of stimuli (E. Gibson, 1969; J. Gibson, 1950; Gibson & Gibson, 1955). As a final example, it is interesting that the phenomenon of synesthesia, which represents a fusion of sensations, such as color and hearing, is much more common among young children than among adults; such sensations are almost invariably reported as separate ones by adults (Marks, 1975).

Thus, whether we are dealing with emotions, cognitive abilities, or modes of perceiving the world, the differentiation principle asserts that the infant has far fewer and less refined capabilities than he will demonstrate when he is older. To return to imitation, our suggestion that attachment and competency motives for imitation are initially fused, that they become increasingly separate with age, and that each becomes itself more differentiated, is compatible with the more general principle of differentiation, which has been widely useful in developmental considerations of many other phenomena as well.

The problem-solving function of imitation is probably its most readily apparent use. Imitative learning—usually observational learning—is indisputably an efficient means for increasing problem-solving competence, perhaps especially so in early childhood, when so much of the environment is unexplored and unfamiliar. A child may successfully learn through imitation that a banana can be eaten and that it tastes good, even though his earlier trial-and-error attempts to explore that banana's properties had mistakenly convinced him that it was a hard, unpleasant-tasting, inedible object. Adults similarly can learn by imitation. This is most apparent when they first attempt to master new activities, such as repairing automobiles, sailing a boat, or skiing. As is well known, new learning of this sort is immeasurably aided by the opportunity to observe how a skilled model behaves.

The very obviousness of the problem-solving advantages of imitation, however, can tend to obscure the fact that competence-related motives are actually quite complex. It is extremely important to note that the relationship between imitation and problem-solving efficacy in very young children, and even in chimpanzees, is often an indirect rather than a direct one. We find ourselves in agreement with Bruner's (1972) interpretation of findings based on observations of chimpanzees in their natural settings. Bruner suggests that imitative responses in young primates are rarely directly applied to problems but instead seem to occur most often at times when there is no pressing need for them and when there is also no reward. That is, imitative and partially imitative responses frequently appear during the activity called play, and it is this play rather than the imitation itself that forms the basis for growth in competence. If this view is accurate, then it would be a gross oversimplification of the actual nature of primate imitativeness and its functions early in development to assume that most early imitation arises simply because the child has a desire to solve a particular problem, watches someone else solve the problem, and then attempts to solve it himself, thereby gaining reward. Such direct imitation certainly exists, but it is probably seen with great frequency only in older children and adults.

The earliest forms of competence motives for imitation, we have argued, are bound up with the infant's emotional feelings about the model. The initial developmental fusion of competence and attachment motives is strongly suggested by observational data on primate imitation and by studies of primate maternal behavior. (The theoretical formulations of Freud and of Mowrer, discussed in chapter 2, also suggest such a combination of motives for early imitation.) As is well known from Harlow's now classic studies of the nature of mothering, the exploratory, playful activity so characteristic of primate infants is unlikely to occur if the infant is isolated from others of its kind (Harlow, 1963). The deserted infant rhesus monkey shows signs of distress and withdrawal and does not explore. However, the introduction of the mother, or familiar mother surrogate, or in some cases other juvenile monkeys, is sufficient to transform a cowering, terrified monkey into an active, almost audaciously exploratory creature (Harlow & Zimmerman, 1959). In general it appears that the infant's emotional freedom to engage in play, which incorporates imitation, is closely related to its feelings of security, feelings that are customarily provided by a close attachment to the mother. Studies with infants (Ainsworth & Bell, 1969; Bowlby, 1969; Rheingold & Eckerman, 1973) suggest that this principle is probably as true for humans as it is for rhesus monkeys or chimpanzees.

With humans the necessary observational data on imitation are rare, but those that exist are compatible with the interpretation that attachment to the model increases the likelihood of infant imitation and that imitation is thus by no means solely determined by the nature and consequences of the modeled act themselves. Valentine (1930), for example, reported that the infants he observed frequently imitated novel acts introduced by their mothers while they did not imitate identical acts performed by other members of the family or by strangers. Matsuda (1973) has more recently reported a similar finding for 5-year-olds. Bruner notes that novel actions playfully introduced by the mother—actions such as crawling about on the floor, throwing up the hands, making odd noises and faces— usually result in enthusiastic glee and sometimes also in imitation by the infant. Interestingly, Bruner (1972) further observes that:

> the capers most likely to produce laughter when performed by the mother are the ones most likely to produce tears when performed by a stranger. The mother seems able to bring the young, so to speak, to the edge of terror. King (1966) has suggested

that this feature of mothering is universal; that. . .the presence of the mother reduces fear of novel stimuli and provides the assurance necessary for exploratory behavior. But it is only among humans that the adult *introduces* the novel, inducts the young into new, challenging, and frightening situations [p. 698, italics in original].

The evidence is thus suggestive that attachment to the mother is not only a significant determinant of early human imitation but is also an inseparable motive initially from problem-solving, exploratory motives.

Subsequent developments in attachment motives for imitating undoubtedly involve a generalization of the affiliative bond with the mother to other nurturant persons. As we have noted earlier, it is often reported that children are more likely to imitate unfamiliar adults if the adults are warm and affectionate than if they are distant and cold. The nature of emotional relationships with others can be negative as well as positive, and it has been suggested that there may also develop negatively motivated imitation, such as imitation of a feared adult (A. Freud, 1946) and deliberate nonimitation of individuals who are disliked or distrusted (Abelson & Zigler, 1975; Zigler & Yando, 1972). In all instances where the nature of the relationship between child and model affects imitation, it is likely that the effects may be relatively age-specific. The exact ages and circumstances under which these attachment-related motives are important for imitation remain to be more fully explored.

In considering how attachment-related motives for imitation change developmentally, the case of nonimitation of distrusted adults can be singled out as an unusual one that has received very little attention thus far. A study conducted by two of the present authors found that asocial children who had been highly deprived and/or abused in their prior experiences with adults engaged in motivated nonimitation (Zigler & Yando, 1972). Many of these children actually verbalized their distrust of adults and their belief that the adult model might be choosing incorrect answers in order deliberately to mislead them. The children's nonimitation is consistent with the conclusion reached by many workers that early social deprivation can result in fearfulness of adults and reduced social responsiveness to them (Sarason & Gladwin, 1958; Shallenberger & Zigler, 1961; Stevenson & Zigler, 1957; Zigler, 1971; Zigler & Harter, 1969). What is of special interest in the present context is whether such motivated nonimitation also occurs among children whose history of interactions with adults has been more normal. The present evidence is very sketchy. In one recent study, however, Fein (1973) suggests that normal children do develop a motive not to imitate and that this motive is more characteristic of older than of younger children. The often-reported negativistic behavior of adolescents may also fit such a pattern of deliberately avoiding parentally approved models (including the parents themselves). As deCharms has noted (1968), adults customarily devalue their behavior when they feel they are merely acting out the wishes of others. Thus a normal developmental pattern may well culminate in a state of substantial resistance toward imitation among adults.

Before leaving the issue of attachment motives, it is worth adding a few more comments on the strength and importance of such motives. We do this because we ourselves have previously tended to overlook attachment in favor of what we believed to be the more obvious competence motives for imitation. We now believe that the attachment functions served by imitation are of great interest and deserve equal attention with competence functions.

Probably the most significant fact about the attachment-imitation relationship early in development is that it appears to be a reciprocal relationship. That is, not only does early imitation appear more likely in the context of an emotional relationship with a model, but also it may serve to strengthen the emotional bonds of attachment. There is a real likelihood that parents themselves take an early active role in stimulating imitation and that they find their infant's imitative responsiveness to be gratifying. As Piaget reports (1962b), one of the most effective means of getting an infant to imitate is to imitate what the infant is doing. This usually precipitates an interaction in which the infant and parent take turns, intensifying their efforts in imitating each other in what is evidently a mutually satisfying experience. The consequences of such interactions may well be the strengthening of the bonds of attachment between parent and child.

There is recent evidence in studies with older children showing that both adults and children find it rewarding to be imitated and that imitation increases feelings of attachment. Fouts (1972, 1975), for example, has found that being imitated by an adult is rewarding to preschool children and to some 11-year-old children as well. Thelen, Dollinger, and Roberts (1975) have reported a similar result for first-grade children, adding that for these children "being imitated increased the subject's attraction toward the person who imitated him and increased the subject's subsequent imitation (reciprocal imitation) of the person who imitated him [p. 471]." In another study, Bates (1975) examined the reactions of adults to being imitated. Bates found that adults rated those children who imitated them higher in intelligence and social abilities than they rated children who were nonimitative. The adults were also more positive and responsive toward the imitative children during face-to-face interactions with them. Bates (1975) thus suggests an interesting reverse side to the common finding that children imitate nurturant adults more than they do nonnurturant adults, namely, that "when the child imitates, the adult becomes more nurturant than when the child does not imitate [p. 850]."

We have argued thus far that early motives for imitation appear to involve a complex mixture of problem-solving and attachment motives that cannot initially be separated from each other. In later years, of course, it is quite possible for a child or an adult to imitate solely for the external reward that such imitation can bring or for the feelings of competence to be gained from performing an act effectively regardless of personal feelings about the model. The medical student who is learning a surgical technique is likely to focus on the acts he is learning rather than upon any feelings about the individual who is demonstrating the technique, and few adults would care about the personality of their golf instructor so long as the instructor was effective in improving their performance. It is also possible to witness the converse—imitation of nonsensical behavior that has no obvious problem-solving value but that is imitated because of strong feelings of admiration for the model—although this fascinating kind of imitation has not yet received the amount of attention it merits.

The path from interdependence to independence of attachment and competence motives is not well charted and is certainly one of the major issues that needs to be addressed in a developmental theory of imitation. There are many important questions about the relationship between such motives that have received little attention to date. At what age can children successfully separate their feelings about the model from their interest in the model's acts and its consequences? If the model's competence is pitted experimentally against the model's nurturance are there age-specific effects? For example, are younger children more likely to imitate a nurturant incompetent model rather than a nonnurturant, competent one? How does the nature of the acts being performed interact with such model characteristics, and at what ages do children become sensitive to task characteristics? For example, are simple, expressive activities such as gestures and mannerisms imitated only if the model is nurturant while acts with problem-solving value are imitated regardless of the model's nurturance? Would such a result be age-specific? There is much to be learned about the function of imitation by exploring such questions.

OVERVIEW OF THE REMAINDER OF THE BOOK

In the next six chapters, we will examine the status of the theoretical and empirical literature on children's imitation and present a developmental study that we have recently conducted. We will consider the theoretical literature first. Our review in chapter 2 will make evident that no one imitation theory seems fully adequate when confronted with the task of explaining imitation across the human life span. We will argue, therefore, that a comprehensive developmental theory might well borrow certain aspects from each of the existing theories, and we will briefly outline such a new theory. In chapter 3 we will discuss the major issues that arise from considering the existing theories, and we will compare positions on those issues that they address in common.

Chapter 4 presents the results of a search for published studies that have examined imitation in children of more than one developmental level. Our conclusion based on this search is that most studies have tended not to explore developmental issues in any systematic way. Often, although children of different ages have been studied, differences in their performance have not been examined for their full developmental implications. Often, too, procedural factors have been confounded with the age of the children so that the kinds of imitative demands made of younger children have been different from those made of older children. Because of the many ambiguities in the empirical picture, we conducted a study of 240 children, ranging in age from 4 through 13 years, in order to illuminate some of the issues raised by the existing literature. In chapters 5, 6, and 7, respectively, we describe the method, provide the results, and discuss the findings of this study.

The final chapter, chapter 8, returns to the issues raised in the present chapter and provides a fuller description of the developmental theory that we sketch briefly in chapter 2. Finally, we suggest directions that might be taken in future research to explore the nature of imitation from a developmental perspective.

2

An Overview of Theoretical Positions
on Children's Imitation

Imitation has been a subject of interest to researchers in many disciplines. Cultural anthropologists have regarded imitation as one of the mechanisms by which complex traditions such as those governing sexual practices, food preparation, and mode of dress are maintained. Imitation has interested students of cognitive development as representing a mechanism for the advancement of intellectual competence. Social psychologists have been especially impressed with the role of imitation in such phenomena as "behavioral contagion" and conformity, especially under those conditions where imitation runs counter to the general social welfare or to an individual's inner convictions (Asch, 1955; Wheeler, 1966). Imitation can also be placed within the context of comparative psychology, where it is often examined under the rubric of "social facilitation." Schooling behavior in fish, aggressive or courtship behavior in response to stimuli from another animal, and panic behavior, all have major imitative aspects, although the exact mechanisms that produce these diverse behaviors in different animals can vary widely (Scott, 1968; Thorpe, 1956; Zajonc, 1965).

Given the breadth of events that show an influence of imitation, it is not surprising that a great deal of specialization has arisen in research on imitation. In the present chapter, we have chosen to limit our consideration to those theoretical positions that deal directly with imitativeness in children. As will be seen, even within this limitation there has been a diversity of theoretical approaches. We will also limit our presentation to a statement of theoretical positions, reserving a presentation of empirical literature until chapter 3.

We begin our discussion with a consideration of the Freudian concept of "identification" and its implications for studies of children's imitativeness. Next we will examine two other large-scale theoretical positions that have had a great deal to say about imitation, the cognitive-developmental position of Piaget, and the social learning theory of Bandura. We then consider several positions that are less associated with any one theorist but can be characterized by their emphasis upon one or another particular aspect of imitative behavior. Such theoretical positions are those that stress (a) the role of external reinforcement for imitation, (b) the significance of affective factors in imitation, and (c) the significance of problem-solving, or effectance, motives in imitation. Table 1 sketches an overview of these positions.

THE PSYCHOANALYTIC CONSTRUCT OF IDENTIFICATION

While Freud did not advance a theory of imitation as such, his construct of identification has provided a widely recognized contribution to the study of imitative behavior. Since the introduction of the concept early in this century (Freud, 1905/1953, 1921/1955, 1914/1957b, 1924/1961a, 1923/1961b, 1933/1964),

TABLE 1

An Overview of the Imitation Theories Reviewed in Chapter 2

Theoretical position	Major age of concentration	Developmental changes?	General description
Psycho-analytic	Infancy through preschool	Yes	Emphasizes significance of the emotional relationship between child and model.
Piagetian	Infancy	Yes	Emphasizes importance of the interplay between the child's cognitive level and imitation.
Social learning	Late preschool and older	No	Conceptualizes imitation as requiring the child first mentally to code the model's performance; imitation is controlled by rewards and punishment.
Reinforcement	Late preschool and older; pathological cases (low mental age)	No	Conceptualizes imitation as requiring only motoric ability; imitation is controlled by rewards and punishments.
Affective	Infancy through preschool	Yes	Stresses importance of emotional gratification in controlling the child's imitation.
Effectance	All ages	Yes	Stresses importance of intrinsic competence motives in guiding the child's imitation.

it has had considerable impact upon other theorists. It has also influenced many studies of the relationship between child rearing and personality development (e.g., Emmerich, 1959; Hetherington, 1965; Hetherington & Frankie, 1967; Mussen, 1961; Mussen & Rutherford, 1963; Payne & Mussen, 1956; Sears, 1957; Sears, Maccoby, & Levin, 1957; Sears, Rau, & Alpert, 1965).

It is nevertheless difficult to define precisely what Freud meant by identification or what the term has meant to those who have subsequently employed it. In a lucid review of the history of this concept, Bronfenbrenner (1960) noted that identification has come to refer to three different classes of events. In some cases it refers to observable similarity between a child and his parents in behavior and attitudes. In some cases it refers to a motive to become like the parent. Finally, it often means a process by which both behavior and motives are learned. As Bronfenbrenner (1960) has observed, however, in all Freud's writings "identification, however described, is invariably based on 'an emotional tie with an object,' typically the parent [pp. 15-16]."

The nature of identification, Freud suggested, varies developmentally. He distinguished between a prototypical state occurring in early infancy when the child cannot yet distinguish self from others, and the emergence of actual identification, occurring after the child has made this distinction. Freud (1905/1953) argued that initially, during the primitive oral phase, "sexual activity has not yet been separated from the ingestion of food. . .the sexual aim consists in the incorporation of the object—the prototype of a process which, in the form of identification, is later to play such an important psychological part [p. 198]." Only later did the desire to possess an object become a differentiated, separate motive from the desire to become similar to the object.

In psychoanalytic theory the initial object choice, and thus the initial basis for identification, focused upon the person responsible for the satisfaction of such basic bodily needs as feeding, care, and protection. In Freud's definition (1914/1957b), "this type and source of object choice. . .may be called the 'anaclitic' or 'attachment' type [p. 87]." Anaclitic identification emerging from the object choice based on caretaking—typically the mother—was assumed to be motivated by the child's fear of losing the love and nurturance provided by the mother. According to Freud (1933/1964), this identification could be likened to:

> the assimilation of one ego to another one, as a result of which the first ego behaves like the second in certain respects, imitates it and in a sense takes it up into itself. Identification has been not unsuitably compared with the oral, cannibalistic incorporation of the other person. It is a very important form of attachment to someone else, probably the very first, and not the same thing as the choice of an object [pp. 62-63].

Identification was thus viewed as follows: as a very broad, sweeping kind of seeking to be equivalent to another person for reasons related to the nature of emotional ties with that person.

Later in childhood, a developmentally more advanced form of identification was based upon a later-developing fear, fear of punishment, arising from changes in the relationship between the child and the same-sex parent. In Freud's formulations, it is easier to trace this process for boys than for girls. For boys, it was presumed to arise toward the end of the preschool years as part of the Oedipal conflict, in which the boy comes to see his father as a potential source of punishment (castration anxiety) for his incestuous libidinal feelings towards his mother. The boy, Freud suggested, is able partially to alleviate his fears of punishment by striving to become like his father. A somewhat analogous process for girls was believed to strengthen the girl's desire to be similar to her mother. An important consequence of this form of identification was believed to be the development of the superego, or conscience, an internalized representation of the parent's ideal standards for behavior. Identification based upon fear of punishment was later elaborated upon by Anna Freud (1946), who termed it "identification with the aggressor," and by Mowrer (1950), who termed it "defensive identification."

In both anaclitic identification and identification with the aggressor, the forces underlying the child's adoption of parental characteristics were presumed to be powerful, sweeping, and emotional ones, operating within the limited logical capabilities of the preschool child. Learning of this sort, it was postulated, may be particularly resistant to change during later development when the child's reasoning processes have come under his own critical scrutiny. Thus the basis exists for the argument that the kind of imitation referred to as identification may be qualitatively different from much of the imitation seen in older children. In summarizing this argument, Bronfenbrenner (1960) observes:

> In short, psychoanalytic conceptions of identification should not simply be equated with any acquisition by the child, through ordinary learning, of characteristics of his parent. Freud's formulations have at least two distinguishing features which, though they may be expressible in terms of learning theory, are hardly conventional attributes of it. First, these conceptions clearly imply the existence of *a motive in the child to become like the parent.* Second, this motive functions in relation not to isolated elements but to a total pattern or Gestalt [p. 27]. (©1960. Reprinted by permission of the Society for Research in Child Development, Inc., Chicago, Ill., and by permission of the author.)

As this brief review suggests, making empirical tests of Freud's formulations on identification is difficult for a number of reasons. As is the case for many Freudian concepts, there is fluctuation and vagueness in definitions of identifcation, and it is difficult to derive clear predictions of what sort of behavior should be expected if Freud's formulations are correct (Sarnoff, 1971).

Partly because of this vagueness of definition and partly because of methodological problems, much of the existing research on identification is difficult to interpret. As Bandura (1969c) has pointed out, attempts to assess similarity between parents and children have been plagued with measurement problems, and there are reasons, other than identification, to expect similarity between parent and child. Naturalistic, longitudinal studies of children in their own homes might, however, yield information pertinent to identification that the usual retrospective studies of child-rearing practices and personality development cannot provide; such studies are therefore of great importance for future research. Evidence for the Freudian position might be found if, for example, children showed marked changes in imitation of their mother following brief periods of separation from her. That is, if identification with the mother is motivated by fear of withdrawal of nurturance, actual loss of nurturance in the form of separation from the mother should have a strong resulting effect upon the child's imitation. Such an effect might well take the form of greater imitation of the mother following her return than was observed preceding her absence. Similarly, the Freudian conceptualization of the Oedipal situation implies that preschool boys might initially imitate their mothers more than their fathers but that this situation should become quite suddenly reversed within a relatively short period of time. At some time between approximately 5 and 7 years, boys should show a marked increase in imitation of their fathers and avoidance of imitation of their mothers.

Regardless of whether further study confirms the empirical usefulness of the concept of identification, certain characteristics of the Freudian point of view seem to deserve inclusion in any theory of imitation. The emphasis on emotional considerations in imitation is an important one which implies that behavior that appeals to the emotions might be imitated very differently from behavior that has a predominantly problem-solving, rational quality. The Freudian analysis also suggests that the nature of the relationship between the observer and the model significantly affects imitation, and that the effect of this relationship may interact with the factor of the content of the modeled behavior. Thus, while children might imitate virtually any model who demonstrated a successful problem solution, such as peeling an orange in order to eat it, they might copy odd mannerisms and expressions only if they liked the model who displayed them. Valentine's (1930) observations of children's greater imitation of their mothers' novel acts than of the same acts produced by others are certainly consistent with this possibility. Finally, a major contribution of Freudian theory is its suggestion that developmental considerations may influence all findings in imitation research. Freud was clear in suggesting that the motives for imitation in infancy may be quite different from the motives for imitation in later childhood, and this aspect of psychoanalytic theory, as we have argued, deserves preservation.

It would unquestionably be strained to attempt to build an entire theory of imitation on the Freudian foundation alone. The present authors agree with Kohlberg (1969) that "psychoanalytic theories of parent identification are obviously unsuitable to deal with the bread-and-butter phenomena of imitation which constitute the basis of much of the child's ordinary situational and reversible social learning [p. 424]." Nevertheless, it seems equally true that other theories seem inadequate in explaining some of the more profound instances of children's imitative behavior and that a comprehensive theory designed to be applicable to all forms of imitative behavior at all ages cannot afford to ignore Freudian perspectives.

PIAGETIAN COGNITIVE-DEVELOPMENTAL THEORY

Like the Freudian approach, the theory of Jean Piaget is a developmental one. The emphasis, however, is upon cognitive rather than emotional factors. For Piaget imitation is, in fact, one of two complementary functions that are essential for human intelligence.

In considering the Piagetian position, it is helpful to recognize that Piaget obtained his early scientific training as a biologist. Piagetian theory is most easily understood when one observes that, in this theory, intellectual development is described as occurring in a manner analogous to the kind of physical development charted by developmental embryologists (see Carmichael, 1954; Gottlieb, 1970; and Waddington, 1957, for descriptions of the principles of developmental embryology). In physical development, organismic structures are constantly changing as a result of interaction with the environment: the appropriate environment for the zygote stimulates it to divide to produce a multicelled organism, which after repeated divisions becomes physically very different from its original state. As a result of changes in structure, the organism interacts with the environment in different ways at different points of its development. Growth thus represents continuing change both in physical structures and in the nature of the interactions between the organism and its environment.

If we consider intellectual, or cognitive, growth in an analogous way, we are in a position to follow Piaget's formulations more readily. Piaget regards intelligence as an adaptive process in which the child must constantly respond to new events in a manner made possible by the currently existing cognitive structures. Since cognitive structures are often inadequate to represent external events, conflict frequently arises: to resolve the conflict the child must either modify his cognitive structures or modify the new events. Piaget has labeled the process of changing cognitive structures as "accommodation." Imitation, in Piaget's formulation, is accommodation in its purest form. The complementary process, "assimilation," is the changing of external stimuli in order better to match the existing internal structures. Piaget characterizes assimilation in its purest form as being play. As Piaget (1962b) has expressed this relationship:

A stable equilibrium between assimilation and accommodation results in properly intelligent adaptation. But. . .if there is primacy of accommodation over assimilation, the activity tends to become imitation. Imitation is thus seen to be merely a continuation of the effort at accommodation, closely connected with the act of intelligence, of which it is one differentiated aspect, a temporarily detached part.

It is clear from the outset that the problem of imitation is linked with that of representation. Since representation involves the image of an object, it can be a kind of interiorized imitation, and therefore a continuation of accommodation [p. 5].

Although the process of accommodation remains the same over the lifespan, the cognitive structures of the child do not. Therefore, the kinds of external events that result in accommodation differ with age.

Imitation in Infancy (Sensorimotor Imitation)

Most of Piaget's (1962b) research on imitation has been concentrated upon very young children from the time of birth to approximately 18 months. Cognitive growth shows a particularly dramatic rate of change during infancy, and it is perhaps for this reason that Piaget has described such clear changes in imitation as a function of changes in a child's level of cognitive development. It is worthwhile to trace these changes in some detail. As was noted in chapter 1, among the most important developmental changes during human infancy is the development of the ability to form interiorized representations of events, an ability that can usually be inferred to exist early in the second year of life. The tracing of the events that mark this development is the aim of the Piagetian stages, which are described as follows.

Piaget has suggested that newborn infants are not capable of true imitation at all. While the possibility of neonatal imitation has not been fully ruled out (Parton, 1976), several other observers who have studied the intellectual and imitative capabilities of the human infant have also commented upon this initial deficiency in imitation (Baldwin, 1906; Décarie, 1965; Guillaume, 1926/1971).

Although neonates do not engage in what Piaget would be willing to call imitation, he has noted that acts that appear to be imitative do occur very early. One newborn infant crying in a nursery is likely to stimulate the other infants to cry also. a circumstance that Piaget argues can most parsimoniously be attributed to the triggering of existing response patterns through external stimulation. (Piaget terms this Stage 1, or "preparation through the reflex.") Guillaume (1926/1971) similarly cautioned against prematurely attributing significance to apparently imitative reactions, such as smiling and expressions of fear, disgust, and other emotions, noting that "before any imitation exists. . .there is a uniformity in the behavior of the infant and the adult that is merely a manifestation of the similarity of organs and instincts [p. 98]." The recent work of ethologists lends support to this caution. The response of smiling, for example, has been found to occur in blind infants as well as sighted infants (Freedman, 1964), and ethologists have suggested that smiling may be a species-wide response elicited by certain releasing stimuli in the environment (Ambrose, 1961; Eibl-Eibesfeldt, 1968).

Such responses, however, can be the basis for what Piaget has termed "pseudo imitation" or "imitation by training," in which consequences to the infant may cause him to continue the activity; Piaget considers the appearance of this kind of imitation as signaling the emergence of a second stage he has labeled "sporadic imitation." Such imitation by training can occur very early in life but,

Piaget argues, does not persist without continual external stimulation. This imitation by training would appear to be equivalent to the operant conditioning of infant responses, as described by reinforcement theorists (Brackbill, 1958; Gewirtz, 1971a, b; Gewirtz & Stingle, 1968).

The third stage, which Piaget calls "systematic imitation," appears at approximately 4½ months of age when the child has succeeded in coordinating his vision and prehension. According to Piaget, when the child has learned how to move objects in order to change their visual appearance, he broadens by this new ability the acts he can imitate. However, Piaget reports that, significantly, while the child can imitate movements of the adult such as opening and closing the fist, he cannot imitate similar movements such as opening or closing the eyes. In order to imitate at this stage of his cognitive development, the child apparently must create a visual impression that matches that which he has seen the model create (as is possible in distinctive hand movements, but not in movements of the face). Piaget (1962b) has stated the principle describing this stage of development more generally: "The intellectual mechanism of the child will not allow him to imitate movements he sees made by others when the corresponding movements of his own body are known to him only tactually or kinesthetically, and not visually [p. 19]."

This principle represents an important example of the manner in which developmental level influences what the child is capable of imitating. Without a consideration of developmental level, there would be no reason to consider the opening and closing of a fist as a significantly different kind of stimulus from opening and closing the eyes or the mouth, yet the effects of these different classes of stimuli are clearly distinguishable in terms of the infant's imitations. Another characteristic of Piaget's third stage of imitation is that the child is said to imitate only those sounds and movements that he has already discovered for himself. According to Piaget, imitation during this stage is thus not employed as a means of learning new modes of behavior. Rather it appears to exist primarily as self-imitation, the major motivation for which is to prolong the continuance of events that the child finds interesting.

The ability to imitate movements that cannot be seen upon one's own body appears to emerge simultaneously with the imitation of acts that are not already known to the child. These qualities of imitation characterize Piaget's fourth stage, which occurs at approximately 8-9 months of age. Solving the problem of imitating what cannot be seen appears to be a major accomplishment for the child. Interestingly, Piaget noted that laughter, smiling, and other signs of pleasure occurred as his children solved the problem of locating the equivalent portion of their own faces in response to a modeled facial activity. When the child can imitate a variety of facial expressions, he seems also to take a keen new interest in all kinds of activities of others around him and he begins to imitate these activities. Piaget (1926b) argues that this occurs because "instead of appearing to be the continuation of his own activity modeled actions are now partially independent realities which are anlogous to what the child himself can do and yet distinct from it. Then and only then do new models have interest for the child [p. 50] ." Thus, the function of imitation, according to Piaget, undergoes a transition from being a means for continuing interesting inputs to being a means for seeking out new ones. (Guillaume, 1926/1971, similarly concluded that such a transition occurs at approximately this age and that "imitation becomes the formative factor in new complex modes of activity that give imitation its educative value [p. 157] .")

The next major developments in imitation involve the systematic use of imitation in a trial-and-error fashion as a means for discovering new properties of objects (Stage 5) and the beginning of representative imitation requiring long-term memory for what was modeled (Stage 6). Piaget (1962b) concludes that the development of conceptual representation—of symbols and images—is first seen in Stage 6, which is attained by the age of 18 months. At this time, he concludes, "imitation is no longer dependent on the actual action, and the child becomes capable of imitating internally a series of models in the form of images or suggestions of actions. Imitation thus begins to reach the level of representation [p. 62] ." It is interesting to note that this is the level of ability taken for granted as existing in human beings by the social learning theorists (Bandura, 1973, p. 42). Among the occurrences that make their first appearance at this time are the immediate imitation of complex new acts, imitation of objects in addition to persons, and deferred imitation. Thus, prior to the emergence of language, a phenomenon to be seen in the human child (and apparently also in certain other primates) is the capacity for some kind of representational imagery, a capacity of great importance in permitting imitation to become freed of constraints of time and specific situations. As we noted in chapter 1, this phenomenon is generally referred to as observational learning.

Imitation in Older Children

Piagetian theory (Piaget, 1962a) is less age-specific about imitation that occurs after the child has completed the sensorimotor period (approximately the first 18 months) of development. Descriptions of imitation by older children are presented by Piaget in the context of his examination of the children's attempts to learn the rules of childhood games.

Piaget has described developmental changes both in the adequacy of imitation as a means for learning and in the apparent motivation for such activity. According to Piaget, long before the child understands the complexities of the play of older children, he shows selective imitation of portions of that play. The young child of 4 or 5 may, for example, play on the fringes of a game such as "tag," imitating such features as running to home base and chanting the ritual words used by older children, but under circumstances when it is inappropriate for him to do so. (Older children sometimes find this behavior aggravating, while adults frequently are amused by it.) Piaget similarly reports examples in which young children may be seen playing with marbles in a manner that resembles a genuine marble game in a few details but in which the children do not take turns, win or lose marbles from each other, or show other signs of having comprehended the basic intent of the game.

Piaget (1962a) has characterized the kind of partial imitation we have been describing, which incorporates aspects of the older child's activities into the essentially solitary play of the younger child, as "egocentric." Egocentric imitation is highly susceptible to the desires and aims of the child; thus the use of a procedure that has been observed among older children may simply be discontinued if it produces adverse results, such as the loss of a marble. Questioning children who are showing egocentric, partial imitation has typically resulted in assurances from the child that he knows the rules of the game and that he has learned them by watching other children.

The shift from egocentrism to the recognition of the existence and legitimacy of other points of view is evidently such a gradual one that no fixed timetable can be assigned for its occurrence. Clearly, however, such a shift does typically occur, and, as games become more social and interactive, there is an accompanying increase in accuracy of imitation as a means of learning the rules of games. Piaget's theory, however, does not merely assert that older children are superior to younger children along some simple continuum such as accuracy, but that they show important qualitative differences as well. Piaget (1962a) has stated, for example, "From two to seven, representative imitation develops spontaneously, often being unconscious because of its ease and egocentrism, whereas at about seven or eight it becomes deliberate and takes its place in intelligence as a whole [p. 72]." There is thus an implication that imitation is an undirected, somewhat casual activity, perhaps under the control of peripheral, environmental factors before it becomes a self-conscious, reasoned strategy for achieving effective solutions to problems.

General Comments on Piagetian Theory

As with Freudian theory, it is sometimes difficult to specify exactly what Piagetian theory predicts. In general it is easier to derive testable predictions for imitation for the sensorimotor period (from birth to approximately 18 months) than for imitation among older children. (In chapter 3 we review several studies that have made tests with infants.)

Piagetian theory provides a global point of view, which has valuable implications for the developmental theory of imitation we are attempting to synthesize. As previously noted, one such implication is that the effects of the environment must be expected to differ depending upon the stage of development that the child has attained. Piagetian theory generates the prediction that exposure to a model as well as many events that have been posited as being of importance for imitation, such as reinforcement, vicarious reinforcement, and punishment, will have different effects when applied to children of different ages.

A commonly drawn implication of Piagetian theory is that a child does not successfully imitate what he cannot yet comprehend. This implication derives from the extensive body of work that has led Piaget (1970) to propose that cognitive growth can be described as progressing through a series of discrete stages. It has been presumed by some critics (Bandura & McDonald, 1963; Siegler, Liebert, & Liebert, 1973; Zimmerman, 1974) that the assumption that cognitive development proceeds in stages necessitates the conclusion that a child cannot be taught by any means, imitative or otherwise, concepts that are characteristic of children at a later stage of development. It is not, however, entirely clear that such a conclusion is a necessary corollary of the theory and it is not clear exactly where Piaget stands on this issue. As in the classic studies in which efforts were made to accelerate the development of physical skills in young children by special training (e.g., McGraw, 1935), it may be that the Piagetian stages are predictive of the amount of effort that will be required to teach a new concept as well as whether such a concept can be taught at all. Thus, while one may be able to teach a 2-year-old to button his coat by investing great effort in the training, one can teach a 5-year-old with ease. By contrast no amount of effort would result in a 6-month-old child's acquiring this skill, through observational learning, operant conditioning, or any other means. If Piagetian stages are generally descriptive of the path of intellectual development, then by analogy it might be possible, though difficult, to teach a 7-year-old child (concrete operational stage) principles that are easily learned by the 11-year-old (formal operational stage), whereas it might be impossible to teach such concepts to a 4-year-old (intuitive stage). We shall examine evidence of this sort in the next chapter.

THE SOCIAL LEARNING FORMULATION OF BANDURA

A third major theoretical approach to children's imitation is represented in the social learning position advanced by Bandura (1962, 1965, 1969a, 1969b, 1969c, 1971a, 1971b, 1973, 1977). The major focus of social learning theory has been upon imitative behavior in older children and adults, that is, in individuals with relatively well-developed verbal and logical abilities. As we shall see, however, many of the social learning principles might easily be adapted to a developmental theory of imitation.

In the social learning formulation, before imitation can occur, an individual must form an internalized representation of the modeled acts. Bandura labels this process "acquisition." According to Bandura, acquisition is partially under the control of stimulus characteristics, especially the fact that the stimulus acts shown by the model occur closely together in time. Since the stimulus acts are contiguous, Bandura suggests that the perceptual responses that occur during observation are also contiguous and give rise to a unified, centrally stored mental image or other representation. The acquisition process is also influenced by characteristics of the observer and by other processes, such as attention and motivation, as we will discuss shortly. In this view, the observer is like a sophisticated camera, making a record of selected aspects of the modeled display for use in subsequent reproductions. The nature of what is and is not recorded is an issue of much interest, since it touches upon the central question of whether the observer is relatively passive during acquisition or whether he takes an active, selective role. We will discuss this issue at greater length later. In either case, it is clear that only part of the model's acts are expected to find their way into the "photograph" made by the observer.

Once the observer has acquired a representation of the witnessed acts, the representation can be retrieved at a later time and used as a guide for reproducing the original behavior. The process of overtly acting out the model's behavior Bandura labels "performance" (we will substitute the term "imitation" for the reasons given in chapter 1). The determining factor in whether the observer does or does not imitate, given that he has acquired the modeled acts, is the nature of the expected consequences for imitating. Generally speaking, if the child believes he will be rewarded, he will imitate; otherwise he will not. Thus, in Bandura's (1969c) formulation, acquisition is a necessary condition for imitation but it is not a sufficient one, and acquisition and imitation "are determined by different sets of variables [p. 219]."

Bandura distinguishes among several kinds of modeling effects, all of which can be explained on the basis of the considerations just described. He applies the term "observational learning" to cases where the observer learns to make novel responses that he would not otherwise have known how to perform. This usage is essentially the same as that employed by other theorists and will be the major focus of our consideration here. Other forms of modeling effects discussed by Bandura are "social facilitation" and "inhibition" or "disinhibition" effects. In these cases, the model's actions are already familiar to the observer. In social facilitation, for example, hearing someone hum a favorite tune may lead the observer to begin humming the tune as well. Disinhibition occurs when a model is not punished after performing an act that is usually punished (such as an aggressive act); seeing this, the observer may lower his customary inhibitions against aggression and may imitate. He has not, however, learned a new act from the model.

Bandura (1977) proposes that four processes are important in considering why acquisition and imitation occur: (a) attention, (b) retention, (c) motor reproduction, and (d) motivation. Each of these is described below in detail.

Attention

Attention is considered to be crucial for acquisition. As Bandura (1969a) has noted:

Simply exposing persons to distinctive sequences of modeled stimuli does not in it-

self guarantee that they will attend closely to the cues, that they will necessarily select from the total stimulus complex the most relevant events, or that they will even
perceive accurately the cues to which their attention has been directed. An observer
will fail to acquire matching behavior, at the sensory registration level, if he does not
attend to, recognize, or differentiate the distinctive features of the model's responses.
To produce learning, therefore, stimulus contiguity must be accompanied by discriminative observation [p. 136].

Acquisition in this formulation requires stimulus contiguity but is not guaran-
teed by it.

A number of variables are postulated as having an important influence upon
attention. Bandura (1969a) mentions properties of the stimuli themselves, such
as "intensity, size, vividness, and novelty [p. 136]." Characteristics of the model
such as competence, age, social power, ethnic status, and sex also appear to
influence attention. Such model characteristics are postulated to be important
primarily because they signify differential probabilities of reinforcement for imitating the models. Bandura (1969a) also mentions the "affective valence of models, as mediated through their attractiveness and other rewarding qualities [p.
136]" which may increase attention to the model and therefore produce greater
observational learning. Finally, characteristics of the observers are postulated to
affect attention. Bandura specifically mentions characteristics such as dependency, self-esteem, level of competence, socioeconomic and racial status, sex,
and a learning history including frequent reward for displaying matching behavior.

Retention

While overt and covert rehearsal are important factors in retention, Bandura
(1969a) particularly stresses the usefulness of symbolic coding operations, which
are "even more efficacious than rehearsal processes in facilitating long-term retention of modeled events. During exposure to stimulus sequences observers are
inclined to code, classify, and reorganize elements into familiar and more easily
remembered schemes [p. 140]." Bandura also assumes that there are two representational systems available to observers—visual imagery and verbal coding—
and that the verbal is more important. According to Bandura (1969c), "most of
the cognitive processes that regulate behavior are primarily verbal rather than
visual [pp. 220-221]."

Motor Reproduction

It is doubtful that theorists of any persuasion would take exception to Bandura's
observations concerning the role of motoric capabilities in imitation: If one lacks
the physical capabilities to perform an action, one cannot imitate. Bandura also
notes that the imitation of a complex action is greatly facilitated if the observer
is already familiar with all of the component actions and has merely to learn
how to sequence or coordinate these activities. Interestingly, Bandura includes

within his discussion of motoric factors an observation similar to one of Piaget's—that the imitation of acts that are not readily visible may be more difficult than imitation of acts that can be readily seen by the imitator. Piaget's example, it will be recalled, involved imitation of facial movements; Bandura's example involves the imitation of acts produced by skilled muscle control as in operatic singing.

Incentives or Motivation

Reinforcement contingencies are presumed to be the only major factor affecting motivation for imitation. The role of reinforcement in Bandura's formulation is not a simple one, however. In addition to overt reinforcement, Bandura's formulation includes self-reinforcement in which the subject rewards himself for a performance and vicarious reinforcement in which the model is shown receiving rewards or punishments following the modeling sequence. The effects of self-reinforcement as Bandura conceptualizes this variable are of much theoretical interest since Bandura makes the important observation that children's preexisting levels of aspiration or standards for achievement may modify or change the salience of an externally given reinforcement. When a child evaluates his own performance in the larger context of his own expectations, a high level of achievement on a task that the child deems too simple often does not serve as a reinforcement. In contrast, a failure on a very difficult task may nevertheless result in self-reinforcement.

Bandura and his colleagues have studied self-reinforcement in nonimitative contexts to demonstrate its existence. They have shown, for example, that self-reinforcement can influence level of exertion in a physical task in much the same way as reinforcement administered by the experimenter can (Bandura & Perloff, 1967). Self-reinforcement has been related to imitative behavior by demonstrating that children will imitate the same standard of self-reinforcement as they have seen modeled (Bandura, Grusec, & Menlove, 1967). The finding does not, however, indicate whether children employ self-reinforcement to reward their own imitations. Thus, while the possibility exists that self-reinforcement of the kind Bandura describes is an important factor governing children's imitation in instances where children imitate but are not rewarded, such a role for self-reinforcement has not yet been clearly demonstrated.

Vicarious reinforcement effects are more directly related to imitative behavior by a large body of research findings. As Bandura (1971b) reports, children often increase their imitation if the model was rewarded and decrease their imitation if the model was punished. He argues that vicarious reward and punishment owe their effectiveness to a number of influences upon both acquisition and imitation. He suggests, for example, that seeing the model rewarded or punished provides the observer with information regarding the types of responses most likely to lead to reward or punishment, and that it serves as a guide to the apparent competence or incompetence of the model. He also suggests (a) that consequences to the model have a "stimulus enhancement" effect, drawing the observer's attention to the events that led to reinforcement, and making them more distinctive, (b) that seeing such consequences influences motivation by setting up expectancies concerning reward, and, (c) that there may be arousal of the observer's emotions (especially in the case of punishment).

To summarize, in the social learning formulation reinforcement is considered to have an important influence on both imitation and acquisition. For imitation, provided the observer has the requisite physical capabilities, it is evidently considered to be both a necessary and sufficient condition. As Bandura and Barab (1971) have stated this position, "performance of imitative behavior is for the most part controlled by anticipated consequences of prospective actions. These anticipated consequences are established through differential reinforcement that is either directly experienced, inferred from observed response consequences of others, or conveyed through verbal explanations [p. 245]." For acquisition, reinforcement effects are also considered important, but in a less direct manner. The anticipation of consequences for imitation, it is argued, leads to selective attention and to selective retention, as the observer makes decisions concerning what should be recorded and/or rehearsed in anticipation of future performance.

Developmental Considerations of the Social Learning Formulation

In principle, social learning theory could lend itself easily to the incorporation of developmental principles, since so much stress is laid upon the capabilities of the observer. The social learning formulation presumes the existence of considerable cognitive abilities, a fact that Bandura (1973) himself employs to distinguish his formulation from theories that propose that behavior is determined entirely by reinforcement contingencies:

> In a vigorous effort to avoid spurious inner causes, [extreme situational determinism] neglected determinants of man's behavior arising from his cognitive functioning. Man is a thinking organism possessing capabilities that provide him with some power of self-direction. People can represent external influences symbolically and later use such representations to guide their actions; they can solve problems mentally without having to enact the various alternatives; and they can foresee the probable consequences of different actions and alter their behavior accordingly. . . . To the extent that traditional behavioral theories could be faulted, it was for providing an incomplete rather than an inaccurate account of human behavior. (Albert Bandura, *Aggression: A social learning analysis,* ©1973, p. 42. Reprinted by permission of Prentice-Hall, Inc., Englewood Cliffs, N.J.)

In turn, however, a similar objection of incompleteness must be raised in describing Bandura's formulation. For the capabilities that Bandura ascribes to "man" are not those possessed by young children. Human cognitive abilities must develop, and as studies of infants and preschool children make especially clear, they develop from a starting place far different from that described in the quotation above.

Interestingly, Bandura has long recognized the significance of variation in cognitive abilities in the context of comparing humans with infrahumans. Bandura (1969a) notes, for example, that differences in the degree to which organisms possess the "capacity for representational mediation and covert rehearsal [pp. 147-148]" will be of major importance in determining successful acquisition and retention of modeling sequences that are complex and lengthy. Yet, while Bandura has recognized the importance of allowing for the fact of phylogenetic variation in any complete theory of observational learning, until his most recent formulation of social learning theory (Bandura, 1977) he has surprisingly failed to consider the significance of ontogenetic variation. His theoretical network has thus included comparative, but not developmental, psychology.

In response to criticism from developmentalists, Bandura (1977) has argued that social learning theory is potentially compatible with a developmental approach, an argument with which the present authors agree. However, it remains to be seen how much influence Bandura's recent addition of developmental considerations to social learning theory will have upon research. It is troublesome to find Bandura (1977) suggesting that researchers might profitably bypass chronological age as a variable and

> study proficiency in observational learning by children who have received different amounts of pretraining in component functions over a period of time. This is an especially effective way of identifying the developmental determinants of observational learning because the critical factors are created directly [p. 30].

The assumption that children can be trained in the component functions of attention, retention, motoric reproduction, and motivation seems to reflect a fundamental misunderstanding of the nature of development. As the training studies of the 1930s (e.g., McGraw, 1935) have demonstrated, and the countless mothers who have attempted premature toilet training have discovered, efforts to accelerate motor development skills in young children are misplaced efforts. Similarly, no amount of pretraining will lead an infant to develop linguistic coding skills or a 3-year-old to display the attentional capabilities of a 7-year-old. Social learning theory can be made compatible with developmental principles, but thus far there is reason to believe that this has not been accomplished.

To date, moreover, studies conducted within the social learning formulation evidence a search for general principles applicable to all ages and generally disregard developmental considerations. For example, such studies typically employ subjects at only one developmental level, but draw conclusions that are considered to be descriptive of human observational learning in general. While many of the findings may indeed be valid across a wide range of developmental levels, others quite probably are not.

Without question, the social learning formulation provides a richly articulated framework for understanding much of the imitative behavior of older children and adults. It has also provided us with what is probably the largest single body of empirical evidence concerning the determinants of such imitation. It would be informative to trace the course of the emergence of the kind of sophisticated observational learning that is characteristic of older children and adults. Clearly, the social learning formulation is ripe for developmental tests of many of its basic principles.

REINFORCEMENT THEORISTS

Many researchers have examined the role that external reinforcement plays in governing imitation (Baer et al., 1967; Baer & Sherman, 1964; Gewirtz, 1971a, b; Gewirtz & Stingle, 1968; Lovaas, Berberich, Perloff, & Schaeffer, 1966; Lovass, Freitas, Nelson, & Whalen, 1967; Metz, 1965; Miller & Dollard, 1941; Parton, 1970; Rosenbaum & Arenson, 1968; Sears, 1957; Skinner, 1953, 1957; Steinman, 1970a, 1970b; Waxler & Yarrow, 1970). This body of research and collection of theoretical papers have as their major goal the explanation of human imitative behavior within the behavioristic principles of operant conditioning. (See especially Skinner, 1953, 1957, for a statement of the basic tenets of operant conditioning.)

Operant conditioning had its roots in the study of animal learning. When applied to human learning, it is not surprising that it has emphasized aspects of behavior that humans and infrahumans share, such as the ability to engage in motoric activity and motoric mediation (an ability we described in chapter 1 as a form of "muscle memory"). The operant conditioning formulation also placed heavy emphasis upon the role of environmental events in controlling behavior. According to this view, when people emit behavior, the consequences that ensue, such as rewards or punishments, have a major causal effect in determining whether the behavior is likely to be repeated in the future under similar circumstances. If positive consequences result, the behavior is said to be "reinforced" and to be more likely to occur again. Applying this to imitative behavior, for example, when a young child imitates, he often receives an enthusiastic response from adults, including hugging, laughter, and other signs of warmth. According to the tenets of operant conditioning, such responses from adults should serve to strengthen, or reinforce, the child's imitative behavior. We will refer to theorists who have attempted to account for all human imitation by the principles of operant conditioning as "reinforcement theorists."

Analyses of imitation within the strict confines of reinforcement theory have been influential both in generating research and in stimulating the growth of other theories that attempt to incorporate and to expand upon them (such as the social learning theory just discussed). The influential work of Miller and Dollard (1941) is a historically important example. Like many who have followed them, Miller and Dollard considered the problem of imitation to be a matter of discrimination learning. Their theory assumed that some primary or secondary drive must be operative in order for the child to learn to imitate and that the child learned to use the behavior of others as a cue for making the response with the highest likelihood of obtaining the reward that would satisfy the initial drive. Thus an imitative response was considered to be simply an instrumental means of obtaining external reward. Miller and Dollard reported the results of a number of experiments with both rats and children showing this kind of imitative behavior. They found, for example, that a rat could learn to turn left or right at a choice point according to the direction chosen by a preceding rat if it was rewarded for doing so. With children, a model's choice of a box on the left- or right-hand side was enacted for the observing child. The position of the model's choice was made the sole basis for predicting which of the two boxes would contain a piece of candy, and many children learned to imitate the model's choice to obtain candy.

Several features of this paradigm are interesting for the purpose of comparison with other procedures. The child was not permitted to see whether the model's choice had been successful; thus no effects of vicarious reward or punishment were operative. Secondly, imitation was studied entirely within the context of a place-learning problem. A third feature was that the child could solve the problem only by observing the model. Finally, the paradigm employed candy as reinforcement with the assumption that some form of extrinsic reinforcement was essential for imitation. Similar treatments of imitation have also been offered by Sears (1957) and by Skinner (1953, 1957).

A more recent theory representing an extension of Miller and Dollard's approach has been advanced by Gewirtz and Stingle (Gewirtz, 1971a, 1971b; Gewirtz & Stingle, 1968). Like Miller and Dollard, Gewirtz and Stingle consider imitation to be a discrimination learning phenomenon. However, they examine imitative behavior that has greater morphological complexity than place learning, suggesting that what an observer has learned to do when he imitates is to select from his already existing repertoire of responses those that match the modeled responses. Thus, instead of selecting simply from location responses (turning right versus turning left), the observer has his entire set of learned behaviors to select from in imitating the model. It is in this sense that the Gewirtz and Stingle position represents a straightforward extension of the Miller and Dollard formulation.

Gewirtz and Stingle also introduce a construct they label "generalized imitation" to explain, without employing constructs such as *intrinsic* or *self-reinforcement,* the occurrence of imitation without reinforcement. According to the generalized imitation formulation, children must learn how to imitate, and this learning process is conceptualized by Gewirtz and Stingle (1968) as follows:

> The first imitative responses must occur by chance, through direct physical assistance, or through direct training. . .When such responses occur, they are strengthened and maintained by direct extrinsic reinforcement from environmental agents. After several imitative responses become established in this manner, a class of diverse but *functionally equivalent* behaviors is acquired and is maintained by extrinsic reinforcement on an intermittent schedule [p. 379, italics in original].

The functional equivalence referred to is established by the reinforcing agent, not by the child, through a process of treating a diverse group of imitative behaviors as equally worthy of reward. Gewirtz and Stingle (1968) argue that "because. . .reinforcers come from a variety of sources, on an intermittent schedule . . .and for diverse imitation behaviors, generalized imitation will be acquired relatively early in the child's socialization, maintained at high strength, and relatively resistant to change [p. 384] ."

The Gewirtz and Stingle formulation goes beyond that of Miller and Dollard in specifically denying that anything new can be learned through observation without overt performance. They argue, rather, that apparent instances of no-trial, nonrewarded observational learning reflect responses the observer had previously learned and that the existence of an adequate learning history for the observer would supply proof for this contention. They further deny that observational learning could occur spontaneously: "We attempt to show how one must *learn* to learn through exposure to model's responses [p. 383] ." Finally, they deny the need for concepts such as intrinsic motivation in explaining imitation, arguing that apparent cases of imitation without reinforcement can be explained on the basis of a generalized tendency to imitate and the observer's failure to discriminate between responses that are and are not likely to be followed by reinforcement.

In summary, the Gewirtz and Stingle formulation represents a clearcut behavioristic theory of imitation. It specifies that learning cannot occur unless responses are performed overtly and unless extrinsic reinforcement has been employed at some phase of the stimulus-response chain. The assumption is made that complex phenomena such as imitation can be adequately accounted for in terms of more basic laws of external reinforcement, and that the organism is fundamentally passive and under the control of the environment. These theorists view their formulation as an alternative to Bandura's; little reference is made to Piagetian theory, although the fact that Piaget and Gewirtz deal with imitation in infancy while Bandura does not would make such a contrast in theories informative. Some points of comparison will therefore be raised in the next chapter.

AFFECTIVE THEORIES

Both Mowrer (1950, chapter 24; 1960, chapter 7) and Aronfreed (1969) have provided theories of imitation that argue that an important motive for imitation is to regain affective or emotional states that were present during the original exposure to the model. Mowrer's basic paradigm is that of Miller and Dollard and stresses the need for physical responses to be made during the learning process; Aronfreed's (1969) contention that the necessary and sufficient condition for observational learning is "learning through cognitive representation during the period of observation [p. 232] " shows similarity to Bandura's formulations.

In arguing that affective factors play a major role in imitation, Mowrer provides the specific example of imitation of speechlike sounds. In seeking to explain the phenomenon of babbling, often overheard when a young child is alone in his crib (Weir, 1962), Mowrer argued that an important motive for engaging in such unreinforced activity was to reproduce events that had acquired secondary reinforcement value through Pavlovian conditioning. Mowrer postulated that since human caretakers frequently talk to an infant while comforting and feeding him, speech sounds may become associated with emotional states of contentment for an infant—just as the sound of a buzzer presented just before food became associated with salivation and visceral responses for Pavlov's dogs. The fact that the infant is capable of making sounds similar to the caretaker's suggests that through stimulus generalization the infant's own sounds will come to be satisfying to him. Thus the child may engage in imitating speech sounds because these sounds have acquired positive affect for him. Presumably this mechanism would also operate in other instances of imitation besides speech. In an extension of his consideration of emotional factors, Mowrer suggested that the child might also be affected simply by observing that a model was rewarded for performing certain acts.

Mowrer's formulation implies that nurturant models should be imitated more than nonnurturant models, that models whose performance is rewarded should be imitated more than those whose performance is not rewarded, and that specific acts that were paired with reinforcement during presentation to the subject should be imitated more than acts that were not paired with reward. The evidence on these issues is mixed. The observation that deaf children begin to babble but cease doing so after a time is suggestive support for Mowrer's position (Mowrer, 1960). Mowrer also cited results from studies with talking birds, which seemed to suggest that the secondary reinforcement phenomenon he had postulated was essential for the birds' imitation of human sounds. A recent study, however, did not replicate this effect, but rather found that myna birds imitated with equivalent frequency both sounds that were consistently paired with food and distinctively different sounds that were never paired with food (Foss, 1964). A study by Paskal (1969) with 6- and 7-year-old girls, designed specifically to test Mowrer's position, provided some support, as the younger children showed more imitation of a nurturant model than of a nonnurturant one. There was no evidence, however, for greater imitation of acts that were specifically paired with nurturance than of acts that were not. In sum, although one should probably be reluctant to consider Mowrer's formulation disproved solely on the basis of data from studies with infrahumans or from studies with children much older than infants, confidence in his formulation is necessarily weakened in the absence of positive findings with such subjects. It does seem clear that conditioned affect, even though it may augment imitation under some circumstances, is not an essential component of imitative behavior under all circumstances. It may be, of course, that conditioned affect has a major influence at early ages but not for older children, a possibility that has not been adequately tested.

Aronfreed's position has much in common with the social learning formulation. He argues, however, that observation of the behavior of others does not occur in an emotional vacuum, and that the affective surrounding in which acts are performed may influence subsequent imitation. As Aronfreed (1969) has summarized his position:

> The behavior of other people in the child's environment is embedded in a context of .. .stimulation that has an affective impact on the child. It will therefore often be true that the changes of affectivity which are induced in the child, in close conjunction with its observation of another person's behavior, become directly coupled to the cognitive template that the child forms for the behavior. The coupling would occur through processes which are essentially like those of Pavlovian conditioning. The child may then reproduce the observed behavior, if the change of affectivity that has become attached to its template has a potential reinforcement value. ... In other words, the overt behavioral reproduction is to some extent under the control of the affective value that has become attached to the template [p. 270]. (© 1969. Reprinted by permission of Academic Press, Inc., New York, and by permission of the author.)

As with Mowrer's formulation, direct evidence pertinent to Aronfreed's arguments is relatively sparse. Several experiments conducted by Aronfreed (reported in Aronfreed, 1969) provide some indication that children are more likely to imitate acts that were paired with positive consequences during modeling. Such experiments, however, have been few and have examined a narrow range of imitative acts. In addition, the Paskal study just noted (1969) failed to find differential imitation of acts paired versus not paired with nurturance during modeling.

Given the similarity of Aronfreed's formulation to Bandura's, it is somewhat surprising that Bandura has regarded Aronfreed's formulation as being in contradiction to the social learning approach. Bandura has cited evidence as weakening to Aronfreed's position that observational learning can occur in the absence of any feedback from the skeletal muscles, as in subjects immobilized by curare. While such evidence is pertinent to Mowrer's position that affect is conditioned to proprioceptive cues (Mowrer, 1960, pp. 112-116), it is less directly related to Aronfreed's position, which stresses central cognitive factors. It is also not the case that curare experiments rule out the potential role of affect. Pavlovian conditioning is primarily a process affecting smooth muscles and glands. While proprioceptive feedback from striate muscles is eliminated by curare, emotional conditioning involving glands and smooth muscles is not, and conditioned emotional responses could become attached to centrally represented cognitive templates. The curare experiments also did not vary the affective context in which the observations occurred, a procedure essential for testing Aronfreed's formulation.

The primary contribution of affective theories appears to be that of providing supplementary considerations to other theories of imitation. Social learning theory and reinforcement theories, for example, present an impression of relatively unemotional organisms consistently behaving in a rational manner to the best of their abilities. Mowrer and Aronfreed have been impressed, as was Freud before them, with the contribution that emotional factors play in human learning and behavior. Differences among theories of imitation with respect to affect again seem to reflect the fact that their domains of inquiry do not overlap. Social learning theorists have relied almost exclusively upon laboratory investigations. Such investigations are perhaps more likely to lead to findings that logical, information-processing abilities are more important than emotional factors, while naturalistic studies might be more likely to find instances of affectively controlled imitation. In short, the potential role of affect in both acquisition and imitation deserves wider and more systematic investigation than it has received to date.

COMPETENCE THEORIES

Another variation in emphasis may be seen in the work of several theorists who have considered the role of competence motives in imitation (Bruner, 1972; Kohlberg, 1969; Zigler & Yando, 1972). Before examining each position in detail, it would be helpful to examine the general theoretical underpinnings that they all share. As Robert White has noted (1960), theoretical interest in competence can be traced to two very different sources: (a) to developments within psychoanalysis that emphasize the role of the ego (Hartmann, 1958; Hartmann, Kris, & Loewenstein, 1949; Loewenstein, Newman, Schur, & Solnit, 1966), and (b) to findings from laboratory studies with animals (Berlyne, 1960; Butler, 1958; Harlow, 1953; Montgomery, 1954; Myers & Miller, 1954), which have indicated "that animals show persistent tendencies toward activity, exploration, and manipulation even when all known primary drives have been satiated" (White, 1960, p. 101).

The ego psychoanalytic movement is interesting in the present context because it indicates a contribution of the Freudian tradition beyond that discussed earlier. A particularly important line of development in psychoanalytic theory derives from the "ego psychology" movement associated with Hartmann. Commenting upon Hartmann's contributions in her comparison of psychoanalytic and Piagetian theories of object constancy, Décarie pointed out the significance of Hartmann's addition to Freudian theory of the ego functions—for example, perceptual activity, use of memory, reality testing. As Décarie (1965) notes, "according to Hartmann, there is not, at birth, an id from which the ego gradually emerges, but an undifferentiated core from which both are progressively formed [p. 81]." Not only did Hartmann argue that adaptive behavior implies the existence of an independent ego, not derived from the id, but also, as White (1960) notes, "that the energy behind ego development is intrinsic, independent of the instincts, and that growth in this sphere yields a pleasure of its own [p. 105]."

The nature of this ego growth and its associated intrinsic pleasure has been described by White (1960) in his provocative theoretical paper as being the search for competence. The significance of exploratory, manipulatory, and curiosity behavior, White argues, is that such activities increase general effectiveness in dealing with the environment. It is of further significance that competence is acquired during times when the organism is not strongly motivated by visceral needs or engaging in activities in which errors might be dangerous. Thus, knowledge of where to find food, of escape routes, or of effective tool use is more efficiently acquired when an organism is not in a state of high primary drive; and the knowledge so obtained is more efficiently employed as a means of drive reduction or safety seeking when the need arises. An implication of this analysis is that play is a significant competence-building activity of young children, a view we discussed earlier in connection with Bruner's (1972) position.

Noting not only the developments in ego psychology but also the research findings concerning competence-related motives in animals and children, White proposed an "effectance" drive, the drive which is the special hallmark of the theories of imitation offered by Bruner, by Kohlberg, and by Yando and Zigler. White (1960) suggests:

> My proposal is that activity, manipulation, and exploration, which are all pretty much of a piece in the infant, be considered together as aspects of competence, and that for the present we assume that one general motivational principle lies behind them. The word I have suggested for this motive is *effectance* because its most characteristic feature is seen in the production of effects upon the environment. . . . The experience that goes with producing such changes I have designated as the *feeling of efficacy*. Effectance is to be conceived as a neurogenic motive, in contrast to a viscerogenic one. . . . Its adaptive significance lies in its promotion of spare-time behavior that leads to an extensive growth of competence, well beyond what could be learned in connection with drive reduction [pp. 102-103]. (©1960. Reprinted by permission of the University of Nebraska Press, Lincoln, Nebraska, and by permission of the author.)

The emphasis on effectance, it should be pointed out, does not deny the importance of other drives. Nor is it asserted by White or others that competency arises from the satisfaction of effectance motivation alone; rather, this formulation also allows for the important role of external rewards in influencing feelings of competence. White also suggests that the role of effectance may be much more clearly seen in young children than in adults, for whom the motive is complexly interrelated with many others. In general, however, White is suggesting that the role of intrinsic motivation for human behavior is often more important than other forms of motivation.

White (1960) traces the role of the effectance motive as it may be seen in each of Freud's psychosexual stages and, in another paper (1959), reviews the empirical evidence for manifestations of various aspects of effectance motivation in both animals and humans. More recently, Harter and Zigler (1974) operationalized the construct by devising tests of four aspects of effectance motivation—curiosity, variation seeking, preference for challenging tasks, and manipulative-structuring tendencies—and administering these tests to several groups of children of different ages. The results of this study confirmed the existence of developmental changes in effectance. Thus, the notion of effectance motivation has both theoretical and empirical support as a construct that may be employed in theories of imitative behavior. Examples of how it has been related to imitation are described in the following discussion of two competence-based theories of imitation. (Bruner's treatment of imitation was discussed in chapter 1).

Kohlberg

Kohlberg (1969) has argued that the primary motive for imitation is the desire to act competently. Like White and Bruner, Kohlberg argues that imitation often occurs in the context of play; unlike these other competence theorists, Kohlberg denies the necessity of any special emotional attachment between model and child. Kohlberg (1969) argues that there is "a primary motivation for competence and self-actualization which is organized through an ego or self whose structure is social or shared [p. 418]." To some extent this is true, Kohlberg argues, because the child needs a model to illustrate what a competent performance is and to provide feedback as to the competence of the child's imitation. Kohlberg also believes, however, that social awareness and empathy are typically gained through imitation and that a child learns the nature of social experiences not only by practicing what he has seen others do but also by noting his own subjective feelings while imitating and subsequently attributing the same feelings to new models who perform the same act.

Kohlberg's theory is a developmental one, and he proposes that there are periods in which children's imitativeness increases with age (3-5 years) and periods during which it declines (5-8 years). He also argues that the child's developmental level determines the effectiveness of task and situational demands in influencing imitation. In discussing the characteristics of acts that children tend to imitate, for example, Kohlberg (1969) argues:

> The one common condition of stimuli that are imitated is that they are interesting
> .... Many of the dimensions of interest or attention have been catalogued...under
> such headings as complexity, novelty, etc.... These dimensions or conditions are
> not located purely in the stimulus, however, since they also include its match to the
> child's behavior structure, as is implied by dimensions like "novelty," or by the di-
> mension of similarity of the model to the self [p. 437].

As Kohlberg notes, much of the activity imitated by very young children includes irrelevant and expressive features of the model's behavior. Kohlberg argues that unselective imitation is characteristic of children during the ages of 3 to 5 and also that during this period increasing imitation of adults occurs in conjunction with an increased belief in the general power and competence of adults. Older children begin selectively imitating skillful models rather than those who are merely powerful, and they selectively imitate only those aspects of a model's behavior that are skillful. If it is assumed that a child's ability to judge the competence of his own performance increases developmentally, then the need to imitate, and particularly the need to imitate task-irrelevent activities in order to obtain social feedback, should decrease developmentally.

It is reasonable to assume that a child who wishes to behave competently will seek to determine the appropriate behavior in ambiguous social situations; a safe judgment will often be to perform as he sees others performing, no matter how odd such behavior may seem. Reliance upon a "when in Rome, do as the Romans do" rule may therefore augment the amount of imitation seen in certain situations, particularly, Kohlberg argues, in experimental laboratory studies of imitation. If the child's own cognitive abilities are sufficient, however, to permit him to solve a task competently, he may do so independently of the model's performance. Thus Kohlberg's formulation predicts an interactive effect of cognitive-level and experimental-demand determinants of imitative behavior.

A final consideration in Kohlberg's theory is that cognitive-developmental status is assumed to be a function of mental age, rather than of chronological age. Thus, bright children should show more imitation than average or dull children at age 4 (in the midst of an age period in which imitation is developmentally increasing) but less imitation at age 6 (in the midst of a period in which imitation is developmentally decreasing. Some evidence for this assertion has been obtained by Kohlberg and Zigler (1967) in a short-term longitudinal study, but in general this assertion has received relatively little attention in the experimental literature.

Outerdirectedness Formulation

In a series of studies designed to investigate the determinants of intellectual functioning in retarded and normal children, Zigler and his associates became impressed with the interaction between imitativeness and problem-solving abilities (Achenbach & Zigler, 1968; Balla, Styfco, & Zigler, 1971; Sanders, Zigler, & Butterfield, 1968; Turnure & Zigler, 1964; Yando & Zigler, 1971; Zigler & Yando, 1972). In particular, these investigators noted that problem-solving strategies based upon observing the behavior of others often interfered with other problem-solving strategies to such an extent that children failed to solve problems that were within their actual level of competence. In some instances, the interfering observational cues consisted of modeled solutions that the children imitated even though they were incorrect and never led to reward (Balla et al., 1971; Yando & Zigler, 1971). In other instances, certain children (institutionalized children of normal intellect) avoided imitation in such a manner that they showed consistently nonimitative behavior (Yando & Zigler, 1971). These investigators described a problem-solving style, which they labeled "outerdirected," that is, "a style of problem solving characterized by reliance on concrete situational cues rather than by active attempts to deduce abstract relationships" (Zigler & Yando, 1972, p. 414). Imitation was thus seen as being one aspect of reliance upon external cues and as having motivational determinants closely related to competence and problem solving.

In studies of the outerdirected style, Zigler and his associates identified four factors as being important in determining imitative behavior. The most central of these factors is the child's level of cognitive development. As Zigler and Yando (1972) have noted, "As the child develops and becomes more cognitively proficient, successful problem solving becomes less dependent upon cues from others and more the product of the internal deduction of abstract relationships among problem elements [p. 421]." The greater the child's actual problem-solving abilities the less motivation he should have to rely upon solutions achieved by others, even if such solutions are rewarded. The outerdirectedness formulation therefore predicts that, if other factors are held constant, the higher the child's cognitive development (as assessed by his mental age) the less the child will imitate.

The nature of the task is also considered to be important. As Yando and Zigler (1971) note, "A major tenet of the outerdirectedness position is that, across all persons, outerdirectedness will increase as a task becomes more difficult and/or ambiguous [p. 286]." Even for highly competent adults, exposure to an unfamiliar situation, such as a social occasion among relative strangers, is likely to increase the tendency to imitate the behavior of surrounding persons. A third factor is the child's prior history of success or failure in the use of his own cognitive abilities. Groups of retarded children, for example, have typically experienced more failure than groups of normal children, and this reason is advanced to explain the finding that retarded individuals are generally more reliant upon external cues than are normal children of equivalent mental age (Achenbach & Zigler, 1968; Balla et al., 1971; Sanders et al., 1968; Turnure & Zigler, 1964; Yando & Zigler, 1971). Finally, the child's attitude toward the model has been found to be significant. Children whose prior experiences with adults have been characterized by many negative encounters (as is often true of institutionalized children) have sometimes been found to show what appears to be a deliberate nonimitative strategy when provided with modeled solutions. Such findings, as Zigler and Yando (1972) have noted, may be relevant to studies employing nurturant versus nonnurturant models, since evidence suggests that many institutionalized children develop an extreme wariness towards strange adults (Zigler, 1971). Such children evidently regard unfamiliar adults as nonnurturant until proven otherwise.

In summarizing the determinants isolated by the series of studies of outerdirectedness, Zigler and Yando (1972) concluded that "the amount of imitation in which a child engages is complexly determined by (a) the cognitive level of the child, (b) his attitude toward the adult who is providing cues which may be imitated, and (c) the nature of the task that confronts him [pp. 423-424];" in addition they suggest that (d) the child's history of success or failure in using his own intellectual abilities is an important factor.

CONCLUDING COMMENTS

As the overview presented in this chapter indicates, a number of different perspectives on the nature of imitation exist, and each of these perspectives provides insights too valuable to be disregarded if we wish to attain a fuller understanding of imitation. In an effort to synthesize these views, we propose a general two-factor theory in which the two factors necessary to explain imitativeness are (a) the cognitive-developmental level of the organism, and (b) the motivational system of the organism. Some of the rationale underlying the choice of these two factors was presented in chapter 1, and we will elaborate more fully upon this two-factor model in chapter 8. For the present, however, it is worth pointing out that the key contributions of each existing theory can be related to these two factors. Within the factor of cognitive-developmental level, for example, one can place the Piagetian descriptions of cognitive stages, Bruner's descriptions of coding methods, Bandura's factors of attentional, retentional, and motoric capabilities, and the general emphasis upon age differences of the outerdirectedness position and several other positions. Within the factor of motivation, psychoanalytic considerations find a ready place, as do the contributions of the social learning, reinforcement, affective, and effectance theories.

Although our emphasis is upon synthesizing from existing theories (and we believe that the two-factor approach permits such a synthesis), a complete overview of existing imitation literature demands that the controversies among the existing viewpoints be described and discussed. A good deal of imitation research has been directed specifically toward contrasting the value of the theoretical constructs and the predictive efficacy of one explanatory system with that of another; in the next chapter we provide a discussion of the main issues of disagreement among the various theories.

3
Comparisons Among Imitation Theories on Major Issues

One of the most central areas of disagreement among theories of imitation has been whether the cognitive level of the observer needs to be considered in order to adequately account for imitation. To phrase this another way, is the "match" between the observer's existing comprehension level and the activities shown by the model important for imitation? Or can the young child, for example, be taught to comprehend complex concepts usually understood only by older children simply by exposing him to an effective model? This is a complex and hotly debated issue; it is also critically relevant to the first factor in our proposed two-factor theory of imitation. We examine the evidence on this question in the first section of the present chapter.

A second issue that has evoked some debate concerns the importance of distinguishing between acquisition (recall for modeled acts) and imitation. Recall is facilitated by coding abilities (such as language): The acquisition-versus-imitation debate is therefore also related to the issue concerning the importance of the observer's cognitive level. We have placed our discussion of this debate as the second section of the present chapter.

With regard to motivational considerations, two particularly controversial issues have been (a) whether the relationship between the model and the observer is a major factor in imitation, and (b) whether extrinsic, overtly administered reinforcement (as opposed to self-, or intrinsic, reinforcement) is essential in order for imitation to occur. In the third and fourth sections of the present chapter we discuss these two issues.

Finally, we will consider one special issue, the significance of task characteristics in determining imitation. Task characteristics were emphasized in our previous outerdirectedness formulation. They are also stressed by Hartup and Coates (1970), whose review of empirical studies led them to conclude that the nature of the task was an important factor in determining whether developmental differences in imitation were found. The issue of task characteristics fits into neither the first nor the second factor of the two-factor theory; rather the effects of this variable can be predicted on the basis of both cognitive and motivational considerations. For example, a child may imitate tasks that are much too easy to satisfy motives different from those he satisfies by imitating tasks that he finds cognitively challenging. In the former case, imitation might be expected only if an external reward is involved, whereas in imitation of the challenging task intrinsic motivation would probably be involved. Since the task factor has been found to be so important in previous developmental research (Hartup & Coates, 1970; Yando & Zigler, 1971; Zigler & Yando, 1972), we included it in the developmental study to be described in chapters 5-7, and we provide a discussion of contrasting theoretical views on this issue in the final section of the present chapter.

THE PROBLEM OF MATCH BETWEEN COGNITIVE-DEVELOPMENTAL LEVEL AND IMITATION

There is no disagreement that the sophistication of the child's physical abilities sets limits on the complexity of the acts he can imitate, but the extension of this principle to include the importance of cognitive abilities is a highly contested matter. At one pole of the controversy, Piagetian theory proposes that a child's existing cognitive schemas play a determining role in the nature of the actions he is capable of imitating. Kuhn's (1973) interpretation puts it strongly: "that the individual only imitates models insofar as he has the requisite cognitive structure to comprehend them and insofar as they bear some relation to his own behavior schemes [p. 163]." At the other extreme, Bandura and others within the social learning theoretical framework have expended considerable research effort toward the goal of demonstrating that "modeling influences alter cognitive functioning of the type described by Piaget and his followers" (Bandura, 1971a, p. 37).

In addition to the infrahuman evidence cited in Chapter 1, evidence pertinent to this issue exists in four main areas: (a) studies of imitation in infancy, (b) studies of linguistic imitation, (c) moral reasoning studies, and (d) studies of children's strategies in problem-solving tasks. As we shall see, evidence for the importance of cognitive level is clearer in studies of younger children (infancy and language studies) than in studies that have concentrated on older children (moral reasoning and conceptual strategies).

Infancy

To some extent, Bandura's argument that modeling influences can "alter cognitive functioning of the type described by Piaget" and his criticisms of Piagetian theory arise from the fact that the age domains of inquiry of the Piagetian and the social-learning-theory investigations of imitation for the most part do not coincide. Bandura's research has focused most heavily upon children of nursery-school age and older. In contrast, while Piaget has extended his investigations of imitation into middle-childhood years, it is predominantly his work with infants that leads to his finely articulated theoretical statements about the interplay between cognitive level and imitation; and it is his work with infants that finds the most consistent support in the work of other investigators (Baldwin, 1906; Décarie, 1965; Guillaume, 1926/1971; Lewis, 1936; Paraskevopoulos & Hunt, 1971; Uzgiris, 1972; Uzgiris & Hunt, 1975; Valentine, 1930). Bandura's theory stresses observational learning, but, as we have argued earlier, young infants appear to lack the cognitive abilities necessary for this particular kind of delayed imitation. It seems likely that if Bandura were to examine imitation in infancy, he would modify his stated position and the apparent disagreements between theoretical positions would vanish.

We do not mean to imply that the nature of infant imitation is fully understood. The sequence of the Piagetian stages has generally been replicated by others, but the ages at which new forms of imitation have been reported to appear (e.g., imitation of novel rather than familiar events) have been variable. Paraskevopoulos and Hunt (1971), for example, have reported much later times of emergence of most forms of imitation than have Piaget (1962b), Guillaume (1926/1971), and Valentine (1930). Differences in subject populations or differences due to the special advantages that parents have in observing children may account for the reported differences in timing, since Paraskevopoulos and Hunt studied Greek infants, some of whom were raised in institutions, while Piaget, Guillaume, and Valentine studied their own children. Further research to determine the representativeness of the Piagetian sensorimotor stages for infants in general would be valuable. Despite these unresolved issues, the basic proposition—cognitive-developmental level plays a major role in determining the kind of imitation seen in infancy—seems well supported.

Language

For children past infancy, the clearest evidence for an important interplay between cognitive level and what can be imitated comes from studies of linguistic imitation. Once a child has mastered most of the grammar of his language, this complex internalized cognitive organization seems to play a major role in his ability to remember and therefore to imitate linguistic stimuli. This principle is seen very clearly in adults, for whom the rules of the native language may be presumed to be a highly overlearned system. In a classic study, for example, Marks and Miller (1964) demonstrated that adults recalled strings of words that conformed to grammatical rules far better than they could recall nongrammatical sequences. This result has been replicated not only with adults (Roberts, 1968; Scholes, 1969), but also with children (see Slobin & Welsh, 1973). The relationship between grammaticality and imitation, in fact, is so compelling that elicited imitation is widely employed as a psycholinguistic tool to determine the level of a child's linguistic development (Anastasiow & Hanes, 1974; McNeil, 1970; Menyuk, 1963a, b, 1964, 1968, 1969; Slobin, 1968, 1973; Slobin & Welsh, 1973).

It is noteworthy that the existence of an established linguistic grammar not only can facilitate the organization of information for better acquisition but also appears to interfere with the acquisition of information that does not conform to the expected rules. Marks and Miller, for example, found significantly poorer recall for nongrammatical sequences than for neutral strings of words. Similarly, school-aged children who speak standard English show poor imitation of sentences that conform to the rules of black, nonstandard English (Baratz, 1969; Hall & Freedle, 1973; Seitz, 1975). This function of grammatical organization might therefore, paradoxically, lead adults and older children to show poorer imitation of certain linguistic stimuli than do younger children. While this remains to be rigorously explored in the laboratory, anecdotal evidence attests that young children have a greater ability to learn a second language than adults, and Guillaume (1926/1971) comments in an interesting passage: "Taine [1871] demonstrates that the child reproduces 'the guttural accents of the beasts' better than does the adult. Attempting to acquire the skill of a ventriloquist, Gutzmann was surprised to note from the very first that his two-year-old son was more adept at this than he [1894] [p. 31]."

The relationship between cognitive development and linguistic imitation for the very young child during the active period of first language learning (before grammatical rules are internalized) is less well understood. It is evident that a child learns to speak the language to which he is exposed rather than some other language, and in this regard imitation must play a very significant role. But the degree to which the child learns by imitating and whether he can imitate only what he understands are matters that are only beginning to become clear.

One source of potential evidence on this issue derives from considering the frequency of spontaneous linguistic imitation at different ages. A number of investigators have reported finding an increase in spontaneous linguistic imitativeness with age until approximately 2 years (Guillaume, 1926/1971; Nelson, 1973; Piaget, 1962b; Stewart & Hamilton, 1976; Valentine, 1930). Slobin (1968), in reviewing early studies of language acquisition, noted a marked decrease in linguistic imitation from 2 through 3 years, at which time overt imitation almost vanishes, having been replaced by conversational interchanges. This finding has also been typical in more recent studies (Nelson, 1973; Reichle, Longhurst, & Stepanich, 1976; Seitz & Stewart, 1975). Such regularity in the frequency curves of spontaneous imitation with age, and other evidence, have led some investigators to suggest that the role of imitation may be greater for the acquisition of vocabulary than for the acquisition of grammatical rules (Nelson, 1973).

It is also possible that there are marked individual differences in the degree to which children employ imitation as a language learning strategy. In a recent longitudinal study of six children during the period between the emergence of single-word utterances and two-word utterances, Bloom and her colleagues (Bloom et al., 1974) made several important observations. First, it appeared that overt imitation was not essential for the acquisition of speech in all children: Two of the six children rarely imitated, yet they learned to speak as adequately as the other children. Second, those children who did imitate were "impressively consistent in the tendency to imitate across time" (Bloom et al., 1974, p. 387). (Such individual differences in imitativeness are consistent with the genetic model we suggested in chapter 1.) Finally, Bloom and her colleagues observed that there were strategical differences in the manner in which imitation seemed to be employed. Some children employed imitation in learning new syntactical constructions (e.g., "car go," an object-action construction) without showing a tendency to imitate when learning single vocabulary words, while the reverse was true for other infants. In summary, these authors concluded that "the important facts were that the children imitated neither linguistic signals that were already well-known to them nor structures that were completely absent from their own spontaneous speech (Bloom et al., 1974, p. 418)." The importance of the interplay between cognitive level and what the child can and will imitate is strongly suggested by these findings, just as it is in the findings concerning linguistic imitation among individuals who have a well-established internalized grammar.

Evidence from elicited imitation studies (in which children are asked to imitate) also suggests the importance of the child's existing cognitive level for imitation. Nelson (1973), for example, employed an ingenious procedure, which included asking children to repeat words that were incorrectly associated with pictures as well as words that were correctly associated. Nelson reported that her subjects, who were 18-21 months old, were unlikely to imitate unfamiliar words, but that "imitation occurred with high frequency whenever the child knew the word to be imitated regardless of whether it was used appropriately [p. 51]." In addition to such evidence of the importance of familiarity, Stewart and Hamilton (1976) have shown that children also differentially imitate words according to the function that the object being named serves for the child. Employing unfamiliar French words with young (14-30 month old) children from English-speaking homes, Stewart and Hamilton found that children imitated these new words most frequently when they designated edible objects, somewhat less frequently when they referred to moving objects, and still less frequently when they referred to passive objects. The results were comparable for both spontaneous and elicited imitation. These results quite clearly support Kuhn's argument for the importance of the match between modeled acts and existing cognitive schemas.

In contrast to the studies just cited, numerous studies of linguistic imitation have been conducted by social learning theorists and interpreted as providing evidence that modeling influences play a major role in language development regardless of the child's existing language proficiency (Bandura & Harris, 1966; Carroll, Rosenthal, & Brysh, 1972; Harris & Hassemer, 1972; Liebert, Odom, Hill, & Huff, 1969; Odom, Liebert, & Hill, 1968; Rosenthal & Carroll, 1972; Rosenthal & White, 1972; Rosenthal & Whitebook, 1970; Zimmerman & Pike, 1972). Such an interpretation might seem at first to require a revision of the conclusion stated earlier that the preponderance of evidence indicates a strong effect of underlying linguistic competence upon linguistic imitation. For example, Bandura (1971a) concludes not only that modeling can influence children's use of linguistic features with which they are already familiar, but also that "children can acquire through modeling an arbitrary ungrammatical rule which they use to generate peculiar sentences [p. 36]."

In the studies just cited, however, the children have been well beyond the age of initial language acquisition. Consequently, it seems likely that many of these children had substantial underlying linguistic competence and may have been merely modifying their style of linguistic output to match the model's without learning any new grammatical principles. Bandura and Harris (1966), for example, showed effects of modeling that increased the imitation of passive voice and prepositional phrase constructions among middle-class, second-grade children. Such grammatical features were probably not novel for these children, as Menyuk (1969) reported that 64% of her sample of 3- to 7-year-old, middle-class children used passive voice constructions and that the use of prepositional phrases had emerged in many cases before the age of 3 years. Menyuk also noted children's use of highly complex sentences before their entrance into school. There are studies that show modification of length or complexity of sentences (Harris & Hassemer, 1972), the use of particular tenses (Carroll, Rosenthal, & Brysh, 1972; Rosenthal & Carroll, 1972), and the use of different styles for asking questions (Zimmerman & Pike, 1972). These studies do not seem to support the broad conclusion offered in a recent review that "modeling procedures ...were found effective in teaching children drawn from diverse populations to respond according to generalized linguistic rules" (Zimmerman & Rosenthal, 1974a, p. 32). Rather, such studies seem to show that children will learn to select from their existing repertoire of linguistic abilities a style that matches a model's.

Surprisingly, the major factor of memory load seems also to have been overlooked in many of the social learning studies of modeling and language. The role of comprehension in imitation seems to depend to a considerable degree upon whether an individual's short-term memory capacity is exceeded by the message. There is evidence, for example, that with very short sequences not exceeding 8 morphemes, imitation ability surpasses comprehension in the young child (Fraser, Bellugi, & Brown, 1963; Lovell & Dixon, 1967; Nurss & Day, 1971). It is only with longer sequences that the facilitative effects of the match between underlying comprehension and successful imitation, as demonstrated by Marks and Miller, appears operative. In the study to which Bandura refers in his conclusion, sentences were never longer than eight words, with all but the final three words occurring in a grammatical sequence. The ability of children to play word games with no memory strain is not surprising. In fact, children during the elementary-school years seem to delight in such word games as pig latin; it seems that these games appear only after the child's grammatical rules are solidly in his control (Stone & Church, 1968).

While the discussion thus far reflects a contrast that has existed between the cognitive-developmental approach to language and imitation, which we have espoused, and the social learning approach, there have recently been encouraging signs of a rapprochement. In a thoughtful review of both naturalistic and laboratory studies of language learning, two social learning theorists, Whitehurst and Vasta (1975), have also advanced the hypothesis that comprehension typically precedes successful imitation. These theorists point to recent studies within the social learning framework that have provided concrete enactment, pictorial models, or training with reinforcement to aid children's comprehension with a resulting enhancement of the children's imitations (I. Brown, 1976; Leonard, 1975; Vasta, 1976; Whitehurst, Ironsmith, & Goldfein, 1974; Whitehurst & Novack, 1973).

In summary, while the role of imitation in language learning is still far from completely understood, there is nevertheless reasonably strong support from studies of linguistic imitation for the importance of the match between the child's cognitive level and what he is likely to imitate well. An important caveat is in order here. The evidence does not suggest that a child *cannot* imitate linguistic input that is not meaningful to him. Rather it suggests that he does so less successfully and less often than he imitates meaningful or partially meaningful material. Brown and Hanlon (1970) have pointed out that any frequently heard stimulus is likely to be imitated by the child:

> We suggest that any form that is produced with very high frequency by parents will be somehow represented in the child's performance even if its structure is far beyond him. He will find a way to render a version of it and will also form a notion of the circumstances in which it is used. The construction will become lodged in his speech as an unassimilated fragment. Extensive use of such an unanalyzed or mistakenly analyzed fragment probably protects it, for a time, from reanalysis when the structure relevant to it is finally learned. Such, we suspect, are the effects of frequency [p. 51]. (©1970. Reprinted by permission of John Wiley & Sons, Inc., New York, and by permission of the authors.)

As cognitive-developmental theorists, our argument is not that such unassimilated fragments do not occur, but that they represent the exception rather than the rule.

Moral Reasoning

Piaget's examinations of the growth of logical abilities (1965a, 1970) and the nature of moral reasoning (1962a) in children have led him to propose that growth in both cases follows a natural sequence that should be difficult to modify by any external means, including modeling and imitation. Many studies have tested this assumption as it applies to moral reasoning. These studies have attempted to change children's level of moral reasoning by exposing them to models whose level of response differed from the stage level that the children originally showed (Bandura & McDonald, 1963; Cowan, Langer, Heavenrich, & Nathanson, 1969; Crowley, 1968; Glassco, Milgram, & Youniss, 1970; Keasey, 1973; Kuhn, 1973; LeFurgy & Woloshin, 1969; Rest, 1973; Rothman, 1976; Schleifer & Douglas, 1973; Sternlieb & Youniss, 1975; Tracy & Cross, 1973; Turiel, 1966; Turiel & Rothman, 1972). A general consensus of these studies is that at least some modification of children's response level is possible through exposure to a model.

Even researchers sympathetic to the Piagetian position have reported some observational learning effects for moral responses. In a careful replication and extension of an earlier study by Bandura and McDonald (1963), for example, Cowan and his colleagues concluded that their findings "provide a great deal of support for Bandura and McDonald's contention that moral responses of children can be modified in either developmental direction by exposure to adult models" (Cowan et al., 1969, p. 272). They also reported, however, that the amount of change and the relative permanence of the new levels of reasoning were not equivalent across all modeling conditions. In more extensive longitudinal studies in which children have been retested after six months (Glassco et al., 1970) or one year (Sternlieb & Youniss, 1975), investigators have similarly found strong immediate effects of modeling but reported permanency of the modeling effect only if the modeling was in the upward (i.e., the normal developmental) direction.

In two studies, which controlled the degree of stage-level discrepancy between modeled responses and children's reasoning level, Kuhn (1973) and Turiel (1966) reported similar findings concerning magnitude and permanence of modeling effects as a function of the degree and direction of the discrepancy. In both studies, the greatest influence was found for modeled responses that were one stage level higher than the child's. Children continued to show imitation of such responses in delayed posttesting sessions whereas children who had been exposed to responses one level lower than their own tended not to maintain the modeling effect but rather to return to their initial level of reasoning. Such results would seem to provide evidence both for Bandura's contention that Piagetian responses can be modified by modeling and for the position that such modification is nevertheless not totally independent of the child's existing abilities. Other studies have reported greater susceptibility to modeling effects for children whose initial moral reasoning was particularly low (Keasey, 1973; Tracy & Cross, 1973), or high (Rothman, 1976; Turiel & Rothman, 1972).

As the above review suggests, the implications of the moral-reasoning studies for the cognitive-level question are ambiguous. A primary difficulty centers upon problems of measuring the level of moral reasoning. This issue is of central importance, since for a Piagetian theorist the choices made in responding to moral dilemmas are of less value in indicating the child's stage level than are the kinds of reasons the child offers in explaining his choices. Social learning experiments have typically confined themselves to a two-level analysis of children's answers, where low-level reasoning is equated with choices based on the objective consequences of wrongdoing and high-level reasoning is equated with judgments based upon the intentionality of the wrongdoer. Thus a child is defined as showing low-level reasoning if he concludes that a little boy who broke 12 glasses while helping his mother set the table is naughtier than another little boy who smashed one glass during a temper tantrum. The Piagetian analysis of children's explanations is necessarily more complex than this scheme, which leads to the likelihood, as Cowan and his colleagues (Cowan et al. 1969) have noted, that if the procedures for diagnosing stage level in their own studies and in the Bandura and McDonald studies were expanded to be fully consistent with Piaget's methodology, they would likely have produced different classifications of moral stage. A potentially more serious problem, however, is that scales for measuring moral reasoning have recently been called into question as lacking standardization, reliability, and possibly validity (Kurtines & Greif, 1974). The fact that moral reasoning studies have been a popular choice of theorists seeking to pit Piagetian formulations against social learning theory formulations does not guarantee that the results of these studies can be employed in this manner. Until clearcut stages can be reliably shown to exist and to be measurable in the same way by different experimenters, the area of moral reasoning seems to provide a very questionable area for a confrontation between theories.

Conceptual Strategies

Another area in which effects of a child's cognitive level upon the nature of his imitation have been examined is in conceptual strategies. Examples of this approach are experiments that attempt to use modeling to teach nonconserving children to conserve (Botvin & Murray, 1975; Charbonneau, Robert, Bourassa, & Gladu-Bissonnette, 1976; Murray, 1974; Rosenthal & Zimmerman, 1972; Samuels, 1976; Sullivan, 1967, 1969; Waghorn & Sullivan, 1970; Zimmerman & Lanaro, 1974; Zimmerman & Rosenthal, 1974b); to teach preadolescents to show formal operations (Kamii & Derman, 1971; Kuhn & Angelev, 1976; Siegler, Liebert, & Liebert, 1973); to modify children's strategies for grouping objects (Kuhn, 1972; Zimmerman, 1974); and to modify children's efficiency in the use of a questioning procedure to solve problems (Denney, 1972; Lamal, 1971; Laughlin, Moss, & Miller, 1969). The conservation, formal operations, and grouping strategy experiments are directly related to the Piagetian descriptions of the development of logical operations in the child (Inhelder & Piaget, 1964; Piaget, 1965a, 1970). The experiments on children's styles of asking questions in solving problems are based upon testing a developmental sequence proposed by Bruner, Olver, and Greenfield (1966). (Their similarity to experiments concerned with Piagetian stages warrants their inclusion here.)

As with the moral reasoning experiments, the results of such studies show the success of modeling in altering the stage-level responses of at least some children; however, the results also suggest that the initial cognitive level of the child is a factor influencing the extent of the modeling influence. The clearest conclusions can be drawn from the conservation experiments. A common procedure in conservation experiments has been to study nonconserving children only, exposing them to various modeling procedures, which sometimes include verbalizations of conservation reasoning and sometimes do not. Almost all of the conservation studies have resulted in influencing at least some children to show conservation following exposure to a model. Several of the investigators have reported individual differences in their samples, however, with some children showing less imitation than others (Charbonneau et al., 1976; Murray, 1974; Samuels, 1976; Waghorn & Sullivan, 1970). Waghorn and Sullivan, for example, found that the brightest and oldest children in their sample of nonconservers were most responsive to modeling effects. Several investigators have also reported that the conservation explanations given by originally nonconserving children who had been exposed to a conserving model appeared somewhat odd and lacking in conviction (Botwin & Murray, 1975; Murray, 1974). Perhaps most importantly, studies that have examined effects of models on both conserving and nonconserving children have shown that while conserving children may show an immediate susceptibility to modeling effects (Rosenthal & Zimmerman, 1972) they are unlikely to show lasting influences of modeling in the "downward" (nonconserving) direction (Murray, 1974; Samuels, 1976).

There have been only a few studies involving attempts to modify children's grouping strategies and attempts to influence preadolescents to show formal operations. These studies have thus far produced contradictory results and no firm conclusion can yet be drawn. In some of these experiments and in several experiments involving children's efficiency in asking questions, the initial cognitive level of the children has not been assessed; rather the children's ages have been taken as rough indicators of probable stage levels (Denney, 1974; Lamal, 1971; Laughlin et al., 1969; Siegler et al., 1973). The possibility that children were not at the assumed stage level and that some children were in a transitional state between stages thus exists for such studies.

The finding that Piagetian conservation responses and grouping strategies can be raised for some children through exposure to a model is consistent with results from studies that have employed other forms of influence. Alterations in conservation responses have been achieved, for example, by training procedures involving discrimination learning and feedback to the child (Brainerd, 1974; Gelman, 1969; Wilton & Boersma, 1974) or participation in discussion groups with peers (Murray, 1972; Silverman & Geiringer, 1973; Silverman & Stone, 1972). However, the fact that a child's response on a Piagetian task can be modified by training procedures or by modeling raises some fundamental questions concerning the significance of such findings for cognitive development. Since conservation, for example, is characteristic of 7-year-olds but not 4-year-olds, one must wonder whether the unstated rationale for an experiment that results in a 4-year-old's demonstrating conservation is to demonstrate that cognitive development can be greatly accelerated by the appropriate uses of principles of learning theory. Alternatively, perhaps, the expectation is that Piaget's theory is fundamentally incorrect and that either there are no important necessary differences between the reasoning processes of 4- and 7-year-olds, or the differences are not as Piaget has described them. Perhaps a clue as to rationale is contained in the conclusion of a recent study by a social learning theorist that the "inability to reverse conceptual sets by 4-year-olds was not a product of the child's physiological or neurological level of development but instead was ameliorable by [modeling influences]" (Zimmerman, 1974, p. 1040). While it surely cannot be the intent of social learning theorists to imply that virtually anything can be taught to anyone through modeling, there is nevertheless the unmistakable vestige of a miniature adult position with regard to the cognitive status of children in the above quote. One cannot help but wonder whether such a conception is an implicit assumption in much of the social learning research.

One also gains the impression that the Piagetians and the social learning theorists may be working with such fundamentally different purposes that criticisms directed against one theoretical position by proponents of the other are unlikely to result in any significant changes in the position being criticized. To any challenge that the younger child can be taught to respond in the manner of an older child, the Piagetian is likely to find refuge—and perhaps deservedly so—in the response that only a superficial change has been achieved. As Piaget (1970) has commented in contrasting normal processes of development (child controlled) with induced processes (experimenter controlled):

> In order to learn how to construct and master a logical structure, the subject must start from another, more elementary logical structure which he will differentiate and complete. In other words, learning is no more than a sector of cognitive development which is facilitated or accelerated by experience. By contrast, learning under external reinforcement (e.g. permitting the subject to observe the results of the deduction he should have made or informing him verbally) produces either very little change in logical thinking or *a striking momentary change with no real comprehension* [p. 714, emphasis added].

Elsewhere, Inhelder and Sinclair (1969) have phrased the matter succinctly: "When a child does not know a fact, you tell him; when he does not understand a concept, you explain [p. 15]."

Thus, although numerous studies of the effects of modeling upon children's levels of conceptual reasoning have been conducted, such studies have been, and are likely to continue to be, inconclusive, since their results are easily accepted by theorists of opposing persuasions. A study by Kamii and Derman (1971), which describes an attempt to teach young children formal operations, provides an excellent example. The results of this study might well satisfy proponents of either the social learning or the Piagetian positions; The children appeared to learn successfully the verbal rules that they were taught, but when they were questioned about their understanding of the underlying concepts, they seemed insecure and showed vacillations in their responses. Evidence of real and permanent comprehension is clearly difficult to define to everyone's satisfaction, and disagreements as to whether changes achieved through modeling are superficial or deep are probably not going to be easily resolved. Because of the findings discussed in the present section, however, it seems appropriate to agree with Charbonneau and his colleagues that "Piagetian scholars may need to increase the potency they assign to current environmental events in their explanatory accounts" (Charbonneau et al., 1976, p. 216).

For the purposes of weighing the evidence on the main issue we have been examining—the importance of cognitive-developmental level for imitating—we would judge the evidence from infrahuman, infant, and linguistic imitation studies to be far more compelling than the evidence from the moral reasoning and conceptual strategy studies. As we suggested in Chapter 1, it may be that no major changes occur in the basic cognitive abilities that underlie imitation once the child has gained the ability to code information symbolically in language. This issue, of course, is still an open, empirical one.

THE ACQUISITION-IMITATION DISTINCTION

Theories of imitation differ considerably with respect to their position on the necessity of distinguishing between acquisition and imitation. Bandura considers such a distinction a critical one, whereas other theorists argue that the use of two separate constructs is unnecessary (Gewirtz & Stingle, 1968; Kuhn, 1973). According to Bandura, the distinction is important because quite different sets of variables influence acquisition and imitation. Specifically, "the acquisition of imitative responses. . .appears to be accounted for more adequately by a contiguity theory of observational learning" (Bandura, 1971a, p. 114), while the performance of these responses (imitation) is more directly under the control of reinforcement contingencies.

Interestingly, theorists who are poles apart with regard to their belief in the importance of cognitive mediational considerations in interpreting behavior object to this distinction. One source of reluctance to accept the distinction appears to reside in an emphasis upon motoric responses and a corresponding exclusion of visual imagery or symbolic coding as being important in learning. Gewirtz and Stingle argue that acquisition is an unobservable construct extraneous to a theory of imitation, which can more adequately be based upon laws of reinforcement. In contrast, speaking for the Piagetian position, Kuhn (1973) argues that acquisition is merely the interiorization of imitation and that both are part of the process of accommodation: "All symbolic representation, in fact, in Piaget's view, has its basis in the interiorization of sensorimotor imitation. The imitative act is functionally the same. . .whether it occurs in an overt form, or an interiorized, representative form [p. 162]." As Piaget (1965b) himself has explained his position, "a close connection seems to exist between the formation of the image and imitation. Thus the image contains an element of active reproduction which makes it into an internalized imitation [p. xiv]."

Without denying the validity of the Piagetian argument, the present authors take the position that the distinction is a useful one for several reasons. While empirical studies rarely report the correlation between measures of imitation and measures of acquisition (which are necessarily measures of recall), it is likely that this value is usually considerably less than the perfect +1 that would justify collapsing the two constructs on empirical grounds. This correlation can, of course, be manipulated. That is, one should not expect to find it existing as a fixed value in nature. If, for example, one were to make observational conditions obscure, as in employing dim lighting, the correlation between acquisition and imitation could be expected to increase. Under most circumstances, however, the correlation is probably positive but not large in magnitude, and there is empirical reason to treat the constructs as separate ones.

There are historical reasons to maintain the distinction as well. The separation of performance upon request from spontaneous performance has a long history in learning theory. Tolman's distinction between learning and performance was clearly a forerunner of the present-day acquisition-imitation distinction (Tolman, 1948, 1949). Tolman not only insisted that learning be distinguished from overt performance—even for rats—but also proposed that learners form "cognitive maps" and that learning perceptually (sign learning) is different from learning motorically (place learning). Guthrie's contiguity learning theory (Guthrie, 1952, 1959) is a predecessor of the social-learning-theory contention that learning may occur purely through the close association of sensory events in time. In an important theoretical advancement of Guthrie's position (a motoric learning theory), Sheffield (1961) argued that observation of events gave rise to perceptual responses that could be conditioned as readily as motoric responses. Through observation, Sheffield argued, the individual could learn the serial association of events, acquiring a representative sequence without ever performing an overt act. In cases where serial order was not important, Sheffield suggested that observers could also form what he termed "perceptual blueprints," which they could later employ in creating external events that provided a match to the blueprint. As Sheffield suggested, such perceptual blueprints were closely related to Tolman's "cognitive maps" (and, perhaps, also to Aronfreed's (1969) more recent "cognitive templates," although the latter are also presumed to have conditioned affective components). An extreme form of such blueprints would be eidetic imagery. As Bandura notes, his own formulation differs from Sheffield's essentially only in the more explicit role it assigns to symbolic (verbal) coding processes, and in the more active role it assigns to observers in discriminatively attending to and coding the events that are most likely to lead to later reinforcement.

The role of motivation in acquisition, and the question of whether the observer is passive or active, has been a controversial matter. Again it is informative to consider the history behind this issue. Tolman presumed that motivation played a role in both learning and performance, but that its role in performance was more direct and important. Motivation, he believed, affected learning only insofar as it guided the learner's selective attention during exposure to the learning situation. In Sheffield's formulation, the observer was not active during acquisition. As Sheffield (1961) noted, much of his theory was "concerned with perceptual behavior and the mediation of overt performance by perceptual responses learned during 'passive' exposure to demonstration materials" (p. 14). Bandura's position has some similarities to both Tolman's and Sheffield's. It is somewhat difficult to determine how active or passive the observer is postulated to be in Bandura's formulation, but on balance the emphasis seems to be on a relatively passive, externally controlled observer. Bandura (1971a) mentions "motivational variables, prior training in discriminative observation, and the anticipation of positive or negative reinforcements contingent on the emission of matching responses [p. 123]" as being important in channeling observing responses. Still, a careful reading of Bandura's description of such factors seems to place the control of attention upon past learning and reinforcement histories rather than indicating signs of active processing by an intrinsically motivated observer.

Liebert and his colleagues are theorists within the social learning framework who offer a somewhat more active interpretation of acquisition. Liebert and Swenson (1971b) have asserted, for example, that "although imitative recall has often been cast as a special case of associative learning...a more advanced and efficient form of learning may occur when the model's responses follow a common dimension or identifiable rule [p. 500]." Under these circumstances, it is asserted, the observer actively abstracts the identifiable rule and may learn more than is observed in the sense that the observer can subsequently predict what the model would have chosen in situations not actually observed. Liebert and his colleagues have also argued that vicarious consequences (reward or punishment administered to the model) can affect acquisition. This position is thus contrary to Bandura's (1971a) suggestion "that the *acquisition* of matching responses may take place through contiguity, whereas reinforcements administered to a model exert their major influence on the *performance* of imitatively learned responses [p. 114, italics in original]."

Liebert and his associates (Allen & Liebert, 1969; Liebert & Fernandez, 1970; Liebert & Swenson, 1971a, 1971b) have proposed what they term an "informational analysis" approach for explaining the effects of vicarious consequences upon acquisition. In this approach, the observer is assumed to be taking an active role while observing the model's behavior and its consequences and using the information provided by the consequences to determine the appropriate behavior he should show. The informational analysis approach has drawn criticism (Peed and Forehand, 1973), however, for technical problems in experiments designed to test it; and the resolution of the empirical question regarding whether vicarious consequences do, in fact, affect acquisition has not yet been achieved.

As Zigler and Child (1973) have noted, the question of whether the child is to be considered an active explorer of his environment or a passive recipient of environmental input is a very basic one for theories of socialization. We believe it is equally basic for theories of imitation. In view of the substantial recent evidence indicating the competent and active nature of even the very young child (see Zigler & Child, 1973, for a review of this evidence), we would argue against any theoretical formulation that postulates a passive observer. A belief in the importance of intrinsic motivation, such as effectance motivation, generates the expectation that acquisition will be strongly affected by motivation and that observers will selectively acquire only certain portions of what they observe. This argument does not deny that stimulus characteristics, such as intensity or frequency, have a general effect for most observers. It does postulate, however, that for more stimulus input observers exercise a considerable degree of idiosyncratic selectivity in acquisition, depending upon their own level of competence, their interest in the activity, and their assessment of its potential for representing problem-solving competence superior to their presently existing capabilities (Yando & Zigler, 1971; Zigler & Yando, 1972). As we have argued earlier, the role of intrinsic motivation in acquisition may also vary developmentally. Thus, instructions and task characteristics related to the demandingness and challenge inherent in the tasks may play a different role at different ages in determining how much children acquire while observing models.

In addition to these considerations, we would finally point out that there is value in recognizing that overt imitation sometimes reflects the existence of an underlying covert representation within the imitator and sometimes does not. While we agree with Bandura that acquisition should be distinguished from imitation, we do not agree that all manifestations of overt imitation must necessarily be preceded by internal coding or representation. Since the ability to form a code, and the kind of code that is formed, are related to cognitive abilities, the concept of acquisition readily finds a place in a developmental theory of imitation. The empirical questions of how extensively young children—particularly those between approximately 1 and 4 years of age—use such mediational techniques and whether their mediations are predominantly in the form of visual imagery or verbal coding are questions richly deserving of future study.

THE SIGNIFICANCE OF THE MODEL-OBSERVER RELATIONSHIP

An historical basis for this issue can be found in the Freudian concept of identification, which suggests that there exists a particularly intense form of imitation based upon significant persons in the young child's life. The question of whether a distinction between identification and other forms of imitation is a useful one is presently an unresolved issue among theorists. Some argue, for example, that *identification* should be used to refer to broad-scale imitation of many of the model's actions or attitudes, while the term *imitation* should be limited to more isolated, discrete cases of matching behavior (Kohlberg, 1963; Parsons, 1955). The distinction has also been made on the basis of underlying motives: It has been argued that the wish to be similar to a model is necessary for identification (Kagan, 1958; Kohlberg, 1963; Mowrer, 1950; Parsons, 1955; Sears, 1957), while extrinsic reinforcement is sufficient to control imitation.

In response to the multiplicity of usage, one reviewer suggested 20 years ago that "a term that can be employed in so many different ways. . .could hardly mean anything very precise. It might be proposed, quite seriously, that we give up the term 'identification' altogether" (Sanford, 1955, p. 107). This sentiment is echoed more recently by Bandura (1969c), who has also noted the methodological inadequacies in much of the identification research. Ratings of parent-child similarity, for example, have been widely employed, although they are subject to known response biases and may lack validity as descriptions of actual behavior. Characteristics that should be found in a child who is strongly identified with the parent, such as guilt following transgression of moral rules and strong sex role preferences, are often uncorrelated. Bandura also points out that the actual parental behavior in child rearing is often not directly assessed but rather is inferred from questionnaires or retrospective ratings.

While the concept of identification unquestionably lacks precision, there is nevertheless a residual core of meaning common to virtually all uses of the term, that is, the notion that the nature of the emotional relationship between the model and the observer is a significant factor for imitative behavior. The Freudian analysis and its derivatives also give emphasis to the role of irrational and primitive qualities in early human learning. The wish to reduce castration anxiety, for example, is an emotion-laden motive that would not meet the logical tests an adult would apply in judging its reasonableness. Developmental considerations are also an important contribution of the Freudian approach, since the nature of the forces that lead a child to imitate are not the same at different ages. The present writers therefore concur with Bronfenbrenner's (1960) argument that certain aspects of the concept of identification are too important to permit its total renunciation:

Admittedly, one could speak of the child's learning of parental behavior, motives, or standards without invoking the term identification . . . . It would also be possible to examine the effects of parental aggression, withdrawal of love, or direct punishment and reward on the child's learning of parental characteristics. What would be lost by a recasting of the problem in such more specific terms?

In this author's view, we would risk losing sight of an important psychological phenomenon, as well as an intriguing theoretical issue. . . In concerning himself with identification, Freud was not asking why and how a child might learn an isolated piece of behavior from his parent. He was interested in what he felt to be a more sweeping and powerful phenomenon—the tendency of the child to take on not merely discrete elements of the parental model but a total pattern. Moreover, as Freud saw it, this acquisition was accomplished with an emotional intensity which reflected the operation of motivational forces of considerable power [p. 27].

We do not take the position that additional effort should be expended in attempting to define the concept of identification to everyone's satisfaction. In our view, the most important influence of the Freudian point of view for the study of imitation would be to refocus attention upon the significance of the model-observer relationship. The major implications—that the imitation of parents may be qualitatively different from the imitation of other persons, that the emotional intensity of the relationship between observer and model is of great importance for imitative behavior, and that the force of this factor may vary developmentally—are valuable hypotheses that deserve a careful test. To date, these hypotheses have simply not received an adequate test. The present authors cannot concur with Bandura's (1969c) conclusion that "there is every indication that essentially the same learning process is involved regardless of. . .the models from whom the response patterns are acquired [p. 219]." Such a conclusion seems particularly premature since there have been so few studies of very young children. Tests of whether identification with parents represents a particularly intense category of imitative behavior should of course meet the standards that Bandura points out, namely, evidence concerning actual parental nurturance and dominance, observations of actual imitation of the parent, and direct measurement of parent-child similarities. Interestingly, where parents have actually been used as models in imitation experiments, there has been some evidence for identification with the aggressor (Hetherington & Frankie, 1967) and for the persistence of parental influence regardless of peer-group shaping (Hetherington, 1965). While such results are not definitive, they do suggest the potential value of research that employs parents as models.

With models other than parents, much research has been directed at the question of whether model characteristics such as nurturance enhance imitation. A number of studies have shown that children's imitation is sensitive to the factor of the model's nurturance or nonnurturance (Bandura, Grusec, & Menlove, 1967; Bandura & Huston, 1961; Hartup & Coates, 1967; Hetherington & Frankie, 1967; Jeffrey, Hartmann, & Gelfand, 1972; Joslin, Coates, & McKown, 1973; Mischel & Grusec, 1966; Mussen & Distler, 1959; Mussen & Parker, 1965; Paskal, 1969; Patterson, Littman, & Brown, 1968; Portuges & Feshbach, 1972; Rosenblith, 1959, 1961; Sgan, 1967; Stein & Wright, 1964; Yussen & Levy, 1975). Although the direction of the influence has not always been consistent, in general there has been greater imitation of nurturant models than of nonnurturant ones (notable exceptions are Aronfreed, 1964; Aronfreed, Cutlick, & Fagan, 1963; Rosenhan & White, 1967). As Yarrow and Scott (1972) have observed, this is a complex problem since model nurturance appears to interact with a number of other variables; we would suggest, in agreement with Aronfreed (1969), that developmental level is probably one of the most important factors interacting with the nurturance factor. In addition to the possible enhancement effect of nurturance, some studies have reported that nonnurturance can result in children's showing active avoidance of imitation (Jeffrey et al., 1972; Patterson et al., 1968; Yando & Zigler, 1971). Such findings suggest the need for a much more extensive exploration of the significance of the model-observer relationship for imitative behavior.

THE ROLE OF REINFORCEMENT IN IMITATION

Theories of imitation differ considerably in the role that they assign to reinforcement. For operant conditioning theorists (Baer et al., 1967; Baer & Sherman, 1964; Brigham & Sherman, 1968; Garcia et al., 1971; Gewirtz & Stingle, 1968; Lovaas et al., 1966; Lovaas et al., 1967; Metz, 1965; Miller & Dollard, 1941; Parton, 1970; Peterson et al., 1971; Peterson & Whitehurst, 1971; Rosenbaum & Arenson, 1968; Sears, 1957; Skinner, 1953, 1957; Staats, 1968; Steinman, 1970a, 1970b; Vasta, 1976), external reinforcement for imitation is considered an essential feature, which must occur at some point in the process of imitation. These theorists do suggest that once imitative habits are established, they can be maintained in the absence of overt reinforcement. Gewirtz and Stingle, for example, argue that imitation of nonreinforced acts occurs through the subject's failure to discriminate such acts from those that lead to reward. Baer and his colleagues suggest that similarity to a model becomes a distinctive stimulus signaling probable reinforcement, that is, that the condition of similarity itself acquires a secondary reinforcement power. In either case, the individual's motivation for imitation is assumed to be related to obtaining external reinforcement. Since these theorists also place emphasis on the physical acting out of an imitative response, the role of reinforcement is seen as the strengthening of a stimulus-response connection.

Bandura's theory makes a sharp distinction between the role of external reinforcement in imitation and its role in observational learning. While essentially agreeing with the reinforcement theorists that overt imitation is controlled by its consequences, Bandura assumes that the role of external reinforcement in acquisition is limited to directing attention to features of the display that are most likely to be rewarded. All features of the display that are attended to, however, are likely to be acquired, and reinforcement is not essential during this process. As previously noted, by introducing perceptual learning into his formulation, Bandura is dealing with a different class of events from motoric performance, and it is not surprising that he should argue that reinforcement plays a different role for these different classes of events. Such a distinction between observational and motoric learning would not be in accord with strict reinforcement theory. Bandura's treatment of reinforcement itself is also considerably different from that of the reinforcement theorists and has provoked criticism from them (Gewirtz, 1971a). As noted previously, in addition to overt reinforcement, Bandura recognizes two other classes of reinforcing events: vicarious reinforcement (given to a model) and self-reinforcement. Self-reinforcement is a complex construct that is difficult to define and verges upon what some theorists would consider intrinsic competence reinforcement. Thus, it is not a simple matter to place Bandura's theory on some continuum concerning the issue of whether external reinforcement is essential for imitation.

Mowrer and Aronfreed differ from other theorists in the role they assign to conditioned affectivity as a form of reinforcement. Mowrer places major emphasis on this factor and has argued that imitation occurs because it results in attaining conditioned emotional states. Aronfreed, like Bandura, evidently assigns external reinforcement a greater role in imitation than in acquisition. If affective changes occur in an observer during observation, however, they are assumed to become part of the "cognitive template" of the event.

The greatest contrast with the position of reinforcement theorists is to be found among competence theorists, who argue that a significant portion of imitation is intrinsically motivated. While not denying that external reward can be a major determinant of imitation, these theorists argue that it is a serious error to attempt to force-fit all examples of imitation into an external-reinforcement-theory explanation, as if external reinforcement were somehow a more basic, scientific explanatory principle than intrinsic motives such as competence. The particular problems of dealing with imitation encountered in the play activities of highly evolved organisms are stressed by these theorists, who believe that the role of reinforcement is more important for some organisms than for others and for some kinds of activities than for others.

It is the present authors' belief that for complex organisms reinforcement is a complex matter. Not only are there external and intrinsic motivational factors for humans, but also their relative importance appears to vary developmentally and to be sensitive to variations in child-rearing practices and life experiences. Havighurst (1970), for example, charted developmental changes in the classes of reinforcers that have been found to be effective with children and noted that there is usually an increase with age in children's preference for more abstract reinforcement, indicating correctness of performance, than for tangible, external reinforcers. In examining the nature of effectance motivation, Zigler (1971) has observed that the biological significance of effectance motivation places it within the category of "life-fulfilling" rather than "life-preserving" needs and that the strength of the motive should therefore be expected to be relatively vulnerable to modification through experience. Zigler presents considerable evidence to suggest that in individuals who have suffered particularly debilitating life experiences, effectance motivation can become subordinated to the need for security, avoidance of strange adults, avoidance of failure, and other such defensive motives. Those who study severely retarded, schizophrenic, or institutionalized children, thus, may find effectance motivation to be a poor explanation for a child's behavior; in contrast, there is evidence that for normal, healthy higher primates engaged in play activity, effectance motivation is a major factor and external reinforcement is a relatively unimportant consideration.

Even where external reinforcers are present, their significance often becomes submerged in favor of satisfactions that are apparently intrinsic to the performance of the acts themselves. As Bruner (1972) has noted, "The play aspect of tool use (and indeed, complex problem solving in general) is underlined by the animal's loss of interest in the goal of the act being performed and by its preoccupation with means–also a characteristic of human children [p. 695]." As examples, Bruner cites Rumbaugh's account (1970) of a chimpanzee who did not consume the banana slices offered to her–one per trial–as reinforcement for solving a problem but instead saved them and returned them to the experimenter on the next part of the experiment, thus reinforcing the experimenter (who therefore continued to experiment). Similar accounts have been given of porpoises who returned fish to their trainers while continuing to perform complex acts (McIntyre, 1975). Bruner emphasizes such factors as a "push to variation" in manipulatory activities as being more important than external reward in cases like these.

There is surprisingly little direct experimental evidence concerning the importance of reinforcement for imitation in the normal preschool child in the age span from birth to 4 years. Where such studies of young children have been conducted, they have yielded provocative results. A recent study by Waxler and Yarrow (1975), for example, examined imitative behavior of 19-month-old infants in a laboratory setting, using the children's mothers as models. The results of this study suggest the existence of considerable variability in children of this age in the importance of reinforcement. Approximately one-third of the children seemed to show the kind of straightforward susceptibility to reinforcement that a reinforcement theorist would expect, increasing their imitation when they were reinforced for imitating. However, a sizeable minority of the children (one-sixth) were never reinforced for imitating, yet showed imitative behavior similar to that of the reinforced children. Many of the remaining children showed bursts of imitative behavior with an interesting reciprocity effect. That is, these infants had mothers who appeared to find it reinforcing to be imitated and who thus participated in a reciprocally reinforcing interaction pattern with their infant. The facts concerning the actual incidence and importance of reinforcement for imitation during development are thus not yet established, and additional evidence, preferably from longitudinal studies, would be of great value in clarifying this issue.

The present authors believe that a synthesis could be achieved across theories by adopting a position that would explicitly take into account both organismic and task factors in specifying the nature of reinforcement that is important in imitation. Since the phylogenetic status of the organism is indisputably important, the role of extrinsic reinforcement could be predicted to be greater in general for rats than for chimpanzees and, in turn, greater for chimpanzees than for humans. Developmental status seems to be important for humans: The mental age of a child would be predicted to be inversely related to the importance of extrinsic reinforcement for imitation. The distinction between motoric, perceptual, and verbal-symbolic-based forms of imitation also seems to be important, and the importance of extrinsic factors versus intrinsic factors would be predicted to vary across these different classes of events.

THE SIGNIFICANCE OF TASK CHARACTERISTICS

Virtually all theories agree that imitation plays an important role in successful problem solving. However, imitation of unusual acts or of task-irrelevant activities that have no obvious problem-solving value remains somewhat of a mystery. Theorists differ in whether they recognize this as an issue and in whether they believe that task-irrelevant imitation may be governed by somewhat different rules than imitation of task-relevant acts.

Among the theorists discussed in this overview, Aronfreed makes the strongest argument for the necessity of such a distinction, particularly for very young children. He suggests that the child's representations of the model's expressive behavior and of the model's instrumental behavior are not only separate but may also be in competition with each other. One basis for the difference, Aronfreed (1969) believes, lies in information load: "a child's cognitive representation [of expressive behavior] may require less information-processing capacity. . .than does its representation of discriminative contingencies among cues, acts, and environmental outcomes [p. 256] ." Since younger children cannot direct the sustained attention that older children can towards learning which criteria and acts are important, they may settle for the amount of learning represented in the expressive acts alone.

Aronfreed also suggests that expressive acts are by their very nature a means of conveying affect. In contrast, instrumental behavior must acquire its effective components as a result of leading to desirable external outcomes. For this reason, sensitivity to expressive cues should be highest in young children, who are more responsive to immediate outcomes than to delayed ones. As children gain proficiency in using symbolic representation, Aronfreed (1969) argues, their behavior "comes increasingly under the affective control of their capacity for symbolic and abstract representation of cues and outcomes [p. 259] " rather than being dependent upon the directly expressed affectivity of expressive cues. Aronfreed concludes that "the common impression that younger children imitate more readily than older children may well be attributable to a developmental decline in children's orientation toward the expressive aspects of other people's behavior [p. 259] ."

Social learning theorists can be presumed to consider any formal distinction between task-relevant and task-irrelevant imitation to be unnecessary. Bandura's position, for example, is that observers learn selectively to attend to actions that are most likely to result in reinforcement for imitation. According to this view, it would not be necessary to postulate different processes affecting relevant and irrelevant imitation. Rather, irrelevant imitation would be presumed to drop out as the observer's ability to discriminate unreinforced acts became more accurate. Learning thus should progress towards ever-more-effective, task-relevant acquisition and imitation. Social learning theorists could also be expected to argue that a salient feature of expressive acts, as Aronfreed has described them, is their physical distinctiveness and the speed with which they are performed. Such actions might therefore fit Walters and Brown's (1964) argument that high-intensity acts are more likely to be noticed simply by virtue of their vigor, a position that found some support in studies of children's imitation (Parton & Geshuri, 1971).

We would argue that the distinction is a useful one, provided that task-irrelevant activity is treated as a more general category, including not only activities that are expressive of emotions but also activities that are simply unrelated to the central task. That is, Aronfreed's distinction appears too restrictive, and, in our opinion, task-irrelevant activities need not be "expressive" ones. While actions such as a model's saying loudly "Sock him in the nose" or "Kick him" while attacking a Bobo doll (Bandura, Ross, & Ross, 1963b) seem to express affectivity, not all critics would be convinced that "a sharp flaring motion of [the] hand" (Aronfreed, 1969, p. 298) does so.

The distinction is useful on empirical grounds. In their review of developmental studies of imitation, Hartup and Coates (1970) reported that the task relevance or irrelevance of modeled acts was a major factor in determining the existence of developmental trends in imitation. The literature on incidental learning also suggests that incidental learning and intentional learning may be independent processes in children (Druker & Hagen, 1969; Hagen, 1967; Hagen & Sabo, 1967; Hetherington & Banta, 1962; Maccoby & Hagen, 1965; Siegel, 1968; Stevenson, 1972). Studies have generally provided evidence for a curvilinear age trend in incidental learning, with an increase until about 11 or 12 years of age and a decrease thereafter (Crane & Ross, 1967; Druker & Hagen, 1969; Hagen, 1967, 1972; Hagen & Sabo, 1967; Hale, Miller, & Stevenson, 1968; Hale & Piper, 1973; Maccoby & Hagen, 1965; Siegel & Stevenson, 1966).

Stevenson (1972) suggests two separate processes that may produce this curvilinearity. First, the increase in incidental learning from preschool years through 11 or 12 years may reflect an increased use of a strategy of examining all parts of a stimulus before responding to it. Part of this strategy may arise from children's increasing ability to ignore distracting external stimuli, such as noises, and to focus their attention on the stimulus at hand, an ability that shows a major improvement between 5 and 7 years of age (Turnure, 1970). Evidence for this argument also comes from investigators who have photographed children's eye movements during learning tasks (Mackworth & Bruner, 1970; Vurpillot, 1968). Vurpillot, for example, found that children younger than 6 consistently examined only part of the stimuli in a learning problem before making judgments about the stimuli. Older children increasingly showed systematic scanning of all features of the stimulus pictures before making judgments. The developmental increase in incidental learning may therefore occur because children are learning more about both the relevant and irrelevant features of stimuli. The decline in incidental learning sets in, Stevenson suggests, as a function of a second process, the ability to judge what is central and what is not and to direct attention selectively in accordance with this judgment.

In addition to cognitive factors influencing whether the child distinguishes relevant from incidental features of a task, motivational factors and personality characteristics of the subjects appear to be important. Nurturance of the model, for example, has been found particularly to facilitate imitation of irrelevant acts and verbalizations (Bandura & Huston, 1961; Chartier & Ainley, 1974; Hartup & Coates, 1967; Mussen & Parker, 1965), and there is also evidence of greater imitation of irrelevant activities by highly dependent preschool children as compared to independent preschool children (Ross, 1966). Stevenson (1972) has suggested:

> The acquisition of the incidental features of the behavior of other persons is influenced by the type of relation that exists between the model and the subjects. . . . Also, if the child generally is dependent upon others for guidance and support, he will be likely to imitate a model's behavior in a broad manner and will fail to attend selectively to those aspects of the model's behavior that are central to the task in which he is participating [p. 221].

The possibility also exists that irrelevant imitation may not be subordinated to relevant imitation but, instead, may continue as a separate form of imitative behavior into adulthood and old age. This possibility deserves exploration. Task-irrelevant imitation may be indicative of a cognitively immature or deficient organism, but it may also characterize normal adults under conditions of reassurance that play activity is permissible or under circumstances involving strong emotional attachments or desires. Imitation of popular entertainers by adolescents is a well-known phenomenon, and, with adequate study, similar examples might be found among adults. Further examination of the interaction between age of subjects, dependency, model nurturance, and relevant versus irrelevant imitation would clearly be informative.

CONCLUDING COMMENTS

In conclusion, it seems evident that a number of debates among imitation theorists can profitably be resolved by adopting the developmental perspective and two-factor theory we suggested in Chapter 2. Much evidence, particularly from linguistic studies and studies of infant imitation, indicates that the developmental status of the child plays an important role in determining the kinds of imitation of which the child is capable. A developmental perspective also requires that we seriously reconsider the Freudian insights concerning the special significance of particular models in the child's development. More research should be directed toward examining the general significance of emotional relationships between models and children in determining imitation and how the importance of this factor changes developmentally. As we have also discussed, task demands and the importance of reinforcement for imitation probably also vary developmentally in their impact.

In the next chapter, we will turn our attention to an empirical overview of developmental studies of imitation. We will examine the nature of age changes in both recall and imitation and the effects of task demands and motivational factors upon such age changes. This empirical overview is intended to further illuminate some of the issues discussed in the present chapter as well as to establish the groundwork for our empirical study to be described later.

4

An Overview of Empirical Studies of Developmental Changes in Imitation

Up to this point we have been examining and comparing theories of imitation, a process that has led us to propose that the two major factors governing imitation are the observer's cognitive-developmental level and his motives for imitating. In the present chapter we shall review the results of empirical studies of children's imitation to see if they support our two-factor theory. We concentrate on those studies of children's imitation that permit comparisons to be made of imitative behavior by children of different ages.

Our decision to limit our review to developmental studies follows from our belief in the central importance of the child's cognitive-developmental level (Factor 1). We do not suggest that there is any simple equivalency between children's ages and their cognitive abilities. However, we join other developmental theorists in pointing out that the regularity of correspondence between age and cognitive development allows one to take age as a useful indicator of probable cognitive abilities when there is an absence of other information. Within this limitation, we will examine studies in terms of procedural variations that might affect motives for imitating. For example, it is possible to classify most studies according to (a) whether the study is one of spontaneous imitative behavior or of prompted recall for the modeled acts; (b) whether the instructions given to the child are likely to arouse predominantly extrinsic or intrinsic motives; and (c) whether the modeled tasks are challenging or not. For many studies, it is also possible to specify other information relevant to motives, such as whether there is any special characteristic of the model that might arouse affect (e.g., the model is the child's parent, a peer, or an adult of the same sex as the child), and whether external rewards were given either to the model (vicarious reinforcement) or directly to the child.

Before examining the results of the developmental studies, it may be helpful to consider what we should expect to find if our two-factor approach is correct.

Our first classification divides studies according to whether they are studies of spontaneous imitation, in which children imitate in the absence of instructions to do so, or studies of prompted recall, in which children are asked to demonstrate their recall of the modeled acts. (This distinction corresponds to the performance-acquisition distinction we discussed in the previous chapter. We will refer to acquisition as "recall" in our discussion of empirical work, since acquisition can be measured only by asking the child directly to demonstrate what he recalls.) Motivation to imitate is probably quite strong in prompted-recall studies, and it would be consistent with our two-factor notion to find that, in general, the greater the child's cognitive-developmental level, the more recall of the model's behavior he will demonstrate upon request. This prediction naturally must be qualified in several ways. For example, when differences in ages are slight, age differences in recall might not be found. Threshold phenomena might also be found such that there is improvement in recall with age up to a certain point with no further improvement thereafter.

In addition to asking the child to imitate, there are other procedures that probably affect motivation in imitation studies. For example, even if a child is not asked to imitate, instructions that imply that his performance is going to be evaluated may lead the child to believe that he is expected to imitate. We would therefore expect to find an age increase in spontaneous imitation in studies where children are led to believe that their performance will be judged. It may be impossible within a laboratory situation to avoid implying some kind of evaluative purpose in an experiment. To the degree that this is true, spontaneous imitation in the laboratory setting might always be greater in older children than in younger children, reflecting their greater ability to recall and therefore to imitate what the model did. Some investigators have attempted to convince children through their experimental instructions that the children are free to play and to behave naturally. Such "no-problem" instructions should reduce extrinsic motives to imitate and should allow the role of intrinsic motives to be seen more clearly.

Intrinsic motives for imitation are probably most directly affected by the nature of the imitation tasks that the experimenter chooses to employ. Challenging, problem-solving activities should be more likely than simple activities to arouse children's intrinsic motivation. We have found it useful to classify the degree of challenge in imitation tasks according to the number of acts the child is expected to remember. Many investigators have studied such relatively simple acts as whether a child does or does not imitate sharing one's winnings after a game has been played. Such modeled activities which fall into a few relatively discrete alternatives probably represent less of a cognitive challenge than do activities in which the child must recall a more continuous stream of behavior. Variations such as these in the amount of challenge in the tasks should become especially important when extrinsic motives are weak. Under such circumstances, children's imitation of challenging tasks should increase with age, while their spontaneous imitation of simple acts should decrease with age.

A final quality of imitation tasks that may affect motivation is the degree to which the imitation tasks appear to be the central purpose of the experiment rather than some incidental, irrelevant part of the procedures. Hartup and Coates, in their earlier review, laid much stress on this distinction (1972). Modeled acts that seem to be the major reason for the experiment (e.g., the model showing the correct solution to a problem) are probably more likely to be interpreted by children as being something they are expected to imitate than are expressive acts, such as shoulder shrugging, or incidental comments that the model makes. Acts that appear to be relevant to some basic experimental purpose are probably more likely to arouse extrinsic motives than are task-irrelevant acts. We would therefore expect age increases in imitation of task-relevant acts. We have no particular expectation for age trends in spontaneous imitation of incidental acts. As Aronfreed has suggested (1969), imitation of such acts may be motivated by affection for the model; at present we know too little about such motives to make predictions of age trends for imitation of this kind of act.

To summarize this line of reasoning, we would expect to find that studies of prompted recall usually result in the finding of increases in recall with age, because extrinsic motives to display imitation are strong in such studies. We would expect to find that studies of spontaneous imitation result in increases with age only if either extrinsic or intrinsic motives for imitation can be inferred to be at high strength on the basis of instructions or task characteristics. With this background regarding our expectations in light of our two-factor notion, we now turn to an examination of studies of imitation and recall, in children of different cognitive-developmental levels.

A DESCRIPTION OF DEVELOPMENTAL
STUDIES OF IMITATION

In an earlier review of the literature, Hartup and Coates (1970) located eight published studies or dissertations in which the investigators had included more than one age group of children and had examined some aspect of imitative behavior with specific attention to developmental trends (Barnwell & Sechrest, 1965; Coates & Hartup, 1969; Hetherington, 1965; May, 1965; McDavid, 1959; Rosenbaum, 1967; Turner & Rommetveit, 1967; Wapner & Cirillo, 1968). Since the time of the Hartup and Coates review, a number of studies that meet their criteria have appeared. Table 2 presents an overview of the 8 earlier studies plus 76 additional and, in most cases, more recent studies located by the present authors as meeting the criteria of Hartup and Coates. Studies were included in this review only if the investigators examined specific imitative actions or verbalizations in a relatively direct manner. Excluded by this criterion were, for example, studies of general attitude change or of diffuse changes in aggressive tendencies following exposure to a model.

Columns 1 and 2 of Table 2 provide information about the investigators, the date of the study, and the number of children involved in each study. Columns 3-5 provide information about the characteristics of the subjects and models in these experiments. Age is the most important single variable and is indicated in column 3. All ages except those of infants have been converted to years and rounded to the nearest half year. Subject characteristics that were examined for each study include sex, socioeconomic status (SES), and ethnicity; in addition, any unusual characteristic of the children, such as residence in an institution, was recorded. Most studies have included equal numbers of boys and girls; therefore, the sex of the children is reported in Table 2 only if the distribution deviated from equal representation of the sexes. SES and ethnic-group information is described only for those studies that reported them. Characteristics of the model are reported in the table in the same manner that these characteristics were reported in the original studies.

Columns 6-8 of Table 2 provide information concerning manipulations of instructions and tasks. Column 6 indicates whether the study examined spontaneous imitation, recall for the modeled acts, or both (denoted "SI" for spontaneous imitation, "PR" for prompted recall, and "SI/PR" for both). This classification was based upon the nature of the instructions given the children: If they were specifically requested to reproduce the model's activities or were alerted before observing the model that they would be asked to recall the activities, such prompting was considered to constitute a test for recall. To be classified as a spontaneous imitation study, a study had to provide a measure of imitative behavior with no request for imitation and with no prior indication having been given to the child that he would later be asked to imitate. Therefore, those few studies that have examined both imitation and recall have necessarily delayed the recall measure until imitation had been assessed or have employed different subjects for the tests of recall and imitation.

The type of instructions given to the child are further classified and reported in column 7 as being problem, no problem, or ambiguous instructions (denoted "P," "NP," and "A"). "Problem" instructions are considered to be those in which children are led to believe early in the experiment that their performance will be evaluated in some manner. In many studies of recall, for example, such instructions take the form of telling the child to remember the model's behavior because they will later be asked to show what the model did. In other studies employing problem instructions, the child is given the general set that he is to find a correct way to behave or a correct solution to a problem, but no specific reference is made to the model as providing cues for such behavior. Such instructions are assumed to arouse an extrinsic motivational set. A few experiments have attempted to eliminate evaluative sets by establishing a play orientation and reassuring children that they are free to perform in any manner they please. We have classified such instructions as "no problem" instructions in Table 2. These instructions are assumed to allow intrinsic motives a relatively greater role. "Ambiguous" instructions are those that neither clearly imply an evaluation of the child's performance nor reassure the child that such an evaluation will not be

Overview of Empirical Studies

Study	N	Subject Age (years)	Subject Characteristics	Model Characteristics	Type of Study: Spontaneous Imitation or Prompted Recall
I. Discrete Verbal					
Bandura & McDonald, 1963	84	5-11[a]	Middle SES	Adult: Female	SI[b]
Bloom, Hood, & Lightbown, 1974	6	1½-2[c]	Middle to upper-middle SES; 2 boys, 4 girls	Adult: Female	SI
Cowan, Langer, Heavenrich, & Nathanson, 1969	80	5½-12½[a]	Lower SES; 42 boys, 38 girls	Adult: Female	SI
DiSimoni, 1975	20	3-5	13 boys, 7 girls		PR
Murray, 1974	120	6½ 7½ 8½	66 boys, 54 girls	Peer: 7-year-old boy (televised)	PR
Nelson, 1973 (full sample)	18	14-24 mo.[c]	Middle SES; 7 boys, 11 girls	Parent: child's mother	SI
(partial sample)	7	18-21 mo.[c]	Middle SES; sex not specified	Parent: child's mother	PR
Sternlieb & Youniss, 1975	63	6-7[a] 10-11	Sex not specified	Adult: Female	SI
II. Discrete Behavioral					
Balla, Styfco, & Zigler, 1971	288	6[d] 7 8 10	Normal IQ/ Familial re-tarded/Organic retarded; 163 boys, 125 girls	Human: Adult Female/Nonhuman: Machine	SI
Barnwell & Sechrest, 1965	60	6[e] 8		Peer: Same sex & ability as child	SI
Bryan & Walbeck, 1970	168	8[e] 9	96 boys, 72 girls	Peer: Same sex as child (film)	SI/PR
Daehler, 1976	48	2½ 3 4	Middle SES, white	Adult: Male	PR
Elliot & Vasta, 1970	48	5 6 7	Lower and lower-middle SES	Peer: Male (film)	SI

Instructions: Problem, No Problem, or Ambiguous	Task Relevance of Acts: Relevant or Irrelevant	Type of Reinforcement	Type of Modeled Acts	Results
NP[b]	R	To child: none[b] To model: direct/none	Moral judgment choices	*Imitation:* No age differences.
NP	R	To child: not specified To model: none	One and two-word verbal utterances	*Imitation:* No age changes in overall imitation. Little imitation of words already familiar to child.
A	R	To child: direct To model: direct	Moral judgment choices	*Imitation:* No simple age function. Magnitude and permanence of imitation dependent on match between child's developmental stage and level of modeled choice.
P	R		Pairs of words differing by one phoneme	*Recall:* Increase with age.
	R		Conservation task choices	*Recall:* No simple age function. Recall dependent on match between child's developmental stage and level of modeled choice.
		To child: not specified To model: none	One-word verbal utterances	*Imitation:* Increase with age.
P	R		One-word verbal utterances	*Recall:* Increase with age for most children.
A	R	To child: direct To model: direct	Moral judgment choices	*Imitation:* No simple age function. Stability of imitation dependent on match between child's developmental stage and level of modeled choice.
P	R	To child: punishment To model: none	Solutions to a discrimination task	*Imitation:* Decrease with age. Organic retardeds imitated more than familials. All retardeds imitated more than normal children.
A	R	To child: none To model: direct/ punishment/none	Preferences among toys	*Imitation:* No age changes.
A	R	To child: none To model: none	An act of sharing	*Imitation:* No age differences. *Recall:* No age differences.
P	R		Solutions to a discrimination task	*Recall:* Increase with age. Modeling alone equivalent to verbal instructions and to modeling plus verbal instructions.
A	R	To child: none To model: direct/ none	An act of sharing	*Imitation:* No age differences.

(continued)

TABLE 2 *(continued)*

Study	N	Subject Age (years)	Subject Characteristics	Model Characteristics	Type of Study: Spontaneous Imitation or Prompted Recall
Fein, 1973	80	6[f] 8	Lower-middle SES	Adult: Female	SI
Grusec, 1972 (Experiment 1)	100	7 11		Adult: Same sex as child	SI/PR
Hetherington, 1965	216	4-5 6-8 9-11		Parent: Mother & Father (half mother-, half father-dominated homes)	SI
Hoving, Hamm, & Galvin, 1969	108	7 10 13	Lower-middle SES	Peer: Same sex as child (responses reported, not directly observed)	SI
Kuhn, 1972	87	4[a] 6 8	Middle SES; sex not specified	Adult: Female	SI/PR
Levy, McClinton, Rabinowitz, & Wolkin, 1974 [Studies 1 & 2]	72	7½ 20½		Adult: Female	SI/PR
	60	4 7½ 9½ 11½ 20		Adult: Female	SI/PR
McDavid, 1959	32	4 5	Upper-middle SES	Adult: Same sex as child	SI
McLaughlin & Brinley, 1973	180	7½ 9½ 12	Middle SES	Adult: Male (film)	PR
Oliver & Hoppe, 1974 [Experiment 3]	119	5[e] 7 9	Approximately one-half boys, one-half girls	Adult: Same sex as child (present/ absent during imitation)	SI
Perry, Bussey, & Perry, 1975	128	7½-8½[e] 9½-10½	Lower SES; boys only	Peer: Same age, sex, and SES as child	SI
Rice, 1976	98	3 4	Lower and middle SES	Puppet	SI
Rothman, 1976	144	12½[a,e] 13½ 14½	Boys only	Adult: Male	SI

Instructions: Problem, No Problem, or Ambiguous	Task Relevance of Acts: Relevant or Irrelevant	Type of Reinforcement	Type of Modeled Acts	Results
P	R	To child: punishment To model: 10%/ 50%/100% direct schedule	Solutions to a discrimination task	*Imitation:* Decrease with age.
	R	To child: none To model: none	An act of sharing	*Imitation:* No age changes. *Recall:* No age changes.
A	R	To child: none To model: none	Preferences among pictures	*Imitation:* No age changes.
P	R	To child: none To model: none	Solutions to a perceptual judgment task	*Imitation:* Decrease for obviously incorrect responses with age. Increase for difficult, ambiguous solutions with age.
A	R	To child: none To model: none	Object-sort on a concept task; explanation of sort	*Imitation:* No simple age function. Magnitude and permanence dependent on match between child's developmental stage and level of modeled act. *Recall:* Same as imitation.
A (to younger) A/P (to older) A	R R	(both studies) To child: none To model: direct/ punishment/both reward and punishment/none	Preferences among pictured objects	*Imitation:* No consistent age functions. Some sex effects. *Recall:* Increase with age to 7½, decrease thereafter.
		To child: direct To model: none	Solutions to a discrimination task	*Imitation:* No age changes.
P	R	To model: direct for correct and punishment for incorrect	Solutions to a discrimination task	*Recall:* No age changes.
A	R	To child: punishment To model: direct/ punishment	Solutions to a discrimination task	*Imitation:* Curvilinear age effect for absent model; lowest imitation by 7-year-olds. No age differences when present.
A	R	To child: none To model: none	Leaving versus remaining with boring task/playing versus not playing with toys	*Imitation:* No age change in remaining with task or playing with attractive toys. Increase with age in playing with unattractive toys.
P	R	To child: random To model: direct/ punishment	Solutions to a discrimination task	*Imitation:* Increase with age.
A	R	To child: none To model: none	Continue or end participation in experiment	*Imitation:* No simple age function. Increase in imitation of decisions based on high-level moral reasons with increase in developmental stage of child.

(continued)

TABLE 2 *(continued)*

Study	N	Subject Age (years)	Subject Characteristics	Model Characteristics	Type of Study: Spontaneous Imitation or Prompted Recall
Rushton, 1975	140	7 8 9 10 11	British "working class"	Adult: Same sex as child	SI
Ryan & Kobasigawa, 1971	87	5½ 7½	Lower-middle SES; Approximately half girls and half boys	Adult: Male (silent/ verbalizing)	SI
Turiel & Rothman, 1972	43	12[a] 13 14 15	Middle and upper-middle SES; boys only	Adult: Male	SI
Ward, 1969	32	6 7½	Middle SES	Adult: Male and Female (two models together; reinforcing/non-reinforcing)	SI
White & Burnam, 1975	192	10 11	Lower-middle SES; all girls	Adult: Female	SI
Williams & Willoughby, 1971	88	9[e] 11	Sex not reported		PR
Wolf, 1972	72	5 7 9	Boys only	Peer (film)	SI
Yussen, 1974	144	5 7½	Middle SES	Adult: Same/ opposite sex as child	PR
Yussen & Santrock, 1974	120	4½ 8	Predominantly middle SES	Peer: Same sex as child	PR
Zigler & Yando, 1972	192	7[d] 11	Institutionalized/ noninstitutionalized	Human: Adult Female/Nonhuman: Machine	SI

III. Continuous Verbal

Study	N	Subject Age (years)	Subject Characteristics	Model Characteristics	Type of Study: Spontaneous Imitation or Prompted Recall
Anastasiow & Hanes, 1974	198	5½[e] 6½ 7½	Lower-SES black/ rural white/middle-SES white; sex not specified	Adult (tape recorded)	PR
Bohannon, 1975	54	6½ 7½ 10½		Adult: Male (tape recorded)	PR
Bohannon, 1976	150	5½ 6½ 7½	Middle SES; 73 boys, 77 girls	Adult: Male (tape recorded)	PR
Denney, 1972	60	6 8 10	Boys only	Adult: Female (film)	SI

Instructions: Problem, No Problem, or Ambiguous	Task Relevance of Acts: Relevant or Irrelevant	Type of Reinforcement	Type of Modeled Acts	Results
A	R	To child: none To model: none	An act of sharing	*Imitation:* No age differences in susceptibility to modeling. Children more influenced by behavior than by preaching.
A	R	To child: direct To model: direct	Solutions to a discrimination task	*Imitation:* Decreased imitation of silent model with age. No age differences with verbalizing model.
P	R	To child: none To model: none	Continue or end participation in experiment	*Imitation:* No simple age function. Increase in imitation of decisions based on high-level moral reasons with increase in developmental stage of child.
	R	To child: chance reward To model: none	Choice of outcomes on a game of chance	*Imitation:* Increase with age. Increase in imitation of same sex model with age.
A	R	To child: none To model: none	An act of sharing	*Imitation:* No simple age function.
P	R		Solutions to a paired-associate task	*Recall:* Increase with age.
	R	To child: none To model: none	Playing versus not playing with toys	*Imitation:* No age changes.
P/A	R	To model: reward/punishment/none	Preferences among objects	*Recall:* Increase with age and with problem instructions. Female model's choices recalled better than male's.
A	R	To model: direct	Solutions to a discrimination task	*Recall:* Increase with age. Girls recalled more than boys.
P/NP	R	To child: chance reward in problem; none in no problem To model: none	Solutions to a discrimination task	*Imitation:* Decrease with age for noninstitutionalized children. For institutionalized children, decrease with age if problem instructions, no age change if no problem instructions.
P	R		Sentences	*Recall:* Increase with age.
P	R		Normal/scrambled word order sentences	*Recall:* No age differences for short sentences. Increase with age for longer and scrambled-order sentences.
P	R		Normal/scrambled word order sentences	*Recall:* Increase with age for normal sentences. No age change for scrambled sentences.
A	R	To child: none To model: direct	Style of seeking information	*Imitation:* No simple age function. Magnitude and permanence dependent on match between child's age and level of modeled act.

(continued)

TABLE 2 *(continued)*

Study	N	Subject Age (years)	Subject Characteristics	Model Characteristics	Type of Study: Spontaneous Imitation or Prompted Recall
Denney, 1975	144	6 8 10	Middle SES, rural	Adult: Female	SI
Entwisle & Frasure, 1974	96	6 7 8 9	Middle to upper-middle SES	Adult: Female (tape recorded)	PR
Frasure & Entwisle, 1973	108	5½ 7 9	Lower-SES black/ Lower-SES white/ Middle-SES white	Adult: Female (tape recorded)	PR
Friedman & Bowers, 1971	72	3-5[e] 5 6	Urban	Adult: Teachers	SI
Hall & Freedle, 1973	360	5 8 10	Middle/lower SES; black/white	Adult (tape recorded)	PR
Hallahan, Kauffman, & Ball, 1974	80	7½ 9½ 11½ 14	Lower-middle to middle SES	Adult: Male (tape recorded)	PR
Harris & Hassemer, 1972	96	7[e] 9	Some children were Spanish-speaking	Adult: Male or Female (One group had Spanish-speaking model)	SI
Lamal, 1971	72	8[e] 10 12		Adult: Same/opposite sex as child	SI
Laughlin, Moss, & Miller, 1969	216	8[e] 10 12		Adult: Same/opposite sex as child	SI
Leifer, Collins, Gross, Taylor, Andrews, & Blackmer, 1971	60	4½ 7½ 10½		(film)	PR
Liebert, Odom, Hill, & Huff, 1969	84	6 8½ 14	Middle SES	Adult: Male	SI?
Love & Parker-Robinson, 1972	24	4 6	Middle SES; 10 boys, 14 girls	Adult: Female	PR
Reichle, Longhurst, & Stepanich, 1976	24	2 3	Middle SES	Parent: Child's Mother	SI
Seitz & Stewart, 1975	18	2 4½	8 boys, 10 girls	Parent: Child's Mother	SI

Instructions: Problem, No Problem, or Ambiguous	Task Relevance of Acts: Relevant or Irrelevant	Type of Reinforcement	Type of Modeled Acts	Results
P	R	To child: none To model: none	Style of seeking information	*Imitation:* Increase with age in 2 of 3 modeling conditions. No changes in third, "cognitive modeling."
P	R		Sentences varied in meaningfulness and correctness of syntax	*Recall:* Increase with age for sentences with semantic or syntactic correctness. No age differences for short strings of random words.
P	R		Sentences varied in meaningfulness and correctness of syntax	*Recall:* Increase with age.
A	R	To child: not specified To model: none	Verbal style in spontaneous classroom speech	*Imitation:* Increase with age. Girls more imitative than boys.
P	R		Sentences varied in grammar	*Recall:* Increase with age.
P	R/I		Serial order of words (relevant task); incidental classes of words (irrelevant task)	*Recall:* Increase with age, greater for relevant than irrelevant material. Differentiated better by older.
A	R	To child: none To model: none	Length and complexity of sentences	*Imitation:* No age differences.
P	R	To child: none To model: none	Style of seeking information	*Imitation:* No age differences.
P	R	To child: none To model: none	Style of seeking information	*Imitation:* Increase with age of an efficient response style. 10-year-olds were most imitative for inefficient style. (Susceptibility to modeling was age related.)
P	R		Sequence of acts in film	*Recall:* Increase with age. (Linear increase with complex sequence; plateau at 7½-10½ for easy.)
P	R	To child: direct To model: direct	Sentences with familiar or unfamiliar grammar	*Imitation:* No age changes for familiar grammar. Increase with age for novel grammar sentences.
P	R		Grammatical/ungrammatical sentences	*Recall:* Increase with age. Effect more pronounced for grammatical than ungrammatical sentences.
	R	To child: not specified To model: none	Natural language phrases and sentences	*Imitation:* Decrease with age.
	R	To child: not specified To model: none	Natural language phrases and sentences	*Imitation:* Decrease with age.

(continued)

TABLE 2 *(continued)*

Study	N	Subject Age (years)	Subject Characteristics	Model Characteristics	Type of Study: Spontaneous Imitation or Prompted Recall
Stewart & Hamilton, 1976	24	1½ 2¼	Middle SES, white	Adult: Female	SI[g]/PR
Turiel, 1966	44	13[a]	Middle SES; boys only	Adult: Male	SI
Turner & Rommetveit, 1967	240	4½ 6 7 8 9			PR
Weener, 1971	90	5½ 6½ 7½ 8½	Lower-middle and middle SES; 49 boys, 41 girls	Adult (tape recorded)	PR

IV. Continuous Behavioral

Study	N	Subject Age (years)	Subject Characteristics	Model Characteristics	Type of Study: Spontaneous Imitation or Prompted Recall
Balla, Butterfield, & Zigler, 1974	70	7-7½[c,d]	Institutionalized organic and familial retarded children	Adult: Male	SI
Brown, 1975	180	5½ 7½	Approximately equal numbers of boys and girls		PR
Coates & Hartup, 1969	72	4½ 7½	Lower-middle SES	Adult: Male (film)	PR
Collins, 1970	168	8[e] 11 12 14	Middle SES	(film)	PR
Collins, Berndt, & Hess, 1974	60	5[e] 7 10 13	Sex distribution not given	Adult: Male (film)	PR
Durrell & Weisberg, 1973	116	5 7½	Lower-middle SES	Adult: 2 Females (previously rewarding/ nonrewarding for imitation)	SI
Fouts & Liikanen, 1975	40	5 8	Middle SES	Adult: Female (televised)	SI
Grusec, 1973	not given	5 10	Sex not specified	Adult: Female (film)	SI
Grusec & Brinker, 1972 [Experiment 3]	144	5 7		Adult: Same/opposite sex as child (film)	PR

Instructions: Problem, No Problem, or Ambiguous	Task Relevance of Acts: Relevant or Irrelevant	Type of Reinforcement	Type of Modeled Acts	Results
A/P	R	To child: not specified To model: none	Foreign (French) words varied in type of activity named	*Imitation:* Increase with age. Higher for edible or moveable than passive objects. *Recall:* Same.
A	R	To child: none To model: none	Level of moral reasoning	*Imitation:* No simple age function. Magnitude dependent on match between child's developmental stage and level of modeled act.
P	R		Sentences varied in grammar	*Recall:* No age changes.
P	R		Sentences varied in meaningfulness and correctness of syntax	*Recall:* Increase with age.
A	R	To child: none To model: none	Picture made from geometric cutouts	*Imitation:* Decrease with age.
P	R		Sequence of acts in a story	*Recall:* No age differences for recall measured behaviorally. Increase with age for verbally measured recall.
P	R and I[h]		Novel ways of playing with toys	*Recall:* Increase with age. Younger children recalled as much as older children with induced verbalization.
NP	R/I		Naturalistic behavior in a filmed story	*Recall:* Linear increase with age for relevant acts. Curvilinear age function for irrelevant acts.
A			Aggressive acts and motives	*Recall:* Increase with age for motives. No age differences for consequences of aggression.
	I?	To child: none To model: none	Ways of playing with toys	*Imitation:* No age changes.
A	R	To child: none To model: none	Novel ways of playing with toys	*Imitation:* Increase with age for "low developmental level" children. No age changes for "high developmental level" children.
		To child: none To model: direct/ punishment/none	Neutral/aggressive acts	*Imitation:* Age differences not reported. Younger children less sensitive to manipulations than older.
A	I		Expressive acts (e.g., rubbing eyes)	*Recall:* Increase with age. More recall for same- than opposite-sex model's acts.

(continued)

TABLE 2 *(continued)*

Study	N	Subject Age (years)	Subject Characteristics	Model Characteristics	Type of Study: Spontaneous Imitation or Prompted Recall
Hamilton, 1973	72	3-5 7 10		(photographs and films)	PR
Joslin, Coates, & McKown, 1973	72	4½ 7½		Adult: Male (nur-turant/nonnurturant) (film)	PR
Paskal, 1969	95?	6 7	Lower-middle and middle SES	Adult: Female (nur-turant/neutral)	SI/PR
Rosenbaum, 1967	144	7-8 9-10 11-12		Peer: Same sex and grade as child	PR
Wapner & Cirillo, 1968	240	8 10 12 14½ 16½ 18			PR
Yando & Zigler, 1971	192	6½[d] 10	Normal IQ/fa-milial retarded/ organic retarded; Institutionalized/ Noninstitutionalized	Human: Adult Fe-male/Nonhuman: Ma-chine	SI
V. Discrete & Continuous					
Eckerman, Whatley, & Kutz, 1975	60	1 1½ 2	Middle SES; 34 boys, 26 girls	Peer	SI
Ervin, 1964 [Study 1]	5	13-25 mo.	1 boy, 4 girls	Parent: Child's Mother	SI
Guillaume, 1971 [1926]	2	0-2[c]	Professional level SES	Parents and Siblings	SI
May, 1965	144	3 5 7	Middle SES	Adult: Same/ opposite sex as child	SI
McCall, 1975 [Study 1]	63	1 1¼ 1½ 1¾ 2	Sex not specified	Adult	SI
McCall, 1975 [Study 2]	not given	1½ 2 3	Sex not specified	Adult (live/ televised)	SI
Paraskevopoulos & Hunt, 1971	233	5 mo.-5 yrs.	Lower SES, Greek; Institutionalized/ raised at home; 147 boys, 86 girls	Adult: Female	SI

Instructions: Problem, No Problem, or Ambiguous	Task Relevance of Acts: Relevant or Irrelevant	Type of Reinforcement	Type of Modeled Acts	Results
P	I		Facial expressions	*Recall:* Increase with age.
A	R and I[h]		Novel ways of playing with toys	*Recall:* Increase with age. Older children more sensitive to nurturance than younger.
	I	To child: none To model: none	Expressive acts	*Imitation:* Younger children imitated nurturant model more than neutral. Older children imitated both equally. *Recall:* No age differences.
P	R		Solution to a maze	*Recall:* Increase with age to age 10. No further increase thereafter.
P			Hand movements	*Recall:* Increase with age.
NP	R	To child: none To model: none	Pictorial design	*Imitation:* Decrease with age. Retarded children imitated more than normal children.
		To child: none To model: none	Free play activities of infants	*Imitation:* Increase with age.
		To child: not specified To model: none	Natural language words and phrases	*Imitation:* Curvilinear age function.
NP		To child: none To model: none	Simple sounds; gestures; play with toys	*Imitation:* Increase with age. Development of deferred and complex imitation.
A	R/I	To child: direct To model: direct	Solutions to a discrimination task; Expressive behavior	*Imitation:* No age changes for relevant acts. Curvilinear age function for irrelevant acts (maximum at 5 years).
A		To child: none To model: none	Novel ways of playing with toys	*Imitation:* Increase with age for both simple, discrete and more complex, continuous acts.
P/A		To child: none To model: none	Novel ways of playing with toys	*Imitation:* Age differences not reported. All ages imitated live more than televised model. No effect of instructions.
		To child: not specified To model: none	Words and gestures	*Imitation:* Increase with age.

(continued)

TABLE 2 *(continued)*

Study	N	Subject Age (years)	Subject Characteristics	Model Characteristics	Type of Study: Spontaneous Imitation or Prompted Recall
Piaget, 1962b	3	0-1½^c	Professional level SES; 1 boy, 2 girls	Parents and Siblings	SI
Uzgiris, 1972	12	1 mo.-2 yrs.^{c}		Adult: Female	SI
Valentine, 1930	5	0-2^c	Professional level SES; 3 boys, 2 girls	Parents and Siblings	SI
Zimmerman, 1974	60	3½ 4 5½	Lower and middle SES; heterogeneous ethnicity	Adult: Female	SI^b

[a] Developmental stages, rather than the ages reported, were the focus of interest in the study.

[b] While testing for imitation was conducted with no-problem instructions and no reinforcement, the children were pretrained with problem instructions and reinforcement for recalling the model's responses.

[c] Longitudinal.

[d] Mental age. (Approximately equal to chronological age for normal IQ children.)

forthcoming. Column 7 is sometimes blank, denoting that the instructions were not reported in the original experiment or that it was otherwise difficult to determine what the child's set was.

Column 8 presents the results of a classifying of modeled acts in terms of their apparent relevance or irrelevance to the major purpose of the experiment. In many studies the model demonstrated a specific task solution or otherwise confined the modeled actions to some single, major activity; such behaviors were considered task relevant (denoted as "R" in column 8). Irrelevant acts (denoted as "I" in column 8) were generally considered to be contextually unusual, expressive behaviors, such as foot stamping or odd verbalizations, or behaviors that were incidental to the central purpose of an evident experimental task. Since the decision as to whether the model provided relevant or irrelevant acts is a difficult one for some kinds of studies, this information is occasionally omitted from the table.

The consequences experienced by the model for performing the modeled activities and the consequences to the child for imitating are described in column 9. The consequences to children for demonstrating recall are not described. As Bandura and Jeffrey (1973) have pointed out, there is a strong demand quality inherent in the practice of waiting for children to perform before continuing the experimental procedures. For this reason, there is probably always an implied set of consequences to the subject in a recall experiment, whether or not formal rewards or punishments are employed. The consequences listed in column 9 are

Instructions: Problem, No Problem, or Ambiguous	Task Relevance of Acts: Relevant or Irrelevant	Type of Reinforcement	Type of Modeled Acts	Results
NP		To child: none To model: none	Simple sounds; gestures; play with toys	*Imitation:* Increase with age. Development of deferred and complex imitation.
		To child: not specified To model: none	Novel and familiar sounds and actions	*Imitation:* Increase with age.
NP		To child: none To model: none	Simple sounds; gestures; play with toys	*Imitation:* Increase with age. Development of deferred and complex imitation.
NP[b]	R	To child: none[b] To model: none	Object sort on a concept task; Explanation for sort	*Imitation:* Decrease with age.

[e] Ages estimated from reported school-grade level.

[f] These two groups were matched on mental age, and thus differed in IQ.

[g] Imitation was assessed several days following recall; demand characteristics may therefore have existed.

[h] The difference between relevant and irrelevant recall was not analyzed.

categorized as direct reward, chance reward, no consequence, and punishment. *Direct reward* and *punishment* are self-explanatory; *chance reward* refers to procedures in which reinforcement was determined according to some chance schedule so that there was no constant, predictable consequence to the child for responding imitatively. Studies in which there was never a reward or punishment for imitation are designated as *none*.

Column 10 describes the overall type of behavior modeled in the study. The studies themselves are also grouped in the table according to the type of behavior that was examined. We have classified modeled activities along two dimensions: first, whether a behavioral act or a verbal response was required, and second, whether the number of responses that were scored fell into a few relatively discrete categories or existed along a relatively more open continuum. The categories are therefore (a) Discrete behavioral acts—the model makes a choice from two or more alternatives, and the child is asked to recall the model's choice or to indicate his own choice from the same alternatives. In some cases the choices denote preferences, as for toys; in other cases they are solutions, as to a discrimination problem; (b) Discrete verbal responses—the model verbalizes a choice among a finite set of alternatives; the child is then asked to name his own choice; (c) Continuous behavioral sequences—the model enacts a series of physical acts, and the child is subsequently asked to show or describe what the model did (recall) or is observed to see if he spontaneously reenacts the model's performance (imitation); (d) Continuous verbal style—the model displays a verbal style unusual for its length, grammatical features, or efficiency in gaining information; the child's subsequent verbal style is examined for evidence of similarity to the model's.

COMMENTS ON THE RESULTS OF DEVELOPMENTAL STUDIES OF IMITATION

A general conclusion that emerges from examining Table 2 is that there is considerable empirical evidence for the importance of both cognitive-developmental abilities and motivational dispositions in determining imitation. In our comments here we will omit consideration of studies that have tested stage-theory formulations, as we discussed such studies in chapter 3. We will also generally limit our comments to those studies that we were able fully to classify in terms of types of instructions and the kind of acts that were modeled.

As expected, for studies of prompted recall the most common finding is increased recall with age. Hartup and Coates commented upon this trend in their earlier review (1970), and their tentative conclusion is strongly confirmed now that there are many more developmental studies of prompted recall available for examination. In the majority of prompted-recall studies, investigators have employed challenging tasks along with instructions that imply that the children's performance will be evaluated. Under these conditions, increasing recall with age has almost always been found (Anastasiow & Hanes, 1974; Bohannon, 1975, 1976; Brown, 1975; Coates & Hartup, 1969; Entwisle & Frasure, 1974; Frasure & Entwisle, 1973; Hall & Freedle, 1973; Hallahan et al., 1974; Leifer et al., 1971; Love & Parker-Robinson, 1972; Rosenbaum, 1967; Stewart & Hamilton, 1976; Weener, 1971). Only in one such study have the investigators reported finding no age differences (Turner & Rommetveit, 1967). In our formulation, studies such as these combine intrinsic motivation (challenging problems) with extrinsic motivation (instructions from the experimenter to recall the model's acts). Motivation to imitate should be high, and the age trends obtained probably are a straightforward reflection of the differences in the children's cognitive-developmental levels.

When we turn to prompted-recall studies that have employed simpler tasks, such as discrete choices among alternatives, the picture is also clear. The methodology has been relatively constant across these studies. Despite some variation in instructions (some investigators have used ambiguous instructions, others problem instructions), all of the discrete-task prompted-recall studies that we located involved task-relevant acts. In most of these studies, we again find that the investigators have reported increasing recall with age (Daehler, 1976; Di-Simoni, 1975; Levy et al., 1974 [curvilinear function] ; Nelson, 1973; Williams & Willoughby, 1971; Yussen, 1974; Yussen & Santrock, 1974). Only two studies in this category have not resulted in age increases (Bryan & Walbeck, 1970; McLaughlin & Brinley, 1973). In both cases, the tasks may have been easy enough to involve ceiling effects. In studies such as the ones we have been discussing, we would presume that intrinsic motives may be low but that extrinsic motives are high; again, the age trends are probably reflecting an increase in cognitive-developmental level.

Only one of the recall studies reported in Table 2 seems to have involved minimal extrinsic motivation (Collins, 1970). Children in this study were not alerted in advance that they would be expected to recall the model's acts or that their performance would be evaluated. Under these nonevaluative conditions, Collins found an age increase in recall for challenging, task-relevant behavior, but he did not find an age increase in recall for incidental behavior. (Interestingly, he reported a curvilinear function in the latter case.) Clearly much more research is needed to determine the nature of developmental trends in recall for tasks under conditions in which extrinsic motives are minimized. The handful of remaining prompted-recall studies have involved task-irrelevant modeled behavior. It would be interesting to know what age trends in recall are like for such behavior when children are not pressured in any way by experimental demands. In the existing studies, however, the investigators have employed either problem instructions (Hallahan et al., 1974; Hamilton, 1973) or ambiguous instructions (Grusec & Brinker, 1972). In all three studies, the authors reported finding increased recall with age.

To the extent that the existing prompted-recall studies provide tests of our predictions, their results are compatible with the expectations that we described earlier in this chapter. It is also apparent, however, that the existing studies do not provide a sufficient and satisfying test of all our predictions. While certain questions have been addressed in numerous studies, others have received only cursory attention. For example, if we consider those studies that we were able to fully classify (and omit studies based on stage theories) there are 27 prompted-recall studies in Table 2. In 21 of these studies, the investigators employed instructions that emphasized evaluation of the children. The results of the prompted-recall studies therefore do not provide us with much information about what determines recall when children are in nonevaluative circumstances. Researchers interested in recall have also tended to concentrate their efforts upon relatively challenging tasks: Of the 27 prompted-recall studies in Table 2, only 8 have involved recall for simple, discrete tasks. The result of such unevenness in the questions that have been addressed is that, while we are able confidently to conclude that cognitive-developmental level is of major significance for recall, we can say almost nothing about how motives to recall modeled acts may operate in children of different ages. We do not know whether children's recall for challenging acts is typically higher than their recall for simple acts, and we do not know whether younger children typically might recall incidental, task-irrelevant behavior better than older children do (reversing the usually found age trend). We will explore these issues ourselves in the next few chapters, where we report the findings of our own study.

Turning to studies of spontaneous imitation, it is immediately evident that the reported age trends are usually different from those reported for prompted recall. The results from these more recent studies thus again replicate the results from the small number of early studies reviewed by Hartup and Coates (1970). Instead of generally increasing age trends, age gradients in spontaneous imitation studies are frequently flat or even decreasing. This pattern of findings suggests that, as we argued earlier, older children often imitate less than they are able to recall. (Stronger evidence for this interpretation would be provided by direct comparisons of children's imitation with their recall of modeled acts within the same study. Few developmental studies to date have included tests of both recall and imitation, however, and in those that have, the investigators have not reported the results of statistical comparisons between the two.)

We suggested earlier that spontaneous imitation should increase with age when children are given instructions that emphasize an evaluative set. There is some support for this expectation in the results of the studies shown in Table 2, but only if the children also received imitation tasks that were challenging. Four of the five studies that combined continuous tasks with problem instructions resulted in increases imitation with age for at least some of the groups of children being studied (Denney, 1975; Laughlin et al., 1969; Liebert et al., 1969; Stewart & Hamilton, 1976; [Lamal, 1971, found no age changes in imitation under these circumstances]). Four of the five studies in Table 2 in which simple, discrete tasks were modeled along with problem instructions resulted in decreasing imitation with age (Balla et al., 1971; Fein, 1973; Hoving et al., 1969; Zigler & Yando, 1972; [Rice, 1976, found increasing imitation with age]).

It is evident that instructions that imply the child's performance will be judged do not motivate the child to imitate to the same degree that direct requests to imitate do. (In prompted-recall studies, age increases were found even when simple tasks were modeled.) The likelihood that problem instructions do arouse some degree of extrinsic motivation is suggested, however, when we compare the results of the studies just discussed with the results of spontaneous imitation studies in which investigators have used no-problem instructions. In such studies, regardless of the degree of task challenge, there have been no reports of increasing imitation with age. Rather, investigators have reported finding either flat age gradients or decreasing imitativeness with age (Bandura & McDonald, 1963; Bloom et al., 1974; Yando & Zigler, 1971; Zigler & Yando, 1972; Zimmerman, 1974).

Most studies of spontaneous imitation have been conducted following what we would consider ambiguous instructions, where children may not be entirely certain what is expected of them. Ambiguous instructions fall somewhere between problem and no-problem instructions, and the results of studies in which ambiguous instructions have been employed also fall somewhere between the results of studies in which problem and no-problem instructions have been used. Where challenging tasks have been modeled, there has been at least a tendency for age increases in imitation to occur. Investigators in two of four such studies reported age increases (Fouts & Liikanen, 1975; Friedman & Bowers, 1971); in one study, investigators found no age changes in imitation (Harris & Hassemer, 1972); and in the remaining study, investigators reported finding decreasing imitativeness with age (Balla et al., 1974). Perhaps the fact that an unusual population (retarded children) were subjects in the study by Balla and his colleagues accounted for the decreasing imitation despite the challenging task. With discrete imitation tasks, there has been one report of age increases in imitation (Perry et al., 1975) and one of age decreases in imitation (Ryan & Kobasigawa, 1971). Most investigators, however, have reported finding no age differences in imitation of simple, discrete tasks following ambiguous instructions (Barnwell & Sechrest, 1965; Bryan & Walbeck, 1970; Elliott & Vasta, 1970; Hetherington, 1965; Levy et al., 1974; May, 1965; Oliver & Hoppe, 1974; Rushton, 1975; White & Burnam, 1975).

As is true for studies of recall, investigators who have examined spontaneous imitation have not systematically explored the effects of task difficulty and of instructions at different ages. It can be seen in Table 2 that researchers who have studied developmental changes in imitation have tended to employ problem or ambiguous instructions and to provide modeled acts that are discrete and task-relevant. There has thus been little examination of the effects of no-problem instructions, which might permit a somewhat more naturalistic view of children's imitation. Similarly, there has been little examination of developmental trends for imitation of the simple, irrelevant behaviors so often modeled for preschool children in nondevelopmental studies. Finally, most researchers to date surprisingly have neglected to compare children's imitation with their recall of modeled acts. Such a comparison has been made by Bandura (1965) in a nondevelopmental study, where he convincingly interpreted the difference in terms of motivational factors affecting children's imitation. Investigators in the few developmental studies in which both imitation and recall have been included, however, have not reported statistical results of such direct comparisons.

In summary, our interpretation of the literature we have reviewed in this chapter is that the results of the prompted-recall studies seem to indicate the effects of Factor 1—cognitive-developmental level—with the effects of Factor 2—motivation—held constant. The fact that spontaneous imitation often does not increase with age and sometimes decreases is support for our contention that motivational factors are also important in governing imitation. This conclusion is frustratingly incomplete, however, because we know so little about which motivational factors are important and when they come into play. In order to assess the relative importance of intrinsic and extrinsic motives at different ages it will be necessary to manipulate instructions and task characteristics in a more systematic way than has been customary.

What is needed at this point is a developmental study in which children are confronted with both challenging modeled acts and simple ones under a variety of instructional conditions, including simply instructing the child that he may play freely. Within each condition, a direct comparison should be made between the children's recall of the modeled acts and their spontaneous imitation of those acts. Such a study would not provide a complete test of all effects and interactions of the two proposed factors; no one study could do so. It would, however, provide a systematic exploratory test of the general validity of the two-factor approach. Positive results of an exploratory study would justify the formal development of the two-factor approach into a theory and the suggestion of a program of research to test that theory. In the next chapter we turn to the description of a study of the kind we have been describing.

5

An Exploratory, Developmental Study of Imitation

As chapter 4's review of the existing developmental studies suggests, there is much to be gained by conducting a study that systematically compares imitation and recall across a wide age range and under experimentally varied task and instructional conditions. The present chapter describes the method of such a study recently conducted by the authors.

OVERVIEW OF THE DESIGN OF THE STUDY

The study was designed in such a way as to explore observer characteristics, task characteristics, and the nature of the incentives for imitation. A description of the factors in the design follows.

Observer Characteristics

Chronological age was the major subject variable in the present study. The difference between adjacent age levels was large, and children were chosen only if their IQ scores were within the normal range, so that the differences between chronological age groups would also reflect differences in mental age (MA) level. These precautions were taken because it is likely that MA, rather than simply chronological age, is the actual predictor of developmental effects.

Ages of subjects were selected to span the period from late preschool through early adolescence. Specific age groups were chosen to permit comparison of preschool children (4 years old), children from two discrete points in the "middle-childhood" period (7 years and 10 years), and children of 13, whose cognitive abilities many theorists have assumed to have reached the asymptotic level shared with adults. We predicted that there would be a general overall decline in spontaneous imitation with age, and an overall increase in recall for modeled acts. On the basis of our earlier arguments that the period of 5-7 years represents a major transition point (see Figure 1 in chapter 1), we predicted that 4-year-olds would differ significantly from the remainder of the children in the study on every dimension that was examined. We also predicted that differences among the other age groups would be significant for some dimensions being examined, but not for others. For example, we predicted that older children would show less imitation of simple, unchallenging modeled acts, but that there would be no age decrease in imitation of challenging, problem-solving acts.

Task Characteristics

The experiment was designed to tap the competence, or effectance, motive directly by employing tasks that focused on problem-solving skills. Several tasks were employed in order to test the generality of the findings across several performance opportunities. All tasks were designed so that a number of plausible solutions might be devised by children, thus providing them with a reasonable alternative to imitation of the model's solution. In addition, construction of the tasks was guided by the desire to achieve novelty without introducing odd or unlikely behaviors. Tasks that had unusual, but plausible, solutions were created; unusualness was defined empirically by showing that control subjects, who had not seen the model, emitted the solutions with very low probability rates.

The effect of task relevance versus irrelevance was studied by including during the modeling of each task a series of incidental behaviors. Such behaviors included, for example, the position in which the model played the game (e.g., sitting or kneeling) as well as distinctive acts such as have frequently been employed in modeling studies with young children (e.g., placing one's hand over one's eyes in a melodramatic and exaggerated manner).

We predicted that task characteristics would play a major role in imitation and recall and that the nature of the role would vary developmentally. It was predicted that younger children would not make the distinction between relevant and incidental learning as well as older children. For example, we predicted that older children would imitate fewer of the irrelevant acts than the relevant ones, while 4-year-olds would imitate equivalently, or perhaps even show greater imitation of irrelevant acts than of relevant ones. We did not make a prediction for recall; our study was exploratory in terms of whether there are different age trends for recall of relevant and irrelevant task characteristics.

Incentives for Imitation

The nature of the incentive for imitation was examined by manipulating the instructions that were given to children before exposing them to the model. In order to maximize a problem-solving set as well as to imply that the quality of their problem solutions would be judged, some children were given explicit problem-solving instructions in which they were informed that the experimenter wished to see if they could figure out the "right way" to solve the problems. Other children were given explicit non-problem-solving instructions, and it was emphasized that there were no right or wrong ways of playing the games, that the examiner simply wanted to know whether the games were enjoyable to children. A third group of children received instructions that were intended to be ambiguous, which is probably often the case in laboratory studies of imitation.

It was predicted that the problem-solving instructions would generally result in an increased level of imitation relative to the no-problem instructions. For the ambiguous instructions, it was hypothesized that children who are not certain of what is expected of them may interpret such ambiguity as signifying that they are probably going to be evaluated in some manner. It was therefore predicted that children given the ambiguous instructions would perform more like children given the problem instructions than like children given the no-problem instructions. It was also predicted that the responsiveness of children to instructional variations would vary as a function of age. Because of the greater number of hypothesized motives for imitating and the greater cognitive resources of older, as compared with younger, children, it was predicted that 13-year-olds would show the greatest variation in imitation as a function of instructional conditions. Under explicit problem-solving instructions, we predicted that 13-year-olds would show high limitation of the model's unusual solutions. Under non-problem-solving instructions, we predicted that 13-year-olds would show much less imitation, preferring to rely upon their own problem-solving abilities to generate a reasonable solution. Younger children were expected to show similar trends, but to show them less strongly.

Imitation Versus Recall

Measures of both spontaneous imitation and recall for the modeled acts were obtained in this study. We predicted that recall would increase with age whereas imitation, under most conditions, would not. We therefore predicted that the difference between the amount of modeled behavior that the child could recall and the amount of modeled behavior that the child actually imitated would become greater in older, as compared with younger, children.

Overview of the Design

The design of the present study employed children of four age groups (4, 7, 10, and 13 years old) who were given one of three kinds of instructions (problem, ambiguous, no-problem) before they witnessed a model. The modeling display systematically presented four different tasks with both task-relevant and task-irrelevant behaviors modeled for each task. Subjects were observed, after the model departed, in order to ascertain the amount of imitation they would spontaneously display. After they had completed playing with the tasks, they were asked to reproduce as much of the modeled activity as they could recall. Thus, both imitation and recall measures were obtained for each subject. In order to determine whether any imitative behavior that was observed might have occurred normally among children who had not observed a model, two control groups, one receiving the problem instructions, the other receiving the no-problem instructions, were allowed to play with the tasks without having observed a model.

METHOD

Subjects

A total of 240 white middle-class children, 120 girls and 120 boys, served as subjects. The population consisted of equal groups ($N=60$) of children at four chronological age levels. The mean ages for the groups were 4, 7, 10, and 13 years. When tested, all subjects were within 6 months of the mean age for their group. The elementary and junior-high-school children were obtained from a suburban public-school system located in the Greater Boston area. The youngest children were obtained from one private nursery school in the same community and six private nursery schools in economically similar suburbs.

Subjects from each of the four age levels were matched by CA and sex for each of five manipulated conditions in the study, yielding an N of 12, 6 boys and 6 girls for each age group in each condition. Prior to sample selection of the school-aged population, principals were asked to exclude any child who evidenced gross motor, sensory, or emotional problems or who had an IQ below 90. Information relative to the cognitive and social functioning of the preschoolers was acquired by means of a rating scale completed by their teachers. Teachers were asked to rate a child, relative to other children in his class, on a 7-point scale for cognitive ability and a 7-point scale for social adjustment. Children were excluded if they received either a rating of below 4 (average) on cognitive ability, or below 3 (slightly below average) on social adjustment.

Materials

Four imitation tasks, designed to provide a multiplicity of plausible solutions, were developed for this study. In addition, a structured interview was utilized in order to gain information concerning the child's understanding of the testing situation and his performance. Figure 2 illustrates the appearance of each of the four tasks.

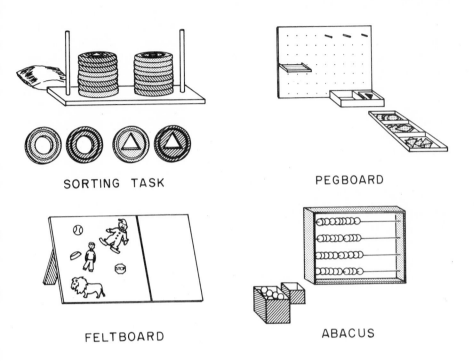

FIG. 2   Four games employed to assess imitation

Sorting Task.   Similar to a ring-tossing game, the apparatus for this task consisted of an 8" X 36" wooden plank with one of two 1" X 15" vertical poles
fastened to the plank 3" from either end. Sixteen wooden rings, 12" in diameter,
were constructed to represent a combination of two of four colors and one of
two shapes. There were eight blue rings, four of which had a 7½" diameter circular center cutout, and four of which had a 9" equilateral triangle cutout. In
addition, two of each of the two types had a 5/8"-wide white stripe placed 1"
from the outer edge of the ring, and two had a similarly placed black stripe.
There were eight red rings, which were identical to the blue rings in shape and
stripe. The rings were stacked in a randomized order on the plank between the
two poles. A 13½" X 13½" red vinyl pillow was placed 12" diagonally behind
and to the left of the plank.

Pegboard.   The pegboard consisted of an upright 24" X 18" wooden panel.
Attached to the lower right-hand corner was a 10¾" X 5¼" X 2" tray with two
compartments. Attached flush to the left-hand side of the board at approximately midline was a 5½"X 2½" rimmed shelf. Five inches from the right of the
shelf and 2" from the top of the panel was a horizontal row of three round pro-
truding pegs (2"X ¼"), each 5" apart. An open 17½" X 5½" X 1" wooden box

with three compartments was placed on the floor perpendicular to the panel and next to the tray.

Thirty-six 4" X 4" white cardboard cards were placed in the right-hand compartment of the tray; a 4" X 4" piece of white tile was placed in the left-hand compartment. Centrally located on each card was a 1½" black outline of either a circle, a square, or a triangle (12 cards per shape). Sorted by shape into the three compartments of the box were six circular, six triangular, and six square cardboard cutouts approximately 4" in size. Two of each type were blue, two red, and two yellow. The colors were randomly arranged within each compartment.

Feltboard. The materials for this task consisted of a 36" X 24" panel of plywood with green felt glued to it, and 15 felt cutouts. A hinge attached to the back of the panel enabled it to stand, easel-fashion, on the floor. A ½" black felt strip running the vertical length of the panel was glued to the green felt, dividing the panel's surface into a large portion on the left side and a smaller 13½" portion on the right. The removable felt cutouts, ranging in size from 2" to 6¾", were randomly placed on the left portion of the panel. Mounted on each cutout was a drawing of an animal, a person, or an object (horse, dog, cat, lion, seal, man, small girl, small boy, policeman, clown, ball, gun, saddle, stop sign, dog dish). In addition, the background felt colors were varied. Each of the five drawings from the three classes was randomly mounted on a background of blue, pink, red, yellow, or orange.

Abacus. The apparatus, resembling an abacus, consisted of a 24½" X 18" X 3" brown wooden frame. Stretched lengthwise across the frame, 4" apart and 3" from each side, were four strips of plastic (strings) with ten 1-1/8" styrofoam balls strung on each one. All balls were located next to one another at one end of the frame, and each was capable of being moved to the other end. The colors of the strings and balls varied from top to bottom as follows: bright orange with light brown balls, bright brown with light orange balls, bright red with light yellow balls, and bright yellow with light red balls. Placed immediately to the left of the frame was an open 4" X 4" X 4" wooden yellow-and-brown felt-covered box. To the left of that box was a similar but larger (6" X 6" X 6") box containing 19 multicolored 1-1/8" styrofoam balls, 5 bright brown, 5 bright red, 5 bright orange, and 4 bright yellow.

Interview. The interview was structured around 25 questions, which focused upon four areas of interest. These were (a) the child's attitudes and feelings about the model and the games; (b) the child's learning set during his performance; (c) the child's verbal recall of the directions, his performance, and the model's performance; and (d) the number of alternate strategies the child could specify for each task. Specifically, all children were asked to recall the instructions they had received before playing the games and to state whether they had enjoyed the games, what their favorite game was, whether they believed their performance in the experiment was related to their schoolwork, whether they believed the experimenter would discuss their performance with their teacher, and how they would feel if their performance were made public. They were also asked to describe the way they had played each game, to suggest other ways each game might be played, and to state what they believed was the "right way" to play each game. Those children who were exposed to the model were asked, in addition, to describe the way the model had played each game, to name the model's favorite game, to give reasons for their imitation or nonimitation on each game, and to state whether or not they had liked the model.

Modeling Sequence

The behaviors that the model enacted for each of the four imitation tasks were selected on the basis of pilot testing in order to reduce the inclusion of behaviors that children were likely to produce spontaneously in response to the stimuli presented. The selected behaviors, however, were considered to be reasonably within the behavioral repertoire of most of the children.

Two categories of behavior were modeled for each task: behaviors relevant to problem solution and behaviors irrelevant to problem solution. A breakdown of these behaviors is presented in Table 3. The sequence of modeled behaviors took approximately 5 minutes. The model demonstrated these behaviors in the manner and order shown in Table 3.

Sorting Task. The purposeful, problem-solving behavior for the sorting task involved demonstrating the solution to a complex discrimination task. Although, as Figure 2 shows, the apparatus resembled a ring-toss game, the modeled solution involved placing a set of rings rather than tossing them. The solution further required that the child classify the rings on the basis of color alone, ignoring other characteristics, and that the child employ an alternation-of-color strategy in sorting the rings onto a single pole. Thus the solution was complex, and the probability of its occurring in the absence of the model was expected to be low.

Approaching the apparatus from the side facing the child, the model walked to the back of the apparatus, picked up the pillow, placed it in front of the rings, and knelt on it. The model then spread the stack of rings and, using a blue-and-red alternation strategy, proceeded to sort them onto the pole to her right. While sorting, the model picked up each ring slowly and deliberately, holding it up for the child to see. Each time the model sorted a blue ring, she tapped the top of the pole with it two times before placing it. The model sorted a total of 10 rings.

Pegboard. The purposeful actions for the pegboard also involved demonstrating the solution to a discrimination task. This solution required the child to attend only to the form, while ignoring the color, of the stimulus cards and to employ a nonmatching strategy based upon the cue provided by a guide card. Again, the modeled solution to the task was relatively complex.

TABLE 3

Description of Relevant and Irrelevant Modeled Acts

Task	Irrelevant behaviors	Relevant behaviors
Sorting Task	Goes to back of game Kneels Uses pillow Spreads rings Taps pole	Places rings Uses one pole Employs a sorting-by-color strategy
Pegboard	Walks around game Semi-sits to right of game Places tile under tray Taps pegs with form Uses rack	Uses white cards as guides Uses one peg Uses a nonmatching strategy
Feltboard	Sits to right of game with legs out Moves finger on black line Removes forms from board Places object upside down in left-hand corner	Uses right side of board Uses a sentence strategy
Abacus	Kneels Places balls on floor Shakes box and places it to left side Covers eyes and doesn't look when picking balls *Tsks* Does not return guide balls to same box	Uses guide ball Uses a numerical-color strategy

The model walked to the front of the apparatus, slowly walked completely around it in a clockwise direction, reversed, and walked around it again in a counterclockwise direction. Moving to the right side of the apparatus, the model seated herself in a distinctive position with both legs to one side. She then removed the tile from the tray and placed it under the tray. Taking the first white card from the stack, the model placed it on the shelf so that the outline of the shape was visible to her and the child. She then proceeded, using a nonmatching strategy, to choose a colored form and place it randomly on a peg. The choice of color was also random. With the first colored form, and only the first form, the model tapped each of the three pegs once before placing it. The model continued the game for a series of 10 trials. Each time, she first placed the white guide card on the shelf, then randomly chose a nonmatched form and placed it on the peg. Only one of the three pegs was used for all forms in any given modeling demonstration.

Feltboard.   The purposeful behavior for the feltboard involved the construction of meaningful sequences of felt cutout figures. The model walked to the front of the apparatus and seated herself with both legs straight out in front of her. Her body was parallel to the panel with her torso to the right of the black felt strip. She then slowly ran her finger down and up the black strip two times. The model next removed all the felt cutouts from the panel and placed them on the floor. She then proceeded, using a sentence strategy, to place three trios of the felt cutouts on the panel to the right of the black strip. Near the top of the panel she first placed the man, gun, and lion cutouts. The cutouts are assumed to represent a sentence such as "The man takes a gun and shoots the lion." Below these she placed the boy, dog dish, and dog ("The boy gives the dog dish to the dog"), and finally, below the second trio, the clown, ball, and seal ("The clown throws the ball to the seal"). The model then took the stop sign and placed it upside down in the far upper left-hand corner of the panel to the left of the black line. The remainder of the forms were left on the floor.

Abacus.   The solution to the abacus task required that the child learn to translate the color of a guide ball into a numerical value and to move an appropriate set of objects according to the correct numerical code. Approaching the end of the frame where the balls were located, the model knelt directly in front of it. She then removed from the larger box, one at a time, a brown, a red, and a yellow ball and placed them in a row on the floor above the boxes. Upon next removing an orange ball, the model began to place it on the floor, stopped, and instead placed it in the smaller box. She then picked up the larger box of balls, shook it, and placed it to the left side of her body out of her line of sight. The model covered her eyes with her right hand and with her left hand took a ball from the large box. The model looked at the drawn ball and, one at a time, moved the similarly colored balls on the abacus according to the following numerical code: brown, move one ball; red, move two balls; yellow, move three balls; orange, move zero balls (corresponding to the order of balls on the floor). She then placed the drawn ball into the smaller box. Using this numerical-color strategy, the model proceeded to draw all the remaining balls (a total of 15) from the large box. On each trial she would, without looking into the box, draw a ball, move the same lighter colored balls on the abacus, and then place the drawn ball into the smaller box. After the first trial, however, she did *not* cover her eyes with her hand. Also, upon drawing an orange ball she would loudly *tsk* and place the ball into the smaller box without moving any balls on the abacus.

PROCEDURES

Two young women with teaching experience were involved in the study. Throughout the entire study, one of these women served in the role of the model, and the other conducted the experiment. Neither of the women was aware of the specific hypotheses being tested. Each child was seen individually for approximately one half hour. Special care was given to the order in which children were tested so as to insure that they could not discuss the testing sessions with each other. This was achieved by juxtaposing schools, grades, and classrooms. (Questioning children after the testing sessions revealed that only one child had heard about the games prior to testing. This child was not included in the final sample reported in this study.)

Children were met at their classroom by the examiner. She introduced herself and explained to the child that his teacher had informed her that he enjoyed helping his teacher, and she was wondering whether or not he might like to do some things for her (the examiner) that day.[1] The examiner then escorted the child into the experimental room and seated him on a chair next to the chair upon which she sat. The four tasks had been prearranged in a diamond-type pattern. Directly in front of the chairs at approximately 3 ft. was the abacus, and at approximately 8 ft. was the sorting task. Approximately 2 ft. to the left and 5 ft. up from the chairs was the feltboard, and an equal distance to the right of the chairs was the pegboard.

Three experimental and two control conditions were employed in this study: problem, ambiguous, no problem, problem control, and no problem control. In each of the experimental conditions, after the instructional set had been given to the child, the model was introduced. The child then played the games, first under the initial instructional set in order to determine imitation, and second, under the direction for recall of the model's performance in order to determine acquisition. Each of these performance periods was approximately 8 minutes in length. During each of the total time periods, the examiner recorded the occurrence of a child's behavior according to a data sheet with predetermined response categories.[2] No attempt was made to score for imitation at that time.

Problem and problem-control conditions. In the problem condition, the child was told that he was to try to figure out how to play each one of the four games. He was also informed that there was only one right way to play the games, and that the examiner wanted to know if he was smart enough to figure out the answers. As the examiner completed the instructions, the model, who had been listening at the door, entered, saying: "Hi, Nancy. I was just going to ask you—Oh, I see you have some new games today. I haven't tried these yet. Do you think I could look at them?" The examiner hesitated and stated that she did

---

[1]Although no child refused to go with the examiner, after being introduced to the tasks 11 children (three male and five female 4-year-olds, one male 7-year-old, one male 10-year-old, and one male 13-year-old) refused to participate. These children were thanked and returned to their classrooms. The noninclusion of these children did not reduce the final sample ($N = 240$).

[2]Prior to experimental testing, the examiner and another observer had been trained in behavior recording. On the basis of 25 pilot testing sessions, the median interrater reliability coefficient was .92 (range=.74-1.00) across the four tasks and the relevant and irrelevant categories of acts. Prior to the sessions employed for obtaining observer reliability, all tasks were piloted in order to assess their appropriateness and to determine modeling behaviors.

not think the child would mind if the model looked at the games. She then told the child he could take his turn when the lady finished. The model proceeded to demonstrate the behaviors described in the previous section. Upon completion, the model thanked the examiner, stated that the game she liked best was the pegboard, and told the examiner she would see her later.

After rearranging the tasks so that they were returned to their starting condition, the examiner restated the directions to the child and the child played the games. During this period the examiner did not reinforce the child nor interact with him in any way. If the child requested attention, the examiner simply stated that he should continue to try to play each of the games.

In order to insure that the child attempted all tasks, a 2-minute time limit for each task was imposed upon the child with the following examiner statement: "Since I'd like you to look at all the games, and we don't have a lot of time, why don't you try another one."

After the child finished playing the games once, the examiner rearranged the tasks and instructed the child to play the games a second time. The examiner then asked the child to show her *everything* the model had done with the games. Verbal reinforcement was given during this period.

The problem control condition was administered with the exact instructional set and procedures employed in the experimental condition. No model was introduced, and the child played the games only once.

No-problem and no-problem control conditions.   In the no-problem conditions, the procedure was identical to the problem conditions with the exception of the instructional set. The examiner explained that she had some games that kids enjoyed playing. The child was informed that he was being asked to play the games for no other reason than that the examiner was interested in knowing which ones he liked best and considered the most fun to play. It was further explained that the child could play the games in any manner that he wanted.

Ambiguous condition.   The instructional set for the ambiguous condition was: "Now, as you can see, there are four games. Although I'd like you to look at each of them, you can do anything you'd like with them." Any attempt by the child to gain further information was met with the simple statement that he could do anything he wanted with the games. The procedure was identical to the other experimental conditions. At the completion of testing, all children were highly praised for the manner in which they played the games and further told that they had played them much better than usual for children their age.

SCORING

On the basis of pilot work for the present study, many of the relevant and irrelevant behaviors listed in Table 3 were subdivided into smaller units. The nature of these units was determined according to the criterion of obtaining the maximum degree of detail consistent with observer reliability. In refining the scoring system, it became evident that for some behaviors, particularly those that were comprised of a series of instances (as in strategy behavior, as opposed to the simple behavior of kneeling on a pillow), a child could be imitating the model even though he did not do so in a continuous fashion. For example, in Task 1, where the child could imitate the model's behavior of tapping alternate rings, a child might do so on 7 out of 8 possible times. It was decided that 80% imitation or more, rather than 100% imitation, should be scored as constituting an imitative response for such behaviors involving a series of identical acts.

Overall scoring. Three types of nonimitative measures were recorded for each of the four tasks: (a) the time in seconds that the child worked, (b) the child's level of attention to the model, and (c) the problem-solving strategy that the child utilized. During the modeling period, the examiner rated the child's level of attention on a 5-point scale ranging from a score of 5 for observing all of the model's actions to a score of 1 for ignoring the model. A strategy score (0 = did not occur, 1 = did occur) was determined on the basis of whether or not 80% of the child's responses on a task fell into a recognizable pattern, containing the possibility of an error. For example, on Task 1 a consistent pattern of sorting by stripe and shape would be considered a strategy.

The imitation measures were grouped into relevant and irrelevant behavioral categories. They are task specific and explained below. In general, an irrelevant behavior was considered to be any of the preestablished behaviors of the model that were irrelevant to the strategy she used to solve the task. Relevant behaviors were considered to be those behaviors of the model that were part of the strategy she used to solve the task. These behaviors were scored as either occurring (1) or not occurring (0). For all four tasks, a total score of 49 irrelevant and 22 relevant behaviors could be obtained. Table 4 provides a detailed description of the scoring rules.

Details of the scoring of the interview are presented in chapter 6 along with the statistical analyses of the children's responses.

Reliability of scoring. In order to determine reliability of scoring, 25 experimental protocols were selected randomly with the restriction that approximately equal numbers of children at each age be included. On the nonimitative scores, the median reliability coefficients across tasks were .97 and .96, respectively, for length of time the child worked on the tasks and level of attention to the model. There was 96% agreement across tasks and children regarding whether the child had used a problem-solving strategy or not. On the imitation scores, reliability coefficients were calculated separately for imitation and for recall, and separately for the relevant and irrelevant acts within each task. The median reliability coefficient was .96 (range = .74.99) for imitation and .99 (range = .81-1.00) for recall scores. On the interview responses, the median reliability coefficient was .96 (range = .78-1.00).

TABLE 4

A Detailed Guide to the Scoring Procedure

Task I: Sorting task

Irrelevant behaviors (N = 10):

Order—S plays this game first.
Back of game—S positions himself on side of game farthest from examiner.
Pillow—S removes pillow from original position.
Kneels—S has both knees touching floor at start of activity.
Spreads—S spreads rings from stacked position over floor.
Taps at all—S taps top or base of either pole any number of times with any part of ring.
Two taps—80% of rings tapped are tapped two times consecutively on the same pole.
Never taps on red—if tapping does occur, S never taps with a red ring.
Taps on same pole as model—80% of rings tapped are tapped on same pole model used.
Taps alternate rings—S taps every other ring any number of times on either pole (80%).

Relevant behaviors (N = 6):

Placing—80% of the rings used are placed on pole(s) as opposed to being tossed or thrown.
One pole—80% of activity (throwing, placing, etc.) takes place on only one (either) pole.
Same pole as model—80% of activity (throwing, placing, etc.) takes place on same pole that
    model used (left of examiner).
Sorts—90% of rings used are sorted by color, shape, and/or stripe.
Sorts by color—90% of rings used are sorted by color (red and blue).
Alternates colors—90% of rings used are sorted in a pattern of red-blue-red-blue or blue-red-
    blue-red.

Task II: Pegboard

Irrelevant behaviors (N = 13):

Order—S plays this game second.
Walks around—S walks around entire game.
Walks around two times—S walks around game two times consecutively.
Clockwise/counterclockwise—S walks around game once clockwise and once counterclock-
    wise (either order).
Semi-sit—S sits on floor with both legs to one side.
Right of game—S is positioned in any way that the major portion of the S is to the right of
    the game.
Tile out—S takes tile out of tray and puts it anywhere, including back into tray.
Tile under—S takes tile out of tray and puts it under tray.
Taps a peg—S taps one or more pegs with anything.
Taps with first form only—S taps any peg with first colored shape used.
Taps each peg—S taps all three pegs with an object.
Uses rack—S puts anything on the rack.
Uses rack for guide cards—S places 80% of white cards used on rack.

Relevant behaviors (N = 4):

One peg—80% of colored shapes used are hung on one peg.
Model's peg—80% of colored shapes used are hung on same peg model used.
Use white cards as guide—80% of colored shapes used are determined by white cards (90% if
    S is nonmatching).
Nonmatch—if guide cards are used, 90% of shapes placed do not match shapes on guide cards.

(continued)

TABLE 3 *(continued)*

Task III: Feltboard

Irrelevant behaviors ($N = 11$):

Order—S plays this game third.

Legs out—S is seated on floor with both legs out straight in front of him.

Blank side—S is seated so that rear end is in front of blank (small) side of board.

Runs finger on line—S moves finger or hand up and/or down black line.

Two times—S moves finger or hand up and down black line two times consecutively.

Forms off—S takes at least one form off the board and does not replace it immediately.

On floor—at least one form is removed from the board and placed on the floor.

All forms—before placing any form, S removes all forms from board.

Form alone on left—S places a form alone on the left-hand side of the board and leaves it. No other forms remain on that side.

Any object upside down—S places any form upside down anywhere on the board and leaves it.

Stop sign left corner—S places the stop sign in the upper left-hand corner of the board and leaves it.

Relevant behaviors ($N = 6$):

Same side—80% of forms placed on board are on right-hand side.

Any sentence—S forms a sentence using three or more forms. A sentence consists of at least three forms—a person or animal, an object, and another person or animal—placed in a horizontal row.

Sentence 1—S places "man-gun-lion" on board.

Sentence 2—S places "boy-dog dish-dog" on board.

Sentence 3—S places "clown-ball-seal" on board.

Order of sentences—S places any two or all three sentences on board in order from top to bottom—Sentences 1, 2, 3. If he uses only 1 and 3, there must be something else between them, and if only Sentences 1 and 2 or 2 and 3 there must be nothing between them.

Task IV: Abacus

Irrelevant behaviors ($N = 15$):

Order—S plays this game fourth.

Kneels—S has both knees on floor at start of activity.

Balls on floor—any balls are taken out of box and placed on floor.

Three balls—any three balls are taken out of box and placed on floor.

Three colors—if three balls are placed on floor, all three are different colors.

Order brown-red-yellow—if three balls are placed on floor, order of balls from S's left to right is brown-red-yellow.

Orange out—if balls are placed on floor, S does not include orange.

Shakes—S picks up box with balls in it and shakes box to mix.

Box to left—S takes box with balls in it and places it to his left.

Covers eyes—S covers eyes when picking balls from box.

First pick only—S covers eyes the first time balls are picked from box and does not cover eyes thereafter.

Doesn't look—S does not look into box while picking balls on at least two picks.

Tsk at all—S indicates negative affect when any ball is chosen from box.

Tsk on orange—S indicates negative affect when orange ball, and no other color, is chosen from box.

Takes guide ball and does not return to same box—80% of balls taken from box are not returned immediately to same box. They are placed somewhere else and/or at least one more ball is picked before they are returned.

(continued)

TABLE 3 *(continued)*

Relevant behaviors $(N = 6)$:

Uses guide color to move—80% of moves on abacus are determined by color of guide ball (includes matching ball to color of string).

Color match—80% of moves on abacus are determined by matching color of guide ball to color of balls on abacus. No other color is moved.

Brown = 1—75% of times brown balls are moved, S moves one brown ball in either direction.

Red = 2—75% of times red balls are moved, S moves two red balls in either direction.

Yellow = 3—66% of times yellow balls are moved, S moves three yellow balls in either direction.

Orange = 0—75% of times orange is chosen from box, S does not move any balls on the abacus; or S has had opportunity within his strategy to move orange balls and has not done so 75% of the time.

6
Results of the Exploratory Developmental Study

CONTROL-GROUP PERFORMANCE

The free-play data for control subjects were scored in the same manner as for experimental subjects in order to determine the base rate of occurrence of the acts modeled for the children in the experimental conditions. The data were analyzed in a 4 X 2 X 4 X 2 analysis of variance (Age X Instructions X Task X Relevance) with repeated measures on tasks (1-4) and relevance (relevant versus irrelevant) with 12 observations per cell.[1] The overall level of these chance imitation scores was low: The mean proportion of acts produced by control subjects that would have been considered imitative if the children had seen a model was .10. Given the small absolute values of the chance imitation scores, only those findings from the analysis of variance of the control children's performance that attained significance at the .01 level of statistical significance or better will be reported. This decision was made in order to preserve the reader from having to consider findings which, although they attained a conventionally acceptable level of statistical significance, represented only very slight differences in actual performance levels.

The analysis yielded a significant main effect for age, F (3, 88) = 6.72, $p <$ .001, reflecting the fact that the amount of chance imitation increased with age (the mean proportion for 4, 7, 10, and 13-year-olds, respectively, was .08, .09, .10, and .12). The main effect for instructions was significant, F (1, 88) = 25.46, $p < .001$: The score for the problem instructions group was higher than that

---

[1] While it is often necessary to transform proportional data using an inverse sine transformation, all analyses of transformed versus untransformed data in the present study yielded identical significance levels and conclusions. Results from untransformed proportions are therefore presented for easier consideration of the subjects' actual level of performance. In addition, the data for this analysis, as well as for all subsequent experimental group analyses, were collapsed across sex, since preliminary analyses showed no effects of this variable.

for the no-problem instructions group (.12 versus .08, respectively). The main effect for task was significant, F (3, 264) = 30.30, $p < .001$: Chance imitation was much higher for the first task than for the remaining three tasks (the mean proportion for Tasks 1-4, respectively, was .16, .08, .07, and .07). A significant main effect for relevance, F (1, 88) = 21.69, $p < .001$, reflected the fact that chance imitation scores were higher for relevant than for irrelevant behaviors (.12 versus .08). The Task X Relevance interaction was also significant, F(3, 264) = 36.98, $p < .001$. This interaction arose because the high chance imitation on Task 1 was found only for task-relevant behaviors (the mean chance imitation of relevant acts for Tasks 1-4, respectively, was .24, .06, .09, and .08). The four Tasks were relatively similar to each other in chance-imitation levels on task-task-irrelevant behaviors (.08, .11, .05, and .07, respectively, for Tasks 1-4).

EXPERIMENTAL GROUP PERFORMANCE

Three dependent measures were of interest in the present study: (1) the proportion of modeled acts spontaneously imitated; (2) the proportion of modeled acts correctly recalled; and (3) the relationship between imitation and recall. (Proportions were analyzed since the number of modeled acts was not the same for different tasks.) The results will be presented in separate sections, focusing on each of the three measures in order. These sections will be followed by a section on task effects. (Since effects of specific tasks were considered of interest only as a test of the replicability of other findings across more than one performance opportunity, task effects are presented in the context of examining the generalizability of the major findings presented in the earlier sections.)

Spontaneous Imitation

The proportion of modeled behaviors that were imitated were analyzed by a 4 X 3 X 4 X 2 analysis of variance (Age X Instructions X Task X Relevance) with repeated measures on tasks (1-4) and relevance (relevant versus irrelevant) with 12 observations per cell (Winer, 1971). Table 5 summarizes the major findings of this analysis as well as those for the analysis of recall (which will be discussed later).

TABLE 5
Summary of Major Findings from Analyses of Variance
of Imitation and Recall

	Significance level	
Main effects	Imitation	Recall
Age	n.s.	$< .001$
Instructions	$< .001$	n.s.
Relevance	$< .001$	$< .001$
Interactions		
Age X Instructions	$< .05$	$< .05$
Age X Relevance	$< .001$	$< .001$
Instructions X Relevance	$< .001$	n.s.
Age X Instructions X Relevance	$< .001$	n.s.

As may be seen in Table 5, the main effect for age was not significant. Children from 4 through 13 spontaneously imitated approximately one-fourth to one-third of the behaviors that were modeled (.27, .26, .31, and .29 for 4-, 7-, 10-, and 13-year-olds). The main effect for instructions was found to be significant, F (2, 132) = 14.95, $p < .001$, reflecting the fact that imitation following the problem instructions was significantly higher ($p < .01$) then imitation following either the ambiguous or the no-problem instructions (.35, .25, and .24, respectively).[2] The difference between the ambiguous and the no-problem groups was not significant. The significant main effect for relevance, F (1, 132) = 149.71, $p < .001$, reflected the fact that imitation of relevant acts was significantly higher than imitation of irrelevant acts (.35 and .22, respectively).

The nature of the significant Age X Instructions interaction, F (6, 132) = 2.58, $p < .05$, may be seen in Figure 3. As Figure 3 shows, 4-year-olds imitated to the same degree regardless of the instructions they had received. For all older children, imitation following problem introductions was significantly greater than imitation following no-problem instructions ($p < .01$ for 7- and 13-year-olds, $p < .05$ for 10-year-olds), and for 7- and 13-year-olds imitation following problem instructions was also significantly greater than imitation following ambiguous instructions ($p < .01$ in each comparison).

Figure 4 shows the nature of the significant Age X Relevance interaction, F (3, 132) = 8.21, $p < .001$. As can be seen in Figure 4, task-relevant acts were imitated at a higher level than were task-irrelevant acts by all age groups. The difference was not significant, however, for the 4-year-olds. For the three older age groups the difference between relevant and irrelevant imitation was significant ($p < .01$ in each case).

The significant Instructions X Relevance interaction, F (2, 132) = 7.42, $p < .001$, reflected the fact that while the proportion of relevant acts imitated was higher than the proportion of irrelevant acts imitated by subjects in all three instructions groups ($p < .01$ in each group), the difference between relevant and irrelevant imitation was particularly large for the problem group. Figure 5 shows the means entering into this interaction.

The nature of the significant Age X Instructions X Relevance interaction, F (6, 132) = 4.04, $p < .001$, is shown in Figure 6. As can be seen in Figure 6, the most clearcut developmental differences in imitation were seen for task-relevant imitation following instructions to the subjects to "find the right way to play the games." Under this combination of conditions, children 7 years old and older imitated much more than did children 4 years old ($p < .01$ for each comparison), while differences among the older groups of children were not significant. Following ambiguous instructions, there was also one significant age difference for task-relevant imitation, with 10-year-olds imitating significantly more than 7-year-olds ($p < .05$). Following the no-problem instructions there

[2]Post hoc comparisons among means were conducted by the Newman-Keuls method in all cases where post hoc comparisons were appropriate.

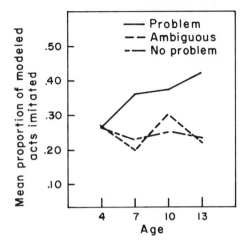

FIG. 3   The nature of the Age X Instructions interaction in imitation

were no significant age differences in imitation. For task-irrelevant imitation, there were no significant age differences regardless of instructional conditions.

Recall

The proportion of modeled behaviors correctly recalled was analyzed by a 4 X 3 X 4 X 2 analysis of variance (Age X Instructions X Task X Relevance) with repeated measures on tasks (1-4) and relevance (relevant versus irrelevant) with 12 observations per cell. (Table 5 summarizes the major findings of this analysis.)

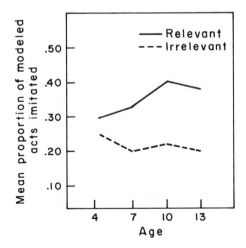

FIG. 4   The nature of the Age X Relevance interaction in imitation

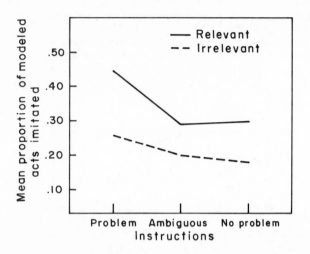

FIG. 5   The nature of the Instructions X Relevance interaction in imitation

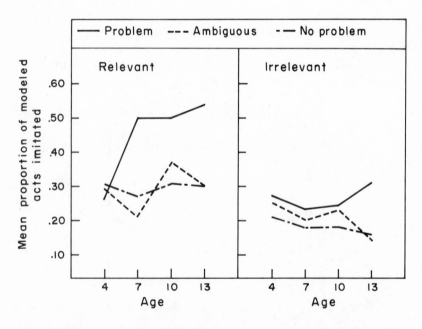

FIG. 6   The nature of the Age X Instructions X Relevance interaction in imitation

A significant main effect for Age was found, F (3, 132) = 53.11, p < .001, reflecting the fact that 4-year-olds recalled significantly less than all older age groups did (p < .01 for all comparisons) and that 7-year-olds recalled significantly less than 10- and 13-year-olds did (p < .01 for both comparisons). The two oldest age groups did not differ significantly in recall. The mean proportion of acts recalled by 4-, 7-, 10-, and 13-year-olds was .28, .46, .57, and .55.

A significant main effect for Relevance, F (1, 132) = 122.35, p < .001, reflected the fact that a significantly higher proportion of relevant than of irrelevant acts was recalled (.53 versus .40, respectively). This finding was qualified by a significant Age X Relevance interaction, F (3, 132) = 5.82, p < .001. The nature of this interaction is shown in Figure 7. Post hoc comparisons showed that for both task-relevant and task-irrelevant acts 4-year-olds recalled significantly less than 10- and 13-year-olds did (p < .01 for all comparisons). The two oldest age groups did not differ significantly from each other. As can be seen in Figure 7, 4-year-olds showed little difference in recall between relevant and irrelevant acts. This difference was not significant. All older age groups recalled significantly more task-relevant than task-irrelevant behaviors (p < .01 for each comparison).

The Age X Instructions interaction was also significant, F (6, 132) = 2.52, p < .05. The nature of this interaction can be seen in Figure 8.

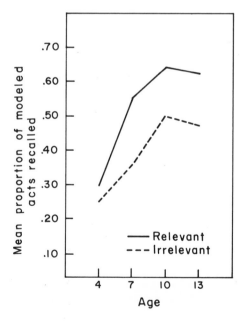

FIG. 7   The nature of the Age X Relevance interaction in recall

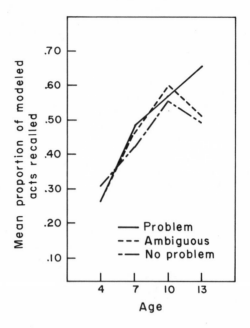

FIG. 8   The nature of the Age X Instructions interaction in recall

As Figure 8 shows, the oldest children showed differential sensitivity to the instructions. For 13-year-olds recall was significantly higher following problem instructions than following ambiguous or no-problem instructions ($p < .01$). Differences among instructional conditions were not significant for any other age group. As Figure 8 shows, the 10- and 13-year-old children did not show a plateau effect for recall, but rather a tendency for a continued increase with age under problem instructions and for a decrease with age otherwise. Examination of the age effect upon recall under each instructional condition separately revealed that under all conditions 4-year-olds recalled significantly less than 10-year-olds. Differences between the 10- and 13-year-olds were nonsignificant except following ambiguous instructions, where 13-year-olds recalled significantly less than 10-year-olds ($p < .05$).

Comparison of Imitation and Recall

In order to compare imitation and recall, the data were reanalyzed. The reanalysis consisted of a 4 X 3 X 4 X 2 X 2 analysis of variance with the first four factors as already described (Age, Instructions, Task, and Relevance), and the final factor of Type of Performance (imitation versus recall). Only those findings involving the new factor of Type of Performance (hereafter called simply

"Performance") are presented here.[3] Table 6 presents a summary of the significant findings of this analysis.

The main effect of Performance was significant, $F(1, 132) = 387.95, p < .001$, reflecting the fact that the average proportion of acts imitated was significantly smaller than the average proportion recalled (.28 versus .46, respectively). Another way of expressing this finding is by saying that children imitated an average of 61% of the acts that they were able to recall.

The Age X Performance interaction was significant, $F(3, 132) = 40.44$, $p < .001$. Figure 9 presents the means entering into this interaction. As can be seen in Figure 9, recall was higher than imitation $(p < .01)$ for all age groups except the 4-year-olds, for whom imitation and recall were not significantly different. Expressing this information as a percentage of acts imitated relative to those recalled, on the average, 4-year-olds imitated 96% of what they recalled while 7-, 10-, and 13-year-olds imitated 56%, 54%, and 53%, respectively.

A significant Instructions X Performance interaction was found, $F(2, 132) = 6.27, p < .01$, reflecting the fact that while imitation was significantly lower than recall under all instructional conditions $(p < .01$ in each case) the difference was smaller following problem instructions than following either of the other instructional conditions $(p < .01)$. Figure 10 shows the means entering into this interaction. On the average, the number of acts imitated relative to the number recalled was 71%, 53%, and 52%, respectively, following problem, ambiguous, and no-problem instructions.

Finally, the Age X Performance X Relevance interaction was significant, $F(3, 132) = 2.90, p < .05$, reflecting the fact that the age differences between imitation and recall were somewhat different for relevant behaviors from those for irrelevant behaviors. Figure 11 presents the means entering into this interaction. As Figure 11 shows, for 4-year-olds imitation was nearly identical to recall for both relevant and irrelevant behaviors. For the three older age groups imitation was significantly lower than recall for both relevant and irrelevant behaviors $(p < .01$ for each comparison). Further comparisons revealed that for the three older age groups the magnitude of the difference between imitation and recall of *relevant* acts was approximately equal and not significantly different. (If the values shown in Figure 11 are expressed as percentages, dividing mean imitation by mean recall, the values for 4-, 7-, 10-, and 13-year-olds on task-relevant behavior were 95%, 60%, 61%, and 61%, respectively.) For task-*irrelevant* behaviors, the magnitude of the difference between imitation and recall was

---

[3]Effects that do not involve the performance factor require averaging across imitation and recall for their explanation. Such an average variable is not a psychologically meaningful one. The separate effects involving imitation or recall alone have already been presented. As for the earlier analyses, there were no significant sex effects, and the presentation of findings relating to specific tasks has been postponed to a later section.

TABLE 6
Summary of Major Findings from Analysis of Variance of Effects
of Performance (Imitation versus Recall)

Effect	Significance level
Performance	< .001
Age X Performance	< .001
Instructions X Performance	< .01
Relevance X Performance	n.s.
Age X Instructions X Performance	n.s.
Age X Relevance X Performance	< .01
Instructions X Relevance X Performance	n.s.
Age X Instructions X Relevance X Performance	n.s.

significantly smaller for 7-year-olds than for 10-year-olds and 13-year-olds
($p < .001$ in each case). (Again expressing this as percentages, the values for task-
irrelevant behavior for 4-, 7-, 10-, and 13-year-olds were 96%, 55%, 44%, and
42%). Thus, as discussed earlier, despite the similarity in level of spontaneous
imitation across ages, younger children were actually much more imitative than
older children as judged by the proportion of behaviors imitated relative to the
proportion recalled. For both relevant and irrelevant behaviors, the 4-year-olds
showed significantly smaller differences between imitation and recall scores than
all groups of older children ($p < .001$ for each comparison).

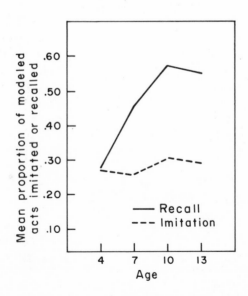

FIG. 9   The nature of the Age X Performance interaction

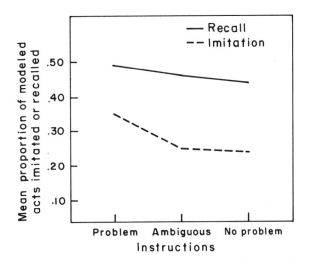

FIG. 10   The nature of the Instructions X Performance interaction

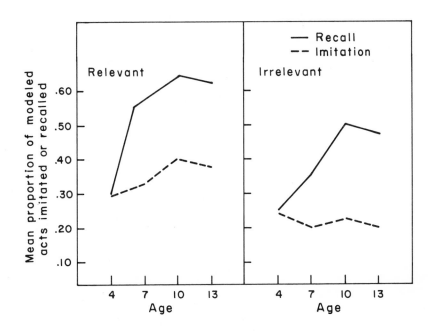

FIG. 11   The nature of the Age X Relevance X Performance interaction

Effects of Tasks

Table 7 presents a summary of the significant findings involving tasks on the analyses of each of the three different measures. Complete tables containing the mean scores for each group on each task for each measure can be found in Appendix A.

Imitation. Table 8 presents a summary of the nature of all significant findings for task differences in imitation. Differences indicated in Table 8 are all significant at the .05 level or beyond. The nature of the findings summarized in Table 8 are described more fully below.

A significant main effect for Task, $F(3, 396) = 20.75, p < .001$, reflected the fact that imitation of Task 1 was significantly higher than imitation of other tasks ($p < .05$ in comparison with Tasks 2 and 4, $p < .01$ in comparison with Task 3), and imitation of Task 3 was significantly lower than of all other tasks ($p < .01$). The mean proportion of imitation for Tasks 1-4, respectively, was .32, .29, .22, and .29.

The significant Age X Task interaction, $F(9,396) = 8.04, p < .001$, reflected the fact that the nature of task differences in imitation was not the same for all four age groups. There was evidence of an order effect for 4-year-olds: The mean imitation shown by 4-year-olds across Tasks 1-4, in that order, was .38, .32, .18, and .18. Comparisons by the Newman-Keuls method showed that imitation on the first two tasks was significantly greater than imitation on the last two tasks ($p < .01$ for each comparison), while the difference between the first and second tasks was not significant.

The significant Relevance X Task interaction, $F(3, 396) = 10.56, p < .001$, reflected the fact that while there was significantly higher imitation of relevant than of irrelevant acts on all four tasks, the difference was smaller for Task 2 than for other tasks. The significant Age X Relevance X Task interaction, $F(9, 396) = 5.31, p < .001$, confirmed the Relevance X Task interaction findings for the three oldest age groups. Four-year-olds, however, were erratic, sometimes

TABLE 7
Summary of Findings Involving the Effects of Tasks

Effect	Significance Level		
	Imitation	Recall	Imitation versus Recall
Task	$< .001$	$< .001$	$< .001$
Age X Task	$< .001$	$< .01$	n.s.
Instructions X Task	n.s.	$< .05$	$< .05$
Relevance X Task	$< .001$	$< .001$	$< .001$
Age X Relevance X Task	$< .001$	$< .001$	n.s
Age X Instructions X Task	n.s.	n.s.	n.s.
Relevance X Instructions X Task	n.s.	n.s.	n.s.
Age X Instructions X Relevance X Task	$< .01$	n.s.	n.s.

TABLE 8
Significant Task Differences in Imitation

Effect	Nature of finding
Task	Task 1 > Tasks 2, 4 > Task 3
Age X Task	4-year-old: Tasks 1, 2 > Tasks 3, 4 7-year-old: Task 2 > Task 3 10-year-old: Tasks 1, 4 > Tasks 2, 3 13-year-old: Task 4 > Tasks 1, 2, 3
Relevance X Task	relevant > irrelevant on all tasks, with difference least on Task 2
Age X Relevance X Task	4-year-old: relevant > irrelevant, Task 1; relevant = irrelevant, Tasks 2, 4; relevant < irrelevant, Task 3 7-, 10-, and 13-year-olds: relevant > irrelevant, Tasks 1, 3, 4; relevant = irrelevant, Task 2

showing more relevant than irrelevant imitation, sometimes the reverse, and sometimes no difference between relevant and irrelevant imitation. Also, while 4-year-olds showed the order effect referred to earlier for both relevant and irrelevant behaviors, the effect was more pronounced for the relevant behaviors than for the irrelevant behaviors.

The higher order interaction for Age X Instructions X Relevance X Task, F (18, 396) = 2.16, $p < .01$, arose partially because of the inconsistent behavior of 4-year-olds across tasks as well as from an occasional tendency of 10-year-olds to respond to ambiguous instructions as if they were problem instructions. The nature of this interaction is complex and will not be more fully interpreted.

In addition to the analyses of variance, correlations of imitation across tasks were also calculated in order to determine whether there was evidence for consistency of imitativeness. Table 9 presents the matrices of intercorrelations for each age group. Total imitation is reported in Table 9 since the correlation matrices for imitation of relevant acts alone yielded essentially the same pattern of conclusions, and the same was true for the correlation matrices for imitation of irrelevant acts alone.

As may be seen in Table 9, the magnitude and the significance of the correlations increased with age. The correlations for the youngest children were low and generally nonsignificant, while all the correlations for the oldest children were moderately high and significant. (The median correlation coefficients for 4-, 7-, 10-, and 13-year-olds were .17, .35, .57, and .68.)

Recall. Table 10 presents a summary of the significant findings for task differences in recall. Differences indicated in Table 10 are all significant at the .05 level or beyond.

TABLE 9
Intercorrelations of Total Imitativeness
Across Four Tasks

		Task	
Task	2	3	4
		4-year-olds	
1	−.02	.35*	.08
2		.14	.26
3			.19
		7-year-olds	
1	.28	.22	.52**
2		.48**	.43**
3			.27
		10-year-olds	
1	.66***	.57***	.57***
2		.40*	.43**
3			.56***
		13-year-olds	
1	.67***	.65***	.68***
2		.77***	.75***
3			.64***

*p < .05   **p < .01   ***p < .001

A significant effect for Task, F (3, 396) = 33.41, $p < .001$, reflected the fact that recall of Task 1 was significantly higher than that for all other tasks ($p < .01$ for each comparison), and recall of Task 3 was significantly lower than that for all other tasks ($p < .01$ for each comparison). The mean proportion of acts recalled for Tasks 1-4, respectively, was .57, .45, .39, and .45.

The significant Age X Task interaction, F (9, 396) = 3.05, $p < .01$, primarily reflected the fact that the 4- and 7-year-olds showed much larger differences in recall across tasks than did the other children, whose recall was relatively constant across the four tasks. (The recall for 4-year-olds ranged from a high of .41 to a low of .18; for 7-year-olds the range was .58 to .36; for 10-year-olds, .62 to .48; and for 13-year-olds, .66 to .51.) For all age groups recall on Task 1 attained the highest absolute value in comparison with the other three tasks.

The significant Instructions X Task interaction, F (6, 396) = 2.48, $p < .05$, reflected the fact that children who had received the problem instructions showed relatively little difference in recall across the four tasks, while children who had received ambiguous or no-problem instructions showed larger task differences in recall. (The problem-group children showed a range of recall from a high of .56 to a low of .45; for ambiguous-group children, the range was .58 to .37; for no-problem-group children, it was .56 to .34.)

TABLE 10
Significant Task Differences in Recall

Effect	Nature of finding
Task	Task 1 > Tasks 2, 4 > Task 3
Age X Task	4-year-old: Task 1 > Task 2 > Tasks 3, 4 7-year-old: Task 1 > Tasks 2, 3, 4; Task 2 > Task 3 10-year-old: Task 1 > Tasks 2, 3, 4 13-year-old: Tasks 1, 4 > Tasks 2, 3
Instructions X Task	Problem: Task 1 > Tasks 2, 3, 4 Ambiguous: Task 1 > Task 4 > Tasks 2, 3 No problem: Task 1 > Task 2 > Task 4 > Task 3
Relevance X Task	Relevant < irrelevant on Task 1; Relevant > irrelevant on Tasks 2, 3, 4
Age X Relevance X Task	4-year-old: relevant > irrelevant on Task 2; relevant = irrelevant on Tasks 1, 3, 4 7-year-old: relevant > irrelevant on Tasks 2, 3, 4; relevant = irrelevant on Task 1 10- and 13-year-olds: relevant > irrelevant on Tasks 2, 3, 4; relevant < irrelevant on Task 1

The significant Relevance X Task interaction, F (3, 396) = 21.22, $p < .001$, reflected the fact that for Task 1 a significantly higher proportion of irrelevant than of relevant behaviors was recalled. For the remaining three tasks significantly more relevant than irrelevant behaviors were recalled. The significant Age X Relevance X Task interaction, F (9, 396) = 5.07, $p < .001$, qualifies the Relevance X Task interaction in that only the two oldest age groups showed the unusual pattern of recalling more irrelevant than relevant behaviors for Task 1. The means entering into this interaction are shown in Figure 12.

Type of Performance. A significant Task X Performance interaction was found: F (3, 396) = 11.04, $p < .001$. This interaction reflected the finding that while imitation was significantly lower than recall for all four tasks, the difference was particularly large for Task 1. To express this finding in another manner, differences across tasks in recall were more marked than were differences in imitation (see the mean values presented earlier to describe the task effects for imitation and for recall).

The Instruction X Task X Performance interaction, F (6, 396) = 2.37, $p < .05$, reflected the finding that children in the problem condition showed approximately the same difference between imitation and recall on all four tasks. It was only the children in the ambiguous and no-problem conditions who showed a larger difference between imitation and recall for Task 1 than for other tasks.

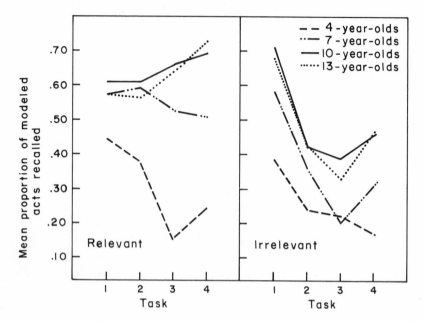

FIG. 12   The nature of the Age X Relevance X Task interaction in recall

The Relevance X Task X Performance interaction, F (3, 396) = 31.20, $p<$ .001, reflected the fact that the unusually large difference between imitation and recall for Task 1 occurred for irrelevant behaviors but not for relevant behaviors. Figure 13 shows the means entering into this interaction.

Correlations of total recall across tasks were calculated; the results are presented in Table 11. As this table shows, 4-year-olds showed no significant consistency in recall across the tasks. For older children, all correlations were positive, but only about half were significant. (The median correlation coefficients for 4-, 7-, 10-, and 13-year-olds were .12, .36, .34, and .30, respectively.)

INTERVIEW DATA

Responses to Interview Questions

Responses to most questions were analyzed using an Age X Experimental Group X Response partitioned chi-square analysis (Winer, 1971, pp. 858-859).[4] Several questions were asked only of those children who had seen the model. For these questions (Numbers 3, 6, 7, 9, and 10) analyses are therefore based upon the answers of the experimental group children alone. In reporting the results, follow-up analyses are reported only if the overall chi-square value was significant, and only those components that were found to be significant are reported.

---

[4]Preliminary inspection of the answers to all questions revealed no indication of sex differences. As in the analyses of overt behavior, therefore, the data were collapsed across sex.

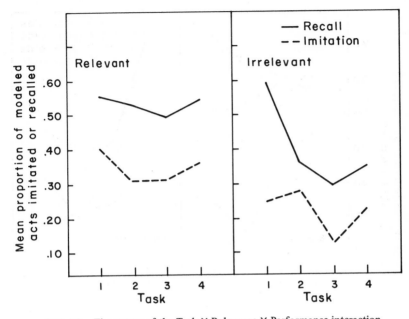

FIG. 13   The nature of the Task X Relevance X Performance interaction

TABLE 11
Intercorrelations of Total Recall Across Four Tasks

	Task		
Task	2	3	4
	4-year-olds		
1	−.10	.22	.14
2		−.24	.26
3			.09
	7-year-olds		
1	.34*	.37*	.32
2		.55***	.21
3			.48**
	10-year-olds		
1	.44**	.33*	.16
2		.34*	.17
3			.42**
	13-year-olds		
1	.24	.14	.24
2		.51**	.35*
3			.42*

*p < .05   **p < .01   ***p < .001

125

1. Enjoyed games. In response to the question concerning enjoying the games, answers were categorized as definitely positive ("yes") or not ("no," "indifferent," or no answer). The Age X Response χ^2 (3) = 38.36, $p < .01$, was significant. The nature of this effect was that older children were less likely to report enjoying the games than were younger children. Of the 120 4- and 7-year-olds, for example, all but one reported enjoying the games, whereas 18% of the 10-year-olds and 33% of the 13-year-olds did not respond positively.

2. Recall of instructions. The analysis of whether subjects recalled the experimental instructions correctly (scored dichotomously as fully correct or not) yielded a significant Age X Response χ^2 (3) = 42.78, $p < .01$. The percentages of children correctly recalling the experimental instructions for 4-, 7-, 10-, and 13-year-olds, respectively, were 42%, 82%, 80%, and 90%. Of the relatively few older children who did not recall the instructions correctly, most had received the no-problem instructions.

3. Recall of model's favorite game. Correct recall of the identity of the model's favorite game (Task 2, the pegboard) revealed a significant Age X Response χ^2 (3) = 23.14, $p < .01$. The percentage of children correctly recalling the model's favorite game among 4-, 7-, 10-, and 13-year-olds was 28%, 75%, 75%, and 67%, respectively.

4. Child's favorite game. The analysis of the child's favorite game response revealed a significant Age X Response χ^2 (9) = 17.43, $p < .05$, and a significant Experimental Group X Response χ^2 (12) = 37.91, $p < .001$. The age effect reflected the fact that 4-year-old children showed a high preference for Task 4 (the abacus), with 40% of the 4-year-old children choosing this game as their favorite, and that the 10-year-olds showed a high preference for Task 3 (the feltboard) and a low preference for Task 2 (the pegboard), with 38% and 10% of 10-year-olds naming each of these tasks, respectively, as their favorite. Other age groups did not deviate significantly from a 25% choice for each of the four games. The effect for experimental group reflected the fact that control children tended to state different task preferences from children who had seen the model. The percentage of control children naming each of the Tasks 1-4, respectively, was 44%, 17%, 26%, and 14%, a distrubution that deviated significantly from the distribution that would be expected if there had been no preferences (χ^2 (3) = 21.25, $p < .001$). Experimental children preferred Tasks 3 and 4: The percentage of experimental children naming each of Tasks 1-4 as their favorite was 14%, 18%, 33%, and 35%, respectively, a distribution deviating significantly from the chance pattern (χ^2 (3) = 18.82, $p < .001$).

5. Descriptions of the child's own performance. Children's descriptions of their own performance on each task were scored on a 4-point scale (1 = no response; 2 = wrong or vague; 3 = correct description of at least one element of strategy; 4 = complete description of strategy). For chi-square analyses these categories were collapsed into two (1 = none or wrong; 2 = partial or complete description). Analyses of children's descriptions of their own performance yielded a significant three-factor Age X Instructions X Response χ^2 for all but Task 1. In accordance with Winer's suggestion, simple chi-square analyses were therefore performed to examine age differences within each instructional group separately (this was also done for Task 1 in the interests of consistency).

Four-year-olds in two of the groups—the problem instructions and no-problem instructions experimental groups—were found to be markedly inferior to all other 4-year-olds and to the older children in describing their own performance. For both of these instructions groups, the Age X Response chi-square values were significant for all four tasks. (For the problem group, for Tasks 1-4, respectively: χ^2 (3) = 8.85, $p < .05$; χ^2 (3) = 28.80, $p < .01$; χ^2 (3) = 28.80, $p < .01$; χ^2 (3) = 21.70, $p < .01$. For the no-problem group, for Tasks 1-4, respectively: χ^2 (3) = 9.97, $p < .05$; χ^2 (3) = 12.70, p .01; χ^2 (3) = 20.70, $p < .01$; χ^2 (3) = 11.50, $p < .01$. In all these cases, the findings reflected poorer self-descriptions by 4-year-olds than by older children. For the 4-year-olds in these two groups, the median percentage of children giving adequate self-descriptions was 42%, with a range of 25% to 58% across the two groups and four tasks, while for the children of 7 and older, the median percentage was 96%, with a range of 75% to 100%.

For the remaining three groups—the ambiguous-instructions experimental groups and the two control groups—the Age X Response chi-square values were almost all nonsignificant, with only one isolated exception (Task 4 for ambiguous group subjects). Even with this exception, the performance of 4-year-olds in these three groups was notably better than for those in the problem and no-problem groups. The median percentage of adequate answers given by 4-year-olds in these three groups was 83%, with a range of 67% to 100%. Considering all five groups of 4-year-olds, thus, it appears that the combination of having witnessed a model and having received the problem or no-problem instructions decreased the accuracy of their self-descriptions.

6. Descriptions of the model's performance. Children's descriptions of the model's strategy were scored in the same manner as their descriptions of their own strategies. As before, dichotomized response categories of inadequate (no answer or wrong) versus adequate (partial or complete) were employed in the analyses. A significant Age X Response χ^2 was found for each task (for Tasks 1-4, respectively, χ^2 (3) = 30.17, χ^2 (3) = 29.62, χ^2 (3) = 38.45, χ^2 (3) = 95.02, $p < .01$ in each case). These findings reflected the fact that 4-year-olds consistently gave poorer descriptions of the model's behavior than did older children. The median percentage of 4-year-olds giving adequate descriptions was 25%, with a range of 8% to 50% across the three groups and four tasks. For older children, the median was 83%, with a range of 58% to 100%.

7. Right way to play games. The response to the question concerning the right way to play each game was scored trichotomously as specifically including the model's way among those that were correct, specifically excluding the model's way as correct, or giving no response. A significant Age X Response χ^2 was found for each task (χ^2 (6) = 22.47, χ^2 (6) = 69.43, χ^2 (6) = 61.89, χ^2 (6) = 59.17, for Tasks 1-4, respectively, $p < .01$ in each case). On all four questions the significant Age effect reflected a greater tendency of 4-year-olds to give no reply to the question. Older children from 7 through 13 tended to respond equivalently, with most of these children answering on Tasks 1 and 2 that the model's way was *not* the right way (79% on Task 1, 82% on Task 2). On Tasks 3 and 4, the older children were approximately equally divided between those answering that the model's way was incorrect and those answering that it was correct (56% of the 7-, 10-, and 13-year-old children believed the model's way was incorrect on Task 3, 54% on Task 4)

8. Number of other ways to play games. An Age X Instructions X Task analysis of variance, with repeated measures on the task factor, of the number of other ways to play yielded significant main effects for age, F (3, 220) = 22.06, $p < .001$, and task, F (3,660) = 19.02, $p < .001$, and a significant Age X Task interaction, F (9, 660) = 4.19, $p < .001$. The age effect reflected the fact that older children suggested significantly more ways to play the games than did younger children, with the differences between all pairwise comparisons of age groups attaining significance at the .05 level or better. (The mean number of ways to play each game suggested by 4-, 7-, 10-, and 13-year-olds, respectively, was .68, 1.05, 1.48, and 1.77.) The task effect reflected the fact that the children suggested significantly more alternate ways to play for Task 1 than for any other task ($p < .01$ for each comparison). The remaining task means were not significantly different from each other (the mean number of ways suggested for Tasks 1-4, respectively, were 1.57, 1.17, 1.19, and 1.05). The Age X Task interaction reflected the fact that the age differences were more pronounced for Task 1 than for other tasks. On all tasks, however, there was a simple monotonic increase with age in the number of suggested ways to play the games.

9. Reasons for imitation or nonimitation. Children gave many different reasons for imitating or not imitating, but several responses occurred with sufficient frequency to suggest that an analysis should be performed relating these responses to age and instructional conditions. Fifty of the 144 children (35%) responded that they imitated because they thought the right thing to do was what the model did. A partitioned Age X Group X Response chi-square analysis of the dichotomized response variable (mentioned this specifically as a reason versus did not mention this as a reason) was performed, yielding a significant Age X Response χ^2 (3) = 9.44, $p < .05$, and a significant Instructions X Response χ^2 (2) = 14.96, $p < .01$. The age effect reflected the fact that younger children were more likely to state that they thought the right thing to do was what the model did: The percentages of 4-, 7-, 10-, and 13-year-olds giving this as a reason were 47%, 44%, 30%, and 17%, respectively. The Instructions X Response effect reflected the fact that problem-group subjects were more likely to give this as a reason than were subjects in the ambiguous and no-problem groups (54%, 33%, and 16% of the children in each group, respectively).

The next most common response was that the child wanted to do it his own way (and therefore did not imitate). Twenty-nine of the 144 children (20%) gave this response. A partitioned chi-square analysis yielded a significant Age X Response χ^2 (3) = 17.06, $p < .01$. The age effect was curvilinear, reaching a peak for 10-year-olds. The percentages of 4-, 7-, 10-, and 13-year-olds giving this as a reason were 0%, 22%, 39%, and 19%, respectively.

Another response was that the child couldn't think of another way to play (and therefore imitated). Twenty-two of the 144 children (15%) gave this reason. A partioned chi-square analysis yielded a significant Age X Response χ^2 (3) = 12.23, $p < .01$, and a significant Instructions X Response χ^2 (2) = 6.55, $p < .05$. The age effect reflected the fact that older children were more likely to give this response than younger children (the percentages of 4-, 7-, 10-, and 13-year-old children giving this response were 0%, 11%, 25%, and 25%, respectively). The instructions effect reflected the fact that this response was least likely to be given by children in the problem condition and most likely to be given by children in the no-problem condition (for children in the problem, ambiguous, and no-problem conditions, respectively, 6%, 14%, and 25% gave this response).

10. Liking the model. Responses to the question of whether the child had liked the model were categorized either as definitely positive ("yes") or not ("no," "indifferent," or no answer). The analysis did not yield a significant overall chi-square value. Most of the children (76%) replied that they liked the model.

11. Related to schoolwork. Responses to the question concerning whether the experimental procedures were related to the child's schoolwork were categorized either as definitely negative ("no") or not ("yes" or no answer). The analysis did not yield a significant overall chi-square value. Approximately half of the children (46%) believed that the experiment was related to their schoolwork and half (54%) did not.

12. Child's performance to be discussed with the teacher. Responses to this question were categorized as definitely negative ("no") or not ("yes" or no answer). The analysis yielded a significant Age X Response χ^2 (3) = 20.69, $p < .001$. The percentages of 4-, 7-, 10-, and 13-year-olds, respectively, who believed that their performance would be discussed with their teacher or who were uncertain were 62%, 70%, 90%, and 53%.

13. Child's feelings if his performance were to be made public. Responses were scored on a 4-point scale (1 = no response, 2 = bad, 3 = indifferent, 4 = good). The chi-square analysis yielded a significant Age X Response χ^2 (3) = 66.67, $p < .001$. The percentages of children replying that they would feel good if others knew of their performance declined significantly with age (52%, 47%, 13%, and 3% for the 4-, 7-, 10-, and 13-year-olds, respectively). Conversely, the percentages of children expressing indifference rose significantly with age (0%,

8%, 28%, and 25% for 4-, 7-, 10-, and 13-year-olds, respectively). Approximately half of the children at all ages gave no response to this question, and very few responded that they would feed bad if others knew (age differences were not significant for these responses).

Relationships Among Questions

In order to determine whether the information contained in the children's responses to the 13 interview questions might be reducible to a smaller number of simple factors, a factor analysis was performed on the responses to the questions. The results of this factor analysis are presented in Appendix B, rather than in the present chapter, since the factor solution indicated that responses to the interview questions could not easily be accounted for by a small number of underlying factors.

Relationship Between Interview Questions and Performance Measures

Analyses of the relationship between interview responses and overall imitation and recall were restricted to responses from those children who had seen the model.

1. Enjoyed games. Since virtually all the 4-year-olds and 7-year-olds reported that they had enjoyed the games, no analyses were made relating this question to performance for the younger children. The overall imitation and recall scores of the 54 older children who reported that they enjoyed the games were compared with those of the 18 older children who reported that they did not enjoy the games. The mean imitativeness of children who enjoyed the games was significantly higher than the imitativeness of children who did not enjoy the games ($\overline{X}$ = .33 versus $\overline{X}$ = .24, respectively, t (70) = 2.32, $p < .05$). The mean recall scores were not significantly related to enjoyment of the games.

2. Recall of instructions. The fact that most of the older children who failed to recall the instructions correctly had received the no-problem instructions suggested the possibility that these children might, in fact, have believed that their performance would be evaluated and might therefore have imitated more than children who recalled the no-problem instructions correctly. Comparisons were particularly appropriate for 7- and 10-year-olds, since approximately half the children within these groups had forgotten, while half had correctly recalled, the no-problem instructions. Comparisons by t tests, however, of the overall imitation and recall scores shown by the children who recalled versus those who did not revealed no significant differences in performance between these two groups.

3. Recall of the model's favorite game. For each age level, the overall imitation and recall scores for children who recalled the model's favorite game correctly were compared with those for children who did not recall the model's favorite game. None of the comparisons attained significance.

4. Child's favorite game. The performance of the 26 children who imitated the model's preference for Game 2 by choosing this game as their own favorite was compared with that of the 118 children who did not choose Game 2. This comparison was made in order to determine whether children who imitated the model's preference might also show higher imitativeness in general. *T*-test comparisons revealed, however, that these two groups did not differ on either overall imitation or recall.

Children's performance on their favorite game was compared with their performance averaged across the remaining three games by a 4 X 3 X 2 X 2 analysis of variance (Age X Instructions X Game X Relevance) with repeated measures on Game (favorite versus nonfavorite) and Relevance (relevant versus irrelevant).[5] The analysis for imitation yielded a significant main effect for Game, $F(1, 131)$ = 6.06, $p < .05$. Children showed significantly lower imitation on their favorite game than they showed on their nonfavorite games ($\overline{X} = .26$ versus $\overline{X} = .29$, respectively). The analysis for recall scores showed no significant differences in recall associated with whether the game was the child's favorite or not.

5. Descriptions of child's own performance. Children's ability to describe their own performance verbally was significantly related to their recall scores. The correlation between the quality of self-descriptions (on a 4-point scale) for each of the four tasks and recall scores on the same task ranged from .17 to .33 and was significant at the .05 level or better for every task. The correlations between self-descriptions and imitation were not significant except for Task 4 ($r = .30, p < .001$).

6. Descriptions of the model's performance. The correlations between children's ability to verbally describe the model's performance in the interview and their recall scores for the acts she had performed ranged from .42 to .65 across the four tasks, with all four correlations highly significant ($p < .001$). The correlations with imitation were near zero for Tasks 1 and 2, but were significant for Task 3 ($r = .26, p < .01$) and for Task 4 ($r = .40, p < .001$).

7. Right way to play games. The relationship between the child's evaluation of the correctness of the model's solution and the imitation and recall displayed by the child was evaluated by comparing the performance of children who had replied that the model's solution was a "right way" with those who had said some other way was correct. The results of these comparisons are shown in Table 12. (The number of children does not always sum to 144 since some of the children, usually 4-year-olds, did not respond to the question.)

---

[5]To avoid duplication, only those findings involving the game factor are reported. The analysis was conducted on 143 children's responses since one 13-year-old declined to state a preference.

TABLE 12
Relationship Between Evaluation of Correctness of
Modeled Solution and Imitation and Recall

	Imitation		Recall	
Evaluation of modeled Solution	$\overline{X}$	t (df)	$\overline{X}$	t (df)
		Task 1		
Correct $(N = 25)$	.36	2.38 (123)**	.64	1.57 (123)
Incorrect $(N = 100)$	.27		.58	
		Task 2		
Correct $(N = 20)$	.31	1.10 (122)	.45	.72 (122)
Incorrect $(N = 104)$	.28		.42	
		Task 3		
Correct $(N = 53)$	.23	2.95 (120)***	.43	2.18 (120)*
Incorrect $(N = 69)$	.16		.35	
		Task 4		
Correct $(N = 52)$	.31	1.93 (121)*	.48	1.81 (121)*
Incorrect $(N = 71)$	.26		.41	

$*p < .05$, one-tailed $**p < .01$, one-tailed $***p < .001$, one-tailed

As may be seen in Table 12, children who responded that the model's way was correct showed significantly higher imitation on 3 of the 4 tasks and showed significantly higher recall on 2 of the 4 tasks.

8. Number of other ways to play games. The correlation between the total number of alternative ways the child could suggest to play the games and his overall imitativeness was low and nonsignificant $(r = .13)$. The correlation between the number of other ways suggested and overall recall was .37 $(p < .001)$.

9. Reasons for imitation or nonimitation. The 50 children who responded that they had imitated because they thought the model's way was right showed significantly higher overall imitation than did the 94 children who did not mention this as a reason $(\overline{X} = .32$ versus $\overline{X} = .27$, respectively, t (142) = 2.21, $p < .05$, one-tailed). The two groups did not differ significantly in recall.

Four-year-olds were omitted from the analysis of the response, "I wanted to do it my own way," since this response never occurred among 4-year-olds. The mean imitation shown by the 29 older children who gave this response did not differ significantly from the imitation shown by the 79 older children who did not give this response. The two groups also did not differ significantly in recall.

Four-year-olds were also omitted from the analysis of the response, "I couldn't think of another way," because of the nonoccurrence of the response among 4-year-olds. The mean imitation shown by the 22 older children who gave this response did not differ significantly from that shown by the 86 older children who did not give this response. The two groups also did not differ significantly in recall.

10. Liking the model. The 109 children who replied that they liked the model did not differ significantly on imitation or recall from the 35 children who did not reply positively to this question.

11. Related to schoolwork. The 66 children who believed that the experiment was or might be related to their schoolwork did not differ in mean imitativeness from the 78 children who responded that the experiment was not related to schoolwork. The two groups differed significantly in recall, however, with children who believed the study was school-related recalling more than children who did not believe it was school-related ($\overline{X}$ = .49 versus $\overline{X}$ = .43, respectively, t (142) = 2.17, p < .05, one-tailed).

12. Child's performance to be discussed with the teacher. The 99 children who thought their performance might be discussed with their teacher did not differ significantly on imitation or recall from the 45 children who did not believe their performance would be discussed with their teacher.

13. Child's feelings if his performance were to be made public. The children who replied that they would feel good if their performance were discussed with others were compared with children who did not respond in this manner. *T*-test comparisons within each age group did not yield any significant differences related to this answer. Similar comparisons were made comparing children who indicated indifference to others' knowing of their performance with children who did not respond in this manner. Again, none of these comparisons was significant.

7
Discussion of the Study's Findings

Our discussion of the results of the developmental study will be presented in an order that parallels the presentation of results in the previous chapter. We begin with a discussion of the control-group children's performance and follow this with discussions of the experimental-group children's performance and of the results of the interview.

SEX EFFECTS AND CONTROL
GROUP FINDINGS

Consistent with the bulk of previous work on imitation, no main effects of sex or significant interactions involving sex of subject were found in the present study. With regard to imitative behavior, the performance of boys and girls on the tasks employed in this study was comparable.

The performance of the two control groups indicated that the dependent measures employed in the present study were not contaminated by a high incidence of imitative responses precipitated either by the demand characteristics of the tasks or by chance imitation. The mean imitation score (averaging across the two control groups) was .10. This value was significantly lower than that found for the experimental children whose overall mean imitation score was .28. Stated in terms of the number of acts imitated, the experimental subjects imitated an average of approximately 20 of 71 modeled behaviors while the control group "imitated" approximately 7. It thus appears that the variations among groups in the present study were not attenuated by ceiling effects. Furthermore this finding indicates that children in the 4-13 age range do not automatically imitate all the behaviors that are modeled for them but rather limit their imitation to something less than a third of the behaviors modeled. Many studies give the impression that children are much more imitative than this. Most such studies, however, either have provided a single act, such as sharing, or have provided a very small number of modeled acts. The percentage of acts imitated is doubtless partially a function of the number of acts modeled, and the level of imitativeness shown by children in naturalistic situations is therefore likely to be less than that suggested by many laboratory studies.

A comparison of the chance imitation scores of the problem and no-problem control groups revealed several unexpected findings. A main effect for age was found, indicating that in both control groups the older children had higher chance imitative scores than did the younger children. It appears that as children mature their information-processing system becomes more and more similar to that of the adult experimenter's. When the older children analyzed the tasks, they evidently devised solutions involving some of the same behaviors selected by the adult experimenters as the behaviors to be modeled. This suggests that in developmental studies investigating imitation across a wide age range some correction factor is required to correct for the greater similarity obtaining between the thought processes of older subjects and experimenters. Such similarity would result in inflated imitation scores for older subjects.

The chance imitation score of the problem control group was found to be higher than that of the no-problem control group. We thus have some suggestive evidence that the instruction manipulation was effective. When instructed that there was a single correct response, the demand characteristics of the tasks probably became more salient and resulted in the problem-condition control children emitting a higher incidence of behaviors designated as modeled behaviors for the experimental children.

Some evidence was found for the effectiveness of the relevance-irrelevance manipulation in the finding that the control group children emitted more chance imitations of the relevant as compared to the irrelevant type. This main effect for relevance must be qualified in light of the significant Relevance X Task interaction which indicated that more relevant than irrelevant chance imitations were not found on each of the four tasks. An important feature of the Relevance X Task interaction is that it indicates that the higher proportion of chance imitation of relevant than of irrelevant acts does not appear to have occurred simply because a smaller number of relevant than of irrelevant behaviors were available to be scored. There was also a significant Age X Relevance interaction found for the two control groups, where the difference between relevant and irrelevant chance imitation was greater in older children than in younger children. This interaction provides further evidence that older children are more sensitive than younger children to demand characteristics.

Some further thought should probably be given to the procedure whereby investigators designate behaviors as being either task-relevant or task-irrelevant. Two procedures immediately come to mind: (1) After a careful examination of the demand characteristics of the tasks to be employed, the investigator can logically designate certain behaviors as task-relevant and certain behaviors as task-irrelevant; (2) on the basis of pretesting, behaviors can be designated as relevant or irrelevant depending upon the actual incidence of various behaviors spontaneously emitted by the pretest children when confronted with the experimental tasks. Employing such an empirical procedure would result in designating as relevant those behaviors having a relatively high incidence of spontaneous emission; behaviors having a very low incidence would be categorized as task-irrelevant. (Behaviors having a very high spontaneous emission rate should not be used as the behaviors to be modeled since this would result in artificially inflated imitation scores.) While the first procedure was employed in the present study to define the relevant-irrelevant dichotomy, the findings with the two control groups indicated that the same behaviors designated as relevant and irrelevant would have been so designated had the second procedure been employed: That is, behaviors designated as "relevant" were spontaneously emitted with a higher frequency than those designated as "irrelevant."

That the demand characteristics of the four tasks differed in intensity was indicated by the significant Task main effect found for the two control groups. This finding reflected primarily the higher incidence of chance imitative behaviors on Task 1 as compared to the other three tasks. Further evidence that the atypicality of performance on Task 1 was due to the demand characteristics of this task was contained in the significant Relevance X Task interaction, which indicated that on Task 1 chance imitation of relevant behaviors was markedly high in comparison with chance imitation of irrelevant behaviors.

All the significant differences obtained in the analysis of the performance of the control groups should be interpreted conservatively since the absolute values of both relevant and irrelevant chance imitation scores were so low. We now turn to the imitative performance of the experimental children.

IMITATION

No main effect for age was found. The failure to find a significant main effect for age is at variance with our prediction of an overall decline in imitation. It is also contrary to a major tenet of the outerdirectedness formulation of imitative behavior, which predicts that imitative behavior should decrease with increasing cognitive development as indexed by chronological age (Achenbach & Zigler, 1968; Balla et al., 1971; Sanders et al., 1968; Turnure & Zigler, 1964; Yando & Zigler, 1971; Zigler & Yando, 1972). It should be noted that in those studies in which the age effects predicted by the outerdirectedness formulation were found (Balla et al., 1971; Yando & Zigler, 1971; Zigler & Yando, 1972), the tasks employed were quite different from those utilized in the present study. As predicted, age effects were found in interaction with all other variables in the study, so the importance of age for imitation appears to have been masked by averaging across all other conditions.

Our prediction of a significant effect for instructions was confirmed. The direction of the effect was only partially as predicted, however: Averaging across all other experimental dimensions of the present study, more imitation was found following the problem instructions than was found following the ambiguous or no-problem instructions. Contrary to expectation, the imitation scores obtained in these latter two conditions were comparable. Within our formulation, emphasis has been placed on the active problem-solving nature of children's imitation. In addition to generating the prediction that the largest imitation scores would be found in the problem condition, this view generates the prediction that there should be higher imitation scores of the task-relevant (and thus problem-solving-related) behavior than of the task-irrelevant behavior. This prediction was confirmed: Averaging across all other experimental dimensions more task-relevant behaviors than task-irrelevant behaviors were imitated.

The finding that age entered into a significant interaction with every other experimental factor confirmed a major prediction of the study and is supportive of the two-factor approach we have been advocating. It is also consistent with the conclusion of Hartup and Coates (1970, 1972) that age is an important determinant of children's imitation (typically in interaction with other determinants of imitation) and is at odds with the relative neglect of the age variable displayed by Bandura (1969a, 1969c, 1971a, 1977). As predicted, 4-year-olds were consistently different from older children.

The significant Age X Instructions interaction reflected the finding that while the problem condition resulted in more imitation for the 7-, 10-, and 13-year-olds, the 4-year-olds displayed comparable imitation in all three instruction conditions. The atypical performance of the 4-year-old group can be attributed to a variety of interrelated possibilities:

1. One potential explanation is that the memory-storage-and-retrieval systems of 4-year-olds have not developed to a level permitting them to retain the instructions given in the three instruction conditions. If all instructions were quickly forgotten by the 4-year-olds, one would expect comparable imitation in each of the three instruction conditions.

2. A second explanation may be that the social learning histories of 4-year-old children are not of the sort that make them conversant with the principle that a task can have but one correct solution. Such a principle is much more likely to be ingrained during the school years than during the preschool period.

3. A third possible explanation is that, given the cognitive immaturity of the 4-year-olds, regardless of their instructional condition, all the 4-year-olds were phenomenologically faced with very demanding tasks and were thus all in an extremely difficult problem condition. If this were so, one would expect the 4-year-olds invariably to display moderately high imitation scores (limited by their attenuated ability to remember the many behaviors that were modeled) but would not expect them to exhibit differing imitation scores as a function of instructional condition.

The significant Age X Relevance interaction parallels the Age X Instructions finding discussed immediately above. While task-relevant behaviors were imitated more than task-irrelevant behaviors by the 7-, 10-, and 13-year-olds, the 4-year-olds did not display significantly less imitation of irrelevant behaviors than of relevant behaviors. The factors just discussed for the atypicality of the 4-year-olds in regard to the instructional condition variable may also hold in understanding why no significant differences between relevant and irrelevant behaviors were found for the 4-year-olds. The present findings thus provide support for Hartup and Coates's (1970) suggestion that "children's imitation of behaviors that are distal to the central task of the experiment may well be different (and the relations of such imitation to age may well be different) from imitation on the salient experimental task [p. 129]." The present findings are also in accord with the argument of Aronfreed (1969) and of Kohlberg (1969) that young children are more influenced by task-irrelevant behavior than are older children.

A significant Instructions X Relevance interaction was found, indicating that the difference between relevant and irrelevant imitation was greater following the problem instructions than following the other two instructions. Again, the children's active problem-solving orientation can be employed to interpret this interaction. When informed that there is a problem to be solved, children should be more motivated to scan and utilize task-relevant behaviors that can be employed in problem solution; children should be much less interested in those behaviors that appear markedly extraneous to problem solution. Whether this effect is mediated by attentional or motivational processes, or some combination of the two, remains an open issue. The fact that no group differences were found on ratings of children's attentiveness to the model suggests that the Instructions X Relevance imitation effect was a function more of motivational than attentional factors. The attention measure in the present study was a relatively gross one, however. If eye movements had been monitored, as has been done in several other studies (Grusec & Brinker, 1972; Yussen, 1974), children who had been given the problem instructions might have been found to be paying especially close attention to the task-relevant acts shown by the model. Such a test might be made in a future study.

In addition to the three simple interactions, a more complex significant interaction was found involving age, instructions, and relevance. Reflected in this interaction is the fact that problem instructions and task relevance of the modeled acts appear to summate in producing the most dramatic increase in imitation with increasing age. Again this finding is certainly consistent with the trend suggested by Hartup and Coates (1970) and by our own review of developmental studies in chapter 4 of this book. Children apparently show increases in imitation with age only if the imitation tasks are challenging ones, and such increases are likely to be found only if children believe that their performance may be evaluated in some way.

RECALL

Not surprisingly, the proportion of modeled behaviors correctly recalled increased with age. The 4-year-olds displayed markedly attenuated recall scores. As our review in chapter 4 indicated, the finding of greater recall with age is usual in developmental studies of modeling influences. The finding of improvement of memory with age is a common one in other kinds of children's learning as well (Flavell, 1970; Flavell, Friedrichs, & Hoyt, 1970; Stevenson, 1972).

Recall was greater for task-relevant modeled behaviors than for task-irrelevant behaviors. Again we see that it is the functional role played by imitation in problem solution that determines the phenotypic pattern of imitation observed. Behaviors related to the solution of the task at hand were more likely to be recalled than were those modeled behaviors irrelevant to generating an acceptable solution to the problems confronting the children. (Parallel findings were obtained with the imitation score as well.) It thus appears that both imitation and recall are influenced by the child's perception that a modeled behavior would be helpful in solving the problem at hand. This finding could be explained without difficulty by social learning theorists, by reinforcement theorists, and by effectance theorists.

As predicted by the two-factor theory, the child's age had a modifying influence upon the effects of task relevance. As found with the imitation score, the difference between the recall of 4-year-olds in the relevant and irrelevant conditions was much less than that observed in the three older age groups. This significant interaction is in agreement with the findings of other studies (Collins, 1970; Hallahan et al., 1974) where comparisons of relevant and irrelevant recall among children of different ages were made. This discrimination between task-relevant and irrelevant behaviors appears to be more difficult for the 4-year-olds than for the older children. For the 4-year-old children, all the modeled behaviors seem to take on a functional equivalence. We would suggest two possible explanations for the failure by the 4-year-olds to discriminate between task-relevant and task-irrelevant modeled behaviors:

1. Older children are more adequate problem solvers than younger children and are probably aware of this greater adequacy. The older children are therefore not as helpless and dependent on external cues as the 4-year-olds are. The inadequacy of the 4-year-olds' problem-solving abilities leads them to be dependent on all of the external behaviors modeled. Stated somewhat differently, the 4-year-olds may feel that any and all behaviors emitted by adults are better guides to action than their own poorly developed problem-solving strategies.

2. The Age X Relevance interaction in recall may be mediated by attentional processes. For the older children, those modeled behaviors that have some logical

relation to the problem at hand (i.e., relevant behaviors) take on greater perceptual salience than those modeled behaviors that have little logical relation to the problem to be solved (i.e., irrelevant behaviors). Within such an attentional explanation, the older children may not only find the task-relevant behaviors to be of greater perceptual salience, they may also be actively suppressing the task-irrelevant behaviors.

These two explanations are not mutually exclusive and may operate in combination with each other. The view that younger children are more dependent than older children and are more the captive of stimuli in their perceptual field is consistent with the literature on field dependence and independence (Witkin et al., 1954; Witkin et al., 1962).

Further evidence of the importance of the children's central mediation in the processing of the modeled cues made available to them can be seen in the significant Age X Instructions interaction found on the recall measure. For the 13-year-olds, as compared with the three younger age groups, the difference in recall scores in the three instruction conditions was much more marked. It is only in the problem condition that one finds a linear increase in recall scores with age. In the ambiguous and no-problem conditions, recall scores actually *decreased* between 10 and 13 years.

Neither the earlier work on imitation nor the work on developmental changes in memory provide any very parsimonious explanation of this decrease in recall scores in the ambiguous and no-problem instructions conditions. In the problem condition the children were challenged by the instructions to find the one acceptable solution to the task. With such a task set, the children probably attended more closely to the modeled behaviors and thus produced ever-increasing recall scores with age. They were evidently motivated to utilize more fully their memory capacity, which increases with age. In the other two instruction conditions, the children were not challenged to produce a single acceptable solution. Since any behavior was acceptable, these children were less motivated to observe and later to recall the modeled behaviors. Freed from such instructional constraints, the 13-year-old children in the no-problem and ambiguous conditions may have felt that their own task solutions were as effective as those indicated by the modeled behaviors. If confidence that one's own solutions are adequate increases with age, say between 10 and 13, the children in ambiguous and no-problem conditions might have attended less and thus displayed the decrease in recall scores found in the present study. (It is interesting that it is within this same age period that studies of incidental learning report a decrease in children's recall of task-irrelevant information.)

Another possible interpretation of this Age X Instructions interaction is that the 13-year-olds accepted the instruction at face value while the younger children attributed some constant purpose to the experiment regardless of the instructional condition they experienced. This interpretation is less than compelling in view of the failure to find a parallel Age X Instructions interaction on the imitation measure. (While there was an Age X Instructions interaction on the imitation score, this interaction took a different form from that found on the recall score.)

THE RELATIONSHIP OF RECALLED BEHAVIORS TO IMITATED BEHAVIORS

While the measure of the relationship between recall and imitation employed in the present study has not heretofore been employed in research on imitation,[1] it appears to be a valuable measure to obtain, inasmuch as it assesses an aspect of imitation gauged by neither the imitation score nor the recall score alone. Conceptually, this score essentially gets at the degree to which behaviors recalled by the child actually appear in the child's imitative behaviors. If recall scores were held constant, the child emitting the greater number of recalled modeled behaviors would be viewed as being more imitative than the child emitting fewer of these modeled behaviors. Imitation behavior is delimited by recall, and recall scores are closely related to age, which is a good index of the quality of the child's memory system. The percentage of recalled acts that are imitated is not so closely tied to the child's age and therefore represents a more age-independent measure of imitation.

The analyses of the relationship between recall scores and imitation scores revealed that:

1. The proportion of acts imitated was markedly smaller than the proportion of modeled acts recalled. In general, averaging across all ages and experimental conditions, the children imitated a little more than half of the modeled acts that they were able to recall.

2. The Age X Performance interaction reflected the finding that the difference between imitation and recall was greater for the three older groups than it was for the 4-year-olds. For the 4-year-olds, the proportion of acts imitated was almost identical to the proportion of acts recalled.

3. The significant Instructions X Performance interaction reflected the finding that the difference between imitation and recall was smaller in the problem than in the other two instructional conditions. It thus appears that the problem instructions caused the child to imitate a greater proportion of the recalled modeled behaviors. The finding on this measure is thus consistent with that obtained on the imitation measure alone.

4. The significant Age X Relevance X Performance interaction reflected the finding that, with increasing age, the difference between recalled and imitated

---

[1]The closest example of a similar measure appears to be the analysis conducted by Bandura (1965), who computed *t*-tests to compare the difference between imitation and recall in a study of children's responses to modeled aggression.

modeled behaviors is due more to the children's suppressing the irrelevant modeled behaviors (not imitating them) than to their suppressing relevant behaviors.

Perhaps the most striking finding of the present study was the performance of the 4-year-olds on this measure, which compares the number of modeled behaviors recalled with the number of these behaviors imitated. The 4-year-olds displayed almost no selectivity. They emitted almost all the acts that they could remember when performing on the tasks. One could interpret this striking finding with the concept of stimulus-boundedness. This would, however, be assigning a name to the experimental behavior observed rather than providing an explanation in terms of those circumscribed processes that mediated the finding in question. As Maslow (1949) cautioned long ago, the process of naming can interfere with explanation since giving an event a name often closes off further investigation. With this caution in mind we would suggest that the behavior of the 4-year-olds may be interpreted in terms of some combination of the following explanations:

1. Considerable biological and developmental work has indicated that the age period from 4 to 7 is a transitional period in which (a) the physiology of the child is changing (White, 1965); (b) the child's perceptual behavior is shifting from the global to the differentiated (Werner, 1940); (c) the child's motor system is coming more and more under the control of his verbal system (Luria, 1957, 1961); and (d) the iconic stage, with its emphasis on visual imagery, is giving way to the symbolic representation of more advanced development (Bruner, 1964). A variety of related cognitive-developmental events are thus taking place in which the child's cognitive apparatus becomes capable of ever-more-demanding cognitive transformations. All of these events lead to a constant developmental progression in which the child becomes less and less a captive of the raw stimuli he encounters and more and more an active transformer, abstracter, and hierarchizer of these perceptual events. Thus the 4-year-old child displays little selectivity. The modeled behaviors he witnesses are represented as individual totalities, and when allowed to do so he simply acts out the modeled representations incorporated into the memory system. In contrast, the older child is much more selective in determining which behaviors he wishes to store in his representational system and utilizes the problem-solving demands of the situation, for example, the instructional condition and relevance dimensions, in determining both storage and imitation rules.

2. Consistent with the theoretical position of Gewirtz and his colleagues (1971a, b; Gewirtz & Stingle, 1968), the imitation behavior of the 4-year-olds may be indicative of the phenomenon of generalized imitation. Perhaps 4-year-olds are more reinforced for imitative acts and therefore imitate all that they can when given the opportunity.

3. Consistent with the position of Bandura (1971a), perhaps 4-year-olds are unable to discriminate between modeled behaviors that will result in reinforcement if imitated and those that will not. In the face of such a discrimination

problem, the young child has little choice but to imitate all those modeled events stored that he is physically capable of reproducing.

4. A further possibility would be based on the effectance concept of White (1959, 1960) and others (Harter, 1974, 1975a, b; Harter, Shultz & Blum, 1971; Harter & Zigler, 1974) in juxtaposition with the evidence that children find operating at the cutting edge of their cognitive ability inherently reinforcing (Harter, 1974, 1975a, b; Shultz & Zigler, 1970; Zigler, Levine, & Gould, 1966a, b, 1967). For the 4-year-old, imitation may represent as cognitively challenging a task as the 4-year-old is capable of producing. Thus, effectance theory also generates a prediction that imitating as much as possible is more likely to be found in 4-year-olds than in older children.

5. Another factor that appears to have been overlooked in earlier work on imitation is what we might label "interference." A common view has been that the child records modeled events in the representational system and plays these events back when given the opportunity to do so, with the fidelity of the playback being particularly enhanced by reinforcement contingencies (see Bandura, 1971a). It is the authors' view that the amount and fidelity of children's imitation may be less a function of reinforcement than of interference in the child's information processing system. The highly artificial and novel imitation situation probably arouses few interfering responses in the very young child. He is exposed to modeled events A, B, C, D, and E. If he has few associations to these modeled events, there is little or no interference and the child produces the events he has witnessed. However, the older the child, the greater the possibility that he has some incongruent associations with the modeled events that he encounters in the modeling situation (associations we will call F, G, H, I, and J). The greater the number of such competing responses, the greater the likelihood that the child's behavior will not be an uncontaminated readout of what the child observed the model do. Thus the child might reproduce some of the modeled acts but also some of his already existing acts to yield A, C, D, F, and J.

The more the child's associations to the imitation tasks are similar to the behaviors the child sees the model perform, the greater the likelihood that the child will emit responses like those performed by the model. However, such fidelity would not be viewed as the child automatically doing what the model does. Rather, it would be an instance of the child thinking like an adult, who arbitrarily designates a finite number of behaviors that are modeled for the child and that the child can either imitate or not imitate. Thus, the interference explanation is capable of incorporating the finding that older children spontaneously emit more responses like those selected by the adult experimenters to be the modeled behaviors. (See Figure 14 for a pictorial representation of the interference model we have been describing.)

The model depicted in Figure 14 can be derived from the two-factor approach. As can be seen, the model in Figure 14 suggests that the major factors

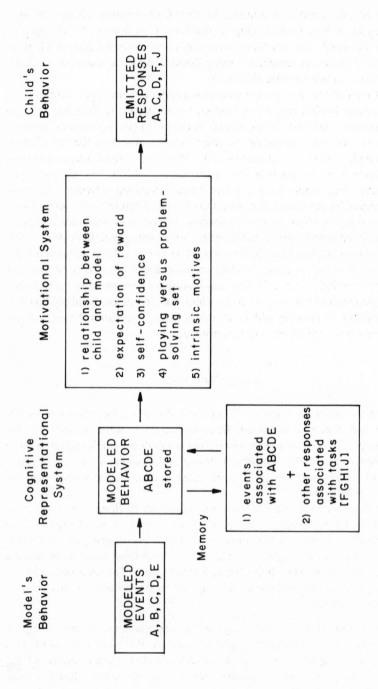

Model's Behavior

Cognitive Representational System

Motivational System

Child's Behavior

MODELED EVENTS A, B, C, D, E

MODELED BEHAVIOR ABCDE stored

Memory

1) events associated with ABCDE
    +
2) other responses associated with tasks [F G H I J]

1) relationship between child and model
2) expectation of reward
3) self-confidence
4) playing versus problem-solving set
5) intrinsic motives

EMITTED RESPONSES A, C, D, F, J

FIG. 14   Hypothesized model of imitation in older children

that must be considered in accounting for children's imitation fall into two general categories: (a) those pertaining to the formal properties of the cognitive system of the child, and (b) those pertaining to motivational factors. (It is assumed that the physical capabilities being demanded by the imitation tasks are not particularly taxing to older children.)

Several tests of the interference model are readily evident. For example, since this explanation implies that direct readout occurs when the child has no competing responses, one test of the model would be to give 4-year-olds, who are presumed to have few competing responses, time to play with the tasks before a model employs them in a modeling task. After such a familiarization period, the interference model predicts that 4-year-olds would be less imitative than usual because they would have acquired some competing activities relative to those displayed by the model. Some support for this interpretation can be found in a recent study of older children examining the effects of prior familiarization with the tasks upon subsequent imitation (Roberts, Santogrossi, & Thelen, 1976).

Another prediction is that children would be more likely to imitate modeled acts that are identical to those the children had themselves demonstrated during the free-play period. Children's free play could also be rewarded or punished with the expectation that reward to the child will strengthen the likelihood that the activities he is showing will be stored in his representational template and thus will interfere with his imitation of novel acts by the model.

TASK EFFECTS

In the present study all three of the behavioral scores were influenced by the particular task that was examined. Whereas four tasks were employed in the present study, the bulk of previous imitation studies have employed but a single task. In view of the marked task effects found in the present study, the question arises as to the generality of findings obtained in those earlier studies that employed but a single task.

A significant main effect for Task was found on all three of the measures. On all three of these measures, the main effect of Task reflected primarily the atypicality of the children's performance on Task 1 (the sorting game). On this task the children had the highest imitation score, the highest recall score, and the greatest difference between imitation and recall scores. The unusualness of the children's performance on Task 1, as compared to the three other tasks, can be interpreted as follows:

1. The sorting game resembled a ring toss and had a greater probability of being familiar to the children than was the case for the other three tasks. This familiarity would result in somewhat inflated imitation scores because of the tendency of children to emit spontaneously some of those behaviors that were modeled. (Support for this interpretation was obtained with the control-group

children, where more chance imitation was found on Task 1 than on the other three tasks.)

2. The higher recall on Task 1 may be due to the children's coming to this task with a relatively well developed schema for it. Presence of such a schema may facilitate recall by providing a cognitive mechanism that can be utilized during the encoding process. Kuhn (1972), for example, has shown that young children are better able to recall modeled strategies that are not markedly discrepant from the strategies the children themselves employ. Bandura (1971a) similarly provides the example that a trained musician is better able than untrained listeners to reproduce the nuances of the musical performances of others because of preexisting familiarity with musical theory and practice.

3. The enhanced recall score may also be due to attentional phenomena. The model always played Task 1 first and it was the authors' impression that the children were still getting their bearings during this first modeled task and therefore watched very closely what the model did on Task 1. (Unfortunately, the attention measure proved to be too gross to provide empirical confirmation for this interpretation.) It may also be true, however, that even with more sophisticated procedures, such as photographing eye movements, it would be difficult to detect an attentional difference between the first task and subsequent tasks. Grusec and Brinker (1972), for example, could find no difference in eye movements to account for a differential recall effect in their study. It may well be, therefore, that the more important locus of attention is central rather than peripheral. Of course, the possibility also exists that eye movements as indicators of attention are age related and that young children reveal distinctive eye movements indicating their focus of attention. The studies by Vurpillot (1968) and by Mackworth and Bruner (1970) cited in chapter 3 suggest that such revealing age differences in eye movements might be found if experimenters looked for them.

A simple test of whether the atypicality of Task 1 was due to the children's being highly attentive because it was the first task in the series or whether the atypicality reflected peculiarities inherent in the task itself could be made in future research by systematically varying the order in which the tasks are presented. (We did not employ such a procedure ourselves in the present study in order not to lose statistical power in examining a relatively large number of other, more major hypotheses.) We would predict that an unusually high recall and an unusual imitation-versus-recall value would generally be associated with the first task in a series.

4. The large difference on Task 1 between imitation and recall may have been due to (a) the high recall scores obtained on this task and/or (b) the interference factor noted above. All other things being equal, the more familiar the task, the greater the interference and, thus, the greater the difference between recall and imitation.

The atypicality of performance on Task 1 was also seen in the significant Relevance X Task interaction on the recall measure. Whereas the children re-called more relevant than irrelevant modeled behaviors on Tasks 2, 3, and 4, they recalled more irrelevant than relevant modeled behaviors on Task 1. This reversal may be due to the fact that on Task 1 the children were less acquainted with the phenomenon of the model performing behaviors that were both task-relevant and task-irrelevant. Certainly the task-irrelevant modeled behaviors were novel and perhaps somewhat surprising. The salience of such acts in conjunction with the great attentiveness of the children on Task 1 could thus have resulted in the recall of more irrelevant acts than relevant ones.

The significant Age X Task interaction on both the imitation and recall measures reflected the finding that the heightened imitation and recall scores on Task 1 were particularly marked for the 4-year-olds. This significant interaction was probably due to some combination of primacy and rehearsal effects. It should be remembered that the 4-year-olds have a poorer memory system than the older children. They may have remembered best what was modeled first, and they may have rehearsed the behaviors that were modeled on Task 1 while the model was performing on Tasks 2, 3, and 4.

The significant Instructions X Task interaction on the recall measure was due to the recall score's being more similar on the four tasks in the problem condi-tion than in the other two instructional conditions. As noted above, this was so probably because the problem condition caused the children to observe the modeled behaviors on all four tasks more closely. That instruction condition moderates Task effects can also be seen in the Instruction X Task interaction with type of performance. The difference between recall and imitation scores on Task 1 was less marked in the problem condition than in the other two con-ditions.

The order effects on both imitation and recall scores for 4-year-olds across tasks, as reflected in the significant Age X Relevance X Task interactions, were found to be somewhat more marked for the relevant as compared to the irrele-vant modeled behaviors. We thus have some slight indication of sensitivity among the 4-year-olds to the relevance-irrelevance distinction.

A current controversy among social psychologists centers about the issue of trait versus situational determinants of behaviors (Alker, 1972; Argyle & Little, 1972; Bem, 1972; Bowers, 1973; Mischel, 1973a, 1973b; Wachtel, 1973). In regard to imitation behavior, the question may be raised of whether individual variations in imitativeness (i.e., a trait of imitativeness) would be expressed across a broad range of situations or tasks. The repeated finding that retarded children are more imitative than normal children of the same mental age (Balla et al., 1971; Yando & Zigler, 1971) suggests that certain life histories give rise to greater general imitativeness.

The correlation matrix of imitativeness across the four tasks throws some further light on the trait-situation controversy. A striking feature of this matrix was the increase in inter-task correlations in imitation with increasing age. Arguments presented to date on the trait-situation controversy appear to have neglected the developmental dimension in the development of personality and/or cognitive style. The correlations across tasks found in the present study suggest that there is a trait of imitativeness but that this trait stabilizes with development and becomes most apparent at the highest age level. This raises the interesting question of whether such trait stabilization with increasing development is unique to imitativeness or is true of all traits.

A case can certainly be made that trait stabilization with age is characteristic of all traits. Although somewhat delimited by his cognitive-developmental level, the young child is capable of learning a variety of styles and strategies. Over the course of development, the child repeatedly tries the various behaviors in his repertoire. Some of these behaviors are reinforced (in the broadest sense of the term) and thus have a higher likelihood of occurring in new situations encountered by the child. Other behaviors are punished and are subsequently lowered in the child's response hierarchy or are totally dropped from the child's behavior repertoire. With the passage of time, then, the child's behavior pattern stabilizes, in that all that is left in the behavior repertoire are those responses that have proved to have some functional value for the individual. The argument here is that it takes time and countless interchanges with the environment for an individual to develop his individuality, which is typically defined by that individual's placement on a number of trait dimensions. Such increasing stability with age is certainly found in regard to intelligence, where the similarity of IQ scores between contiguous age periods is much lower in the early childhood years than in the later ones (Bayley, 1949; Bloom, 1964; Honzik, Macfarlane, & Allen, 1948). In any case, the view that trait constancy across situations would be greater at older than at younger ages is a hypothesis eminently open to test.

INTERVIEW FINDINGS

On the Value of Interview Data

The interview data further illuminate the children's imitative behavior. In light of the interesting findings obtained on the interview measure, one wonders why so few self-report data have been collected for those children who have now participated in previous countless studies of children's imitation. It is the authors' conviction that the increase in our knowledge concerning children's imitation has been frustrated by the reluctance of so many investigators to ask children the simple questions of what the children thought was going on in the experimental situation and why they behaved as they did.

The distrust of verbal report data by so many experimental child psychologists would appear to be a continuing residual inheritance of American behaviorism.

Zigler (1975) has pointed out the empirical and theoretical costs of adhering to this metatheoretical and methodological inheritance and the value accruing to those behavioral scientists who choose to ignore this behavioristically based delimitation of the investigation of children's behavior. Perhaps the most obvious example of this cost to be found in the recent history of developmental psychology is the fact that so many American developmentalists chose to ignore Piaget's work during his early and most productive period. This choice probably was predicated on the discomfort many American workers felt in regard to Piaget's *méthod clinique.*

The reluctance of many American workers to collect and utilize children's self-report data partially reflects their realistic awareness of the methodological difficulty of evenly collecting such reports across the entire life span. There appear to be two other, more metatheoretical, reasons:

1. All too frequently, American developmentalists approach the children who are subjects in their experiments as though the children were little adversaries who were doing all they could to throw up a smoke screen in order to make the investigator's work as difficult as possible. The investigator who adopts such a view has little recourse other than to trick and wheedle the children into disclosing their natures. This point of view has, of course, also been common in research with adults. In an interesting recent commentary, Argyris (1975) has documented the extent to which this viewpoint has been prevalent in social psychology and its cost in terms of failing to provide us with an adequate conceptualization of nonlaboratory human behavior.

2. Continuing to be prevalent is the point of view that children's verbal reports are contaminated by an uninteresting verbal-glibness factor that either does not reflect underlying cognitive structures or else camouflages them. (The reader is referred to Witkin et al., 1954, and Witkin et al., 1962, for examples of such a point of view and to Zigler, 1963b, for criticism of this position.)

One need not be totally for or totally against the use of children's verbal reports. One can collect both verbal and nonverbal measures of behavior (as was done in the present study) and employ the views of Garner (1974) concerning converging operations in measurement and then utilize both sources of information to formulate conclusions. (See Harter & Zigler, 1974, for another example of such a converging-operations approach to children's behavior.)

Responses to Interview Questions

Several of the interview questions gauged primarily the children's memory and/or their verbal ability in articulating and explaining the modeled behaviors they had observed or performed. On Questions 2, 3, 6, 7, and 8, with increasing age the children were able to remember and describe more adequately the behaviors they had observed and performed. On Question 5, while the 4-year-olds in the problem and no-problem experimental conditions were less able to describe the strategy they had employed than were older children, 4-year-olds in the ambiguous conditions and the two control conditions were better able to describe their performance. It is difficult to explain this result. We can probably rule out explanations based on cognitive differences among the different groups of 4-year-olds, however. There were no significant differences among groups of 4-year-olds in teacher's ratings of their intellectual abilities, nor did the three experimental groups of 4-year-olds differ on other measures such as the ability to describe the model's behavior. The fact that control-group 4-year-olds, who had not seen a model, were better able than experimental-group 4-year-olds to describe their own performance would certainly be a reasonable finding, since there would be less to interfere with the control-group children's recall of their own performance. The differences among the three experimental groups of 4-year-olds may perhaps be just an isolated, chance finding, since no such differences emerged in any other comparisons of these three groups.

In regard to Question 1, a greater percentage of 4- and 7-year-olds than 10- and 13-year-olds reported enjoying the games. The tasks did seem to be more appropriate for 4- and 7-year-olds and such age-appropriateness undoubtedly influenced the enjoyment experienced by the children when performing the tasks.

Responses to Question 4, concerning the child's favorite game, showed that exposure to the model influenced the children's rank order of preferences for the games. Most notably, control-group children showed a distinct preference for Task 1, the sorting game, while this was the least preferred task among experimental-group children. Since this game appeared to be a ring-toss game, it was probably the most familiar-appearing of the four tasks to the children. The fact that the model's performance violated the usual procedures associated with this familiar apparatus may have been the basis for the loss of popularity of this game among the experimental-group children.

Questions 9a and 9b inquired about why the child imitated when he did imitate and why he did not imitate when he failed to imitate. The children's answers supported the authors' basic tenet that imitative behavior is often best understood within the framework of children's active efforts to achieve a solution to the problems posed by the tasks with which the children are confronted. This problem-solving, effectance orientation of the children was seen clearly on Question 9a ("Why did you imitate?") where the two most frequent responses were "I thought it was right" and "I couldn't think of another way to do it." Thinking that the way the model performed was right was most marked in the 4-year-olds and decreased with age. Thinking that the model's behavior was right was also more marked in the problem condition than in the other two conditions. These findings generate the prediction that across many tasks (and controlling for the memory factor), 4-year-olds should be more imitative than older children, and especially so when they perceive the experimental situation as one in which there is a circumscribed problem to be solved. The fact that no such simple effect of age was found in the present study is likely due to the fact that memory load was not controlled. Interestingly, for Task 1 alone there was such an effect of decreasing imitation with age.

The prevalence of the second most common reply to Question 9a ("I couldn't think of another way") increased as the children became older. There is thus some support here for the interference factor emphasized earlier. That is, if the child can generate a competing response to the modeled act, he is less likely to imitate. The fact that there was also a significant effect of Instructions upon this response further suggests the effectiveness of the instructional manipulations. Children who had received the problem instructions were very unlikely to give this reason for imitating, while one quarter of the children who had received the no-problem instructions indicated that they had imitated because they could not think of any other way to play the games.

This almost-voiced yearning for some way other than the modeled way to perform on the tasks was seen even more clearly in Question 9b ("Why didn't you imitate?"). The three most common replies to this question, in order of their incidence, were: "I wanted to do it my own way," "I thought the model's way of doing it was wrong," and "Doing it the model's way would be cheating." No 4-year-olds stated that they wanted to do it their own way or that they thought the model's way was wrong. The 4-year-olds thus appear to have a lesser need to produce an original response than do the older children.

The "cheating" response is an interesting one and highlights an unresolved issue in imitation research. As noted earlier, imitation research to date has spoken only minimally to the phenomenon of motivated nonimitation. Classically, the responses that have been of interest to imitation researchers have been imitation and nonimitation. Our research indicates that three categories should be utilized: imitation, nonimitation, and *avoidance* of the modeled responses. Any complete theory of imitation must encompass the behavior of those children who (a) observe the model very closely, (b) can recall perfectly what the model did, and (c) make a point of emitting behaviors other than the modeled behaviors. The dynamics of such a phenomenon must certainly be complex and they have gone virtually unexplored. The children's interview data provide at least two interpretations of such motivated nonimitation. (1) For the well-socialized school-aged child, copying the responses of another may be viewed as "cheating" and thus be a behavior to be avoided. It would be interesting in this regard to see whether measures of moral development (Kohlberg, 1964) would be related to imitative behavior. (2) Children may view the modeled responses as placing unfair constrictions on their behavior and may rebel by generating their own behaviors while actively avoiding the emission of the modeled behaviors. This hypothesis shares some features with the reactance theory of Brehm (1966, 1972), which has been utilized in the attitude-change area. This interpretation can be most succinctly referred to as the "Mother, I'd rather do it myself" phenomenon. (See Zigler & Yando, 1972, for a third interpretation couched in terms of the children's social histories and their resulting general attitudes towards strange adults and the behaviors these adults emit.)

Question 10 did not prove to be a discriminating inquiry owing to the tendency of all the children to report that they liked the model. Whether this was an honest evaluation or politeness (a socially desirable response) is open to conjecture.

Although no significant overall effect was found on Question 11, it was clear that the 4-year-olds were much more ready to believe that their performance was unrelated to schoolwork than was the case with the older children. Given the skepticism of the older children that the experimental tasks were unrelated to schoolwork, the question arises as to the effectiveness of the often-employed deception of assuring subjects that experimental task performance is a private matter between experimenter and subject.

Question 12 also did not appear to be discriminating since, contrary to the experimenter's description, approximately two-thirds of the children felt that the experimenter would discuss the child's performance with the child's teacher. It would appear to be beyond the child's acceptance to believe that the adults he encounters are not in league with one another. One cannot but wonder about the significance of the children's view of the world as a place where adults are not to be believed and where adults continually conspire against children. Certainly there is some evidence that television viewing teaches children to be skeptical of the pronouncements of adults (Kaye, 1974).

The responses to Question 13 indicated a diminished enthusiasm with age for making public the nature of one's performance. If we assume that all of the children felt that they had played the games well, the age effect on Question 13 suggests that younger children are more motivated to have their successful performance revealed so that they might receive social approbation. The older child appears to need social reinforcement less and probably has a greater capacity than younger children to administer self-reinforcement. Veroff (1969) has discussed a similar distinction between two forms of achievement—social comparison versus autonomous achievement. While Veroff does not draw such a conclusion, the responses to Question 13 suggest that social-comparison achievement motivation is more characteristic of the younger child and autonomous-achievement motivation is more characteristic of the older child. It would be interesting to discover whether the age progression discovered in the children's desire to make their performance public would also be found on nonimitation tasks. Stated most broadly, the question raised here is this: Exactly what are the task characteristics that determine a child's desire to make performance on the task public? Bulletin boards in school classrooms all over the country attest to the fact that teachers think that they know a very important performance attribute that motivates the child to have his performance made public, namely, correctness. If a child wants to see his performance publicized, the school culture teaches him to produce a 100% correct paper, which is then posted for the world to admire. The thinking here is that such a reward motivates all children to better performance. This may or may not be true and would certainly appear to be worthy of study in its own right. Might there not be some children who are embarrassed by such a naked show of social comparisons and thus become less motivated to perform perfectly?

Relationship Between Interview Responses and Performance on Tasks

A number of relations were found between children's responses to the interview questions and their performance on the imitation and recall measures. These relations further illuminate the dynamics of children's imitation.

Evidence that the amount of imitation was influenced by the child's attitude toward the tasks was obtained in the finding that children who reported that they enjoyed the tasks imitated more than did children who reported that they did not enjoy the tasks. (This finding was obtained only for the 10- and 13-year-olds, the only two groups in which a sufficient number of the children reported that they did not enjoy the games.) This positive relationship between enjoyment and imitation scores represents something of a mystery. It may be that enjoyment of the games motivated the child to want to do better on them, with the child feeling that superior performance involved imitating the modeled behaviors.

A frequently employed measure of imitation has involved allowing a model to express a preference between two or more objects and gauging children's imitativeness on the basis of their expressing the same preference. Although such a measure of imitation was not directly employed in the present study, the interview data do indicate what the outcome would have been had such a measure been employed. Although many children recalled the identity of the model's favorite game, at all ages few selected the adult model's choice when naming their own favorite game. This suggests that the common preference measure of imitation may be a relatively insensitive one. This conclusion must be qualified somewhat by the failure of many of the 4-year-olds to remember which task the model preferred. The possibility thus remains that the matched preference measure of imitation is a good one with young children provided that the preference task is so arranged that the young child's poor memory does not contaminate the measure.

An interesting finding on Question 4, which appears to have no parallel in the earlier imitation literature, was the finding that children showed less imitation on their favorite game than they did on their nonfavorite games. (We see here again the value of using an array of tasks rather than a single task in studies of children's imitation.) Some conjecture is necessary to explain why children display attenuated imitation on tasks that they particularly like. What determines how much a child likes a task? The general literature on children's preferences for games suggests that children will be attracted to games that involve some novelty but not so much novelty that the child has no schema into which the game can be assimilated (Berlyne, 1969). How might such preferences mediate the finding of diminished imitation on most-liked tasks? If the child prefers those tasks for which he already has at least a minimal cognitive representation, he would be less likely to imitate on such a task since he feels that he already knows how he might perform on it in a manner that is at least acceptable to himself. The hypothesis being advanced here could be tested by assessing children's imitation on tasks varying on the dimension of familarity.

Not surprisingly, the quality of the children's descriptions of their own behavior on the tasks was related to their ability to recall the model's behaviors on the tasks. These two abilities partake of the same cognitive processes (attention, memory, retrieval) and both clearly improve with age. The significant correlation discovered between the children's recall score and their ability to enumerate various ways to play the games was probably also mediated by the age variable. A third finding that was probably also age-mediated was that the children's ability to describe the model's performance in their interview was positively related to their ability to act out the model's behavior during the assessment of recall. This relation raises the interesting question of the directionality of this effect. It is not clear whether the child's verbal report of what the model did represents a script (Schank, 1976) that a child then uses when acting out the model's behavior on the recall measure or whether it is the motor behavior and the proprioceptive and kinesthetic cues to which this behavior gives rise that is utilized by the child to produce the verbal descriptions of the model's performance during the interview. A related question here is whether whatever directionality is finally discovered would be constant for different ages. The developmental literature on the relation between the motor and verbal systems (e.g., Luria, 1957, 1961) suggests that while the verbal system directs the motor system at later ages, this would be less true at younger ages.

The problem-solving emphasis stressed in the authors' approach to children's imitation was supported by the findings obtained on the relation between Question 7 on the interview and the children's imitation. Children who felt that the model's behavior was the "right way" to play the game displayed both higher imitation and recall of the model's behavior. This finding was also obtained on Question 9, where children who explained their imitation as having occurred because the model "did it the right way" were more imitative than children who did not mention this reason. Thus these two different questions both yielded similar conclusions concerning the relationship between the children's opinions of the correctness of the model's solution and their imitativeness.

The only other interview question that showed a significant relationship to the children's performance measures was Question 11 concerning whether the children believed the experiment was related to their schoolwork. The children who believed the study was school related recalled more than did children who did not believe it was school related. It is interesting that this was found on the recall measure but not on the imitation measure. This makes some sense if we can assume that when a child is confronted with a task he considers to be school-related he employs those abilities and behaviors that he has come to associate with successful school performance. Remembering and reporting—which go into the recall measure—are just such school-salient abilities, whereas unmodulated imitation is not.

8

A Two-Factor Theory of Imitation and Suggestions for Future Research

In the first chapter we suggested that much would be gained if we examined imitation from a developmental perspective. We have now considered a substantial amount of information germane to this endeavor and a brief summary might be of value.

In our review of the literature we took the position that imitation is an important cognitive tool not unlike language in its value for enhancing human competence and the strength of attachment among human beings. Because imitativeness appears to have been advantageous in the evolutionary history of the species, we suggested that it is probably at least partially genetically determined. We examined and compared a number of theoretical approaches to imitation and advanced a two-factor theory stressing the cognitive-developmental level of the observer and motivation for imitation as the essential factors for understanding imitation. We next reviewed empirical studies of developmental changes in imitation and reported the findings of our own developmental study. In support of our suggested two-factor approach, the results of this study indicated that the cognitive-developmental level of the children (as assessed by their age) was a major factor in determining the amount and kind of imitation that the children showed. We also found, as predicted, that motives for imitating appeared to differ significantly with age. We are now ready to elaborate upon the two-factor approach we suggested at the end of chapter 2 and to offer suggestions for future research.

A TWO-FACTOR THEORY OF IMITATION

Figure 15 presents a pictorial representation of the two-factor theory that we are proposing. We will discuss each factor in turn.

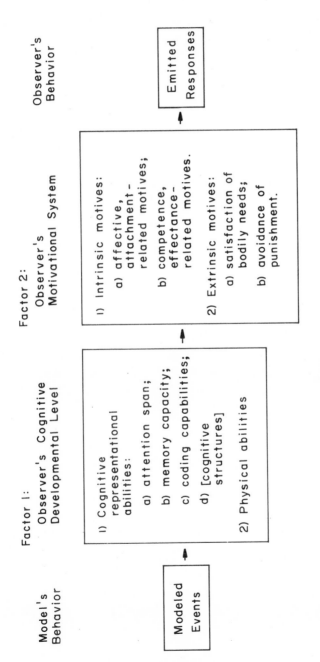

Model's
Behavior

Factor I:
Observer's Cognitive
Developmental Level

Factor 2:
Observer's
Motivational System

Observer's
Behavior

Modeled
Events

1) Cognitive
   representational
   abilities:

   a) attention span;

   b) memory capacity;

   c) coding capabilities;

   d) [cognitive
      structures]

2) Physical abilities

1) Intrinsic motives:

   a) affective,
      attachment-
      related motives;

   b) competence,
      effectance-
      related motives.

2) Extrinsic motives:

   a) satisfaction of
      bodily needs;

   b) avoidance of
      punishment.

Emitted
Responses

FIG. 15   A two-factor theory of imitation

Factor 1: Cognitive-Developmental Level

The most crucial consideration in accounting for imitation is the nature of the observer's abilities. Can the observer form mental images? Can he employ language? Does he possess neuromuscular control over fine motor skills, or is he limited to gross muscular movements? The very obviousness of these questions might lead one to wonder whether they need to be raised at all. Yet as we have seen, many theorists have taken at least the cognitive abilities of the observer for granted.

Both physical and cognitive abilities are important in determining imitation, and both are aspects of the factor we choose to call *cognitive-developmental level,* referring to a number of capabilities that are known to change developmentally in human beings. Foremost among these is the cognitive, information-processing system. The formal properties of the cognitive system include its capacity (attention span and the number of elements that can be encoded) as well as the nature of the coding that can be employed (e.g., motoric, perceptual, symbolic-linguistic). They may also include Piagetian "cognitive structures," reflecting structural changes in the system undergoing stage transformations during development. Since the evidence is not compelling that such structural changes underlie changes in imitation, we point out that it not necessary to embrace Piagetian theory in order to accept the two-factor theory. We merely indicate where Piagetian constructs can be placed with in the two-factor framework.

While we have been emphasizing cognitive changes, it is equally true that physical changes occur during development and that such changes are important determinants of the kinds of imitation that can occur. In our theoretical formulation physical level is simply an analog of cognitive level and both are aspects of the organism's overall developmental level.

Factor 2: The Motivational System

The second major factor that determines imitation is the observer's motivational system. While the first factor of cognitive-developmental level controls the imitative skill of the observer, the second factor controls the amount of imitation actually produced given that the observer is capable of producing it.

An initial distinction must be made between motives that we would consider deep motives for imitation (intrinsic motives) and those that appear to be more transient and situationally determined (extrinsic motives). Deep motives are those that reveal the probable evolutionary significance of imitation. We have earlier suggested that these intrinsic motives fall into two categories according to the basic function they serve: (a) an attachment function, in which imitation serves to increase or decrease the emotional ties to others, and (b) a competence function, in which problem-solving abilities are modified by imitation. Not all imitation arises from such fundamental, pervasive functional systems. An individual may also imitate in order to gain rewards controlled by others related to the satisfaction of bodily needs or the avoidance of punishment. We refer to these motives as extrinsic since they are based upon externally controlled consequences for imitation and since they refer to situations in which the observer takes a relatively passive role.

The specification of the motives for imitation in any particular instance can present a challenging problem, as there are numerous issues to be considered when examining motivation. Among these are the child's emotional relationship with the model, qualities of the model such as nurturance and competence, the child's expectation of reward for imitating, the child's past history of reinforcement for imitation, the child's confidence in using his own abilities (a factor that is often very low for certain subpopulations, such as retarded children), whether the child is actively solving a problem or simply playing, and the importance that intrinsic motives play relative to extrinsic motives in the child's reinforcement hierarchy.

General Comments on the Two-Factor Theory

Differentiation. The differentiation principle, which we discussed in chapter 1, underlies the entire two-factor theory. In our emphasis upon differentiation we join many other theorists who have employed the principle to describe development in a number of domains (see Santostefano & Baker, 1972, for a review of these applications). We presume that the neonate possesses a relatively global, undifferentiated system in which thought, physical action, and motivation are closely interwoven. It is only as the infant matures and gains experience with the environment that it becomes possible to separate ability from motivation in considering how and why imitation occurs. The two factors in our theory are therefore presumed to be initially fused but to become separate enough to warrant independent consideration early in the child's life.

Each factor in turn is also assumed to undergo differentiation. The cognitive-developmental factor, for example, must become differentiated into physical and cognitive aspects. The fact that these are originally closely connected is readily apparent in young children, whose direct physical expression of their desires and inability to inhibit physical activity once begun are well known (Luria, 1957, 1961). The process of separating thought from physical action is a slow one and considerable research has been directed towards illuminating the course of this action-thought distinction in development (e.g., Hill & Zigler, 1964; Katz, Zigler, & Zalk, 1975; Luria, 1957, 1961; Phillips & Zigler, 1961, 1964).

The second factor must similarly undergo differentiation. It is possible to make a clean distinction between intrinsic and extrinsic motives, for example, only as the child grows older. In the infant it is easier to regard imitation as satisfying a combined need of attachment, competency, and the satisfaction of bodily needs than to try artificially to separate these facets. It is difficult to conceive of attachment, for example, as being separate from considerations of providing for an infant's physical needs; similarly, the animal literature (see Bruner, 1972) and research with human infants (Ainsworth & Bell, 1969; Bowlby, 1969; Rheingold & Eckerman, 1973) show the close relationship between attachment and effectance-motivated, exploratory, problem-solving behavior. As Bridges showed long ago (1932), emotions and motives undergo differentiation in development. It is as the child becomes older that the separation of motives becomes meaningful and that it becomes necessary for the investigator to explore the relative strength and the interplay among these motives.

Relationship to other theories.   Many contributions of other viewpoints on imitation are incorporated into the two-factor model. The psychoanalytic stress on the particular importance of parents as models for children is preserved in the motivational factor. The more general emphasis of the affective theorists upon the warmth of the model-observer relationship is incorporated into the motivational factor as is the emphasis of effectance theorists upon competence motives. The Piagetian stress upon the cognitive level of the observer is incorporated into the first factor, as is the more general emphasis on cognitive level in the Aronfreed, Bruner, Kohlberg, and Yando-Zigler formulations. The contributions of reinforcement theorists are preserved in the extrinsic reinforcement aspect of the motivational factor. Finally, the four constructs of social learning theory—attention, retention, motoric capabilities, and motivation—are retained in the two-factor theory with the first three considered to be aspects of the cognitive-developmental level of the organism. We treat these constructs differently than does Bandura in giving them a specifically developmental cast, but we are in agreement that all four constructs are important for imitation.

We do not mean to imply that other theories of imitation can be included in any wholesale fashion in the two-factor theory. We do not necessarily agree that the particular stage constructs advanced by Piaget need be employed in understanding imitation, for example, and our emphasis upon intrinsic motives necessarily places our theory decidedly outside the bounds of any explanatory system that would be advanced by theorists such as Gewirtz. What we are suggesting, rather, is that the two-factor theory is a synthesis of contributions from widely diverse theoretical perspectives, a synthesis directed by taking a developmental approach to imitation. This two-factor theory can be regarded as a prescriptive outline for a number of kinds of research. In the remainder of this chapter we suggest examples of such research.

SUGGESTIONS FOR FUTURE RESEARCH

The Observer's Cognitive-Developmental Level and Imitation (Factor 1)

Existing evidence now quite strongly supports our designation of the first factor. In addition to the infancy and language studies described in chapter 3, the results of our own developmental study confirmed the value of information regarding cognitive-developmental level for predicting imitation. What remains to be accomplished, however, is to progress beyond a general recognition of the importance of developmental level to a specific understanding of how its effects are manifested in children's imitation at different ages. In chapter 1 we presented a hypothesized relationship between age and imitative skill (Figure 1) and we suggested that there are several periods during which imitative skill changes particularly rapidly. We will discuss three especially promising issues for future research: (a) the nature of imitation in infancy; (b) the interplay between language development and imitation; and (c) the nature of the 5-7 age shift.

Infant imitation. We agree with Parton (1976) that infancy remains one of the most interesting and important periods in which to examine imitation. While a great deal of detailed observation of infant imitation has been conducted, Piaget's postulates regarding shifts in imitative capacity during infancy (1962b) deserve replication with large samples of infants. There seems little question that many of the developments suggested by Piaget do occur, such as the slow acquisition of the ability to engage in delayed imitation, earlier imitation of familiar than of novel events, and relatively late emergence of the ability to imitate events where the results of imitation cannot be directly observed. What is at issue is the age at which new forms of imitation appear. Widely varying ages of emergence have been reported, and accurate, normative information about the invariance of the sequence Piaget has proposed and the timing of this sequence would be valuable. The existence of such norms could make possible more sensitive tests of the genetic hypothesis we suggested earlier. Comparisons of identical with same-sex fraternal twins, as in Matheny's (1975) study, would be more richly informative if longitudinal observations based upon a well-established typology of infant imitation could be employed.

There is also some mystery as to whether infants might show imitation earlier than has generally been supposed. In a recent article, Bower (1976) has suggested that "the ability to imitate . . . seems to disappear early, reappearing only near the age of one year [p. 40] ." Both Bower (1976) and Gardner and Gardner (1970) have reported obtaining imitation of tongue protrusion from 6-week-old infants and failing to obtain such imitation when the same infants were subsequently retested some weeks later. If this effect can be widely replicated, it would not necessarily be surprising. As McGraw demonstrated long ago (1943), many mature behaviors such as walking may be seen in rudimentary reflex form early in infancy only to disappear for a time and to reappear under the child's voluntary control when he is older. Imitation might well follow the same pattern. In illuminating the relationship between earlier and later manifestations of imitation, analyses of the behavior in fine-grained detail might be useful. If the immature forms and the mature, voluntary forms were subjected to close scrutiny they might be found to be alike only in gross, topological form with many differences between them.

Parton (1976) has also suggested that imitation may exist earlier than we have recognized since adults may not classify stimuli along the same dimensions as do infants. He suggests, for example, that if a 7-month-old infant habitually imitates the intonation but not the articulation pattern of a vocalization, an adult might not realize that imitation has occurred. As Parton (1976) notes, "During the first year of life . . . there is a substantial possibility that our view of the development of imitation hinges on the extent to which the infant's judgments of stimulus equivalence agree with adult judgments [p. 26]." More fine-grained analyses of infant imitation might help to clarify the issues that Bower and Parton have raised. It is our expectation that many of the Piagetian principles will continue to be confirmed (e.g., the late emergence of delayed imitation) while others (e.g., the absence of neonatal imitation) may need to be modified in light of what is learned.

Language studies. Several investigators who have examined young children's imitation during language acquisition have provided valuable new insights into the relationship between the child's sensorimotor abilities and his emerging linguistic abilities (Nelson, 1973; Stewart & Hamilton, 1976). In terms of our two-factor theory, such studies are exploring the relationship between the more primitive motoric and iconic coding systems and the more advanced linguistic-symbolic coding system. Not surprisingly, in light of the differentiation principle, it appears that emerging language is initially closely tied to the child's sensorimotor-based concepts: the child seems to use his understanding of the physical world as the basis for constructing his higher-order thought processes (Nelson, 1973, 1974). A recent study by Stewart and Hamilton (1976) provides an excellent example of the kind of research needed to further illuminate the effects upon imitative skills of the early interplay between motoric and linguistic coding systems. These investigators found a relationship between young children's motorically based concepts (e.g., edible versus nonedible objects, moving versus stationary objects) and the words the children successfully imitated. Unfamiliar words referring to edible or moving objects were imitated more readily than were equally unfamiliar words referring to nonedible or nonmoving objects. Further studies designed to specifically test the role of motoric coding abilities in linguistic imitation in children at different ages would be most informative.

The 5-7 age shift. In the study that was reported in chapters 5-7, we found differences between the 4-year-olds and the 7-year-olds in almost every aspect of imitativeness we examined. It is clear that some kind of change with significant implications for imitative skill occurs during this period (a possibility consistent with our hypothesized age function depicted in Figure 1). The basis for such a change may lie in the nature of the interplay between the iconic and symbolic coding systems.

It seems likely that a significant aspect of the 5-7 age shift is that the child learns to employ language in preference to visual imagery, whereas the younger child relies more upon imagery. Several investigators employing tasks other than imitation tasks have obtained results consistent with this suggestion (Conrad, 1971, 1972; Cramer, 1976). For adults, language plays a major role in mediating even gestural imitation, as shown in an important study by Gerst (1971), but it is not likely that it plays such a role in the gestural imitation shown by the very young child.

In order to chart the course of developments leading up to the 5-7 age shift more studies are needed to examine the interplay of language and visual imagery in the imitation shown by children at different ages. There is considerable evidence to indicate that iconic or visual-image encoding is relatively well developed in children considerably earlier than is symbolic, linguistic encoding (Bach & Underwood, 1970; Brown, 1973; Brown & Campione, 1972; Corsini, 1972; Corsini, Jacobus, & Leonard, 1969; Cramer, 1973; Daehler, 1976; Jones, 1973; Perlmutter & Myers, 1974, 1975; Underwood, 1969). Few of these studies have involved imitation, however, and a particularly important area for future research is the comparison of gestural and linguistic imitation in young children. Some examples of such studies have been provided by Corsini (1969a, 1969b; 1972) and Daehler (1976). Daehler, for example, in studying children whose ages ranged from 2½ to 4 years, found that gestural imitation was recalled equally well whether or not it was accompanied by verbal descriptions. Five-year-olds, however, have been found to show better recall when both gestural and linguistic models are provided than for either alone (Corsini, 1972). The results of these studies suggest that changes typically occur in the child's use of different coding abilities during the preschool years. Additional comparisons of gestural and linguistic imitation in children from 1 to 5 years of age would be valuable in illuminating the nature of these changes and their impact upon the child's imitation.

The Motivational System for Imitation (Factor 2)

Many questions remain to be explored in clarifying the role of the second factor in the two-factor theory. We will discuss our suggestions for research in the following order: (a) the role of competence motives; (b) the role of attachment motives; (c) the role of extrinsic reinforcements; and (d) interaction among different motives.

Competence motives.   A key question in considering competence is whether the strength of this motive remains constant with development or whether it diminishes as the child becomes generally more effective. The child has so much to learn in infancy and early childhood that the drive for competence may be particularly strong in younger as compared with older persons. It is also possible, however, and perhaps more likely, that the need for competence remains a constant force in an individual's life and that this need is satisfied by solving problems that present a challenge to existing abilities. Stated another way, children probably imitate most when they are confronted with a problem that is just beyond the "cutting edge" of their abilities. The rationale here is that if a child has the resources to solve a problem himself he should prefer to do so rather than to imitate because of the feelings of competence engendered by his own successful efforts. He should readily imitate solutions to problems that are somewhat too difficult because in so doing he actually advances his level of competence. The child is unlikely to imitate solutions to problems that are far beyond his abilities because he does not understand them.

This "cutting-edge" hypothesis can be tested with individuals of any age by providing them with imitation tasks that vary in the ease with which children at that age are able to solve them without the benefit of a model. The results of the study we reported in chapters 5-7 are consistent with an explanation in these terms, although we did not preassess the difficulty of the tasks. Future research in which such preassessment is a part of the design would be valuable. The fact that there is a curvilinear function relating age and spontaneous linguistic imitation is also consistent with the cutting-edge hypothesis. As we have noted, spontaneous linguistic imitativeness typically reaches a peak at some time between the first and second birthdays and subsequently declines. The implication is that very young children find language too difficult to imitate while older children find it too easy to imitate. More studies of the kind conducted by Bloom and her colleagues (1974), by Nelson (1973), and by Stewart and Hamilton (1976) would be most informative in clarifying the relationship between task challenge and imitation.

Attachment motives. When we consider how attachment needs change with age, we are immediately confronted with the fact that detachment is also a critical part of successful relationships with others. Children must become attached to parents, but must then accomplish a successful degree of detachment in establishing their own identity. Because this is so common a pattern in human relationships, we might expect to find that responsiveness to parents as models is strongly positive at some times, whereas it is much less positive, and possibly even negative, at others.

In general the special role of parents as models is one deserving much more examination than it has heretofore received. The studies of Matsuda (1973) and Valentine (1930) suggest the greater salience of mothers as models for preschool children. Comparisons of the salience of other family members (e.g., fathers and siblings) with unfamiliar models of similar sex and age would also be interesting. Do children—especially young children—imitate novel acts more readily if such acts are introduced by trusted family members (as Bruner suggested)? Or is it possible that a modified form of a relationship between attachment and imitation exists such that young children will readily imitate strangers but only if their mothers are nearby? The work of Harlow with rhesus monkeys (1953, 1959, 1963; Harlow & Zimmerman, 1959) and of Rheingold and Eckerman with infants (1973) suggests that children employ their mothers to obtain the security necessary to explore their surroundings with confidence. Imitation of strangers might therefore be enhanced in the presence of the mother.

With older children there is also evidence that parents may be more influential models than are strangers. In a recent study with 7-, 10-, and 14-year-olds, Rothbaum (1976) examined imitative decision making where the child believed the models to be either his own parents or unfamiliar adults, and where the models either agreed or disagreed in their judgments. Rothbaum found that children at every age tested showed substantial imitation of parents whose judgments coincided. In contrast, young children were unlikely to imitate strangers even when the strangers appeared to agree with each other. When the judgments of the models did not coincide, children showed an increasing tendency with age to imitate the choice of one parent or the other, but children at all ages showed little imitation of decisions of disagreeing strangers. Rothbaum's findings suggest that parents who present a united front in their judgments may be especially potent models for children at all ages. Since Rothbaum's oldest subjects were 14, it would be informative to examine this issue with still older persons such as college students.

It would also be interesting to follow up on the research of Hetherington (1965) and Hetherington and Frankie (1967) relating personality characteristics of the parents to their children's imitation. In addition to employing controlled observations, as these investigators have done, naturalistic observations of young children's interactions with their parents over a period of several months would be informative. Do children typically imitate a loved parent more following a brief separation from the parents as Freud's notion of anaclitic attachment might suggest? Do preschool boys show a shift from the mother to the father as the preferred model sometime during the period of 5- to 7-years-of-age? Longitudinal studies would be useful in exploring such possibly changing roles of parents as models for their children. Studies of adolescents are also promising in this regard. If adolescence is a time of detachment, the phenomena of motivated nonimitation (imitation below the level expected by chance) and counterimitation should be evident in the behavior of teenagers towards their own parents.

In addition to parents, there are other significant persons in an individual's life, and the role of such persons as models should be explored. As with parents, it should be the case that during periods in which a relationship is being established there will be considerable imitation, and during the dissolution of a relationship there should be motivated nonimitation and counterimitation. In childhood and adolescence the establishment of friendships, peer groups, cliques, and gangs should provide a naturally existing basis for selecting models appropriate for studying the degree to which the emotional relationship between the observer and the model affects imitation. Among adolescents and adults, lovers and marriage partners should assume a role of special significance, and the nature of imitation in such relationships is worth investigating.

Another issue deserving much more exploration is the effect of being imitated. It would be consistent with our thesis that imitation serves an attachment role to find that the effects of imitation are often reciprocal. Ties of attachment are usually bidirectional. Mothers become attached to their infants as their infants become attached to them, and the widespread existence of phenomena such as friendship, love, and marriage also demonstrate the commonness of reciprocal attachments. We are suggesting that both imitating and being imitated by one's parent, child, friend, or marriage partner may increase the strength of the attachment. Several studies provide evidence that being imitated can indeed increase the attractiveness of the person who is imitating in the model's evaluation (Bates, 1975; Fouts, 1972, 1975; Seitz & Stewart, 1975; Thelen et al., 1975). Even for infants, there have been reports of positive emotional responses to being imitated (Haugen & McIntyre, 1972; McCall, 1975; Piaget, 1962b). The effects of being imitated are not necessarily positive, however. There is also some evidence that in certain instances being imitated can be negatively evaluated by the model. Thelen and Kirkland (1976) found that children who were imitated by an older child showed increased liking for that older child, whereas they did not show increased liking for younger children who imitated them. Fein (1973) has also commented on children's negative evaluations of imitation as representing cheating, especially in school settings. It is clear that being imitated can have effects upon the degree of attachment between the model and the imitator. The conditions which determine whether the effect will be a positive one of increasing attachment versus a negative one of decreasing attachment remain to be more fully explored.

Being imitated can also act as a reinforcement, increasing the child's performance of the acts that are imitated, and being counterimitated can act as a punishment, leading the child to discontinue the activity (Fouts, Waldner, & Watson, 1976; Miller & Morris, 1974; Morris & Miller, 1973). The degree to which being imitated operates to influence attraction (an intrinsic motive) and the degree to which it operates as an extrinsic reinforcer could be explored in children of different ages. We would expect that younger children might not be able to show such a distinction. Thelen and his colleagues found, for example, that third- and fourth-grade children changed both their overt behavior and their feelings about the model as a result of being imitated or counterimitated. Among older children and adults, for whom motives are presumed to be better differentiated, it would probably be possible to demonstrate separate motivational effects of being imitated. Being counterimitated by a neutral adult in a problem-solving task might lead the older child to discontinue his activity without changing his feelings about the adult. The preexisting relationship between the older child and the person who imitates him is probably the critical determinant in whether feelings of attraction will be aroused: For example, counterimitation by a close friend should be much more emotionally arousing than counterimitation by an unknown person. Counterimitation by a disliked person might even be reinforcing.

External reinforcement. A great deal is known about the effects of external reinforcement upon imitation. The social learning theorists and the reinforcement theorists, in particular, have been responsible for many valuable research findings. Much work remains to be done, however, in attempting to determine the separate contributions of extrinsic and intrinsic motives for imitation. In this regard, we would urge investigators to describe very fully the exact nature of the reinforcement that they employ in their studies. It is particularly important to know whether the reward is a tangible consequence such as food, a social reinforcement such as hugging the child, or feedback as to the correctness of the child's performance. The frequent failure to specify the precise nature of the reinforcement probably reflects a common assumption that social reinforcement and competence-based reinforcement are derivative from more basic primary reinforcers. As is doubtless evident by now, our position is most closely aligned with motivational theorists who have stressed intrinsic motives. Although we do not deny the importance of external rewards, along with many other theorists we do not believe it necessary to attempt to describe all other motives by reference to the satisfaction of tissue needs (Bruner, 1972; Harlow, 1953; Hunt, 1965, 1971; Montgomery, 1954; White, 1959, 1960).

It would be informative to study infants longitudinally in an attempt to determine their actual reinforcement histories. The generalized-imitation hypothesis of Gewirtz and his colleagues requires such an approach in order to determine on observational rather than theoretical grounds the degree to which infants are externally reinforced for imitating. Several recent studies suggest that many children imitate despite the absence of reinforcement or are reinforced but rarely imitate (Bloom et al., 1974; Waxler & Yarrow, 1975). These results suggest that external reinforcement does not play a constant role for all children. In the studies just cited, however, the children were past their first year of life; without knowing each child's prior history it is not possible to rule out the generalized-imitation explanation. On the basis of the animal and human infant literature we have examined, we would argue against this hypothesis, but the matter is clearly an empirical one and an important one for future research.

The relationship among motives. Untangling the relationships among motives for imitating is one of the most challenging tasks for future research. As we have suggested, these relationships should not be constant across the life span but should change developmentally. The notion of a reinforcement hierarchy is useful here: At any given time, certain motives have greater strength than others, and the kinds of reinforcement that will be effective can be rank-ordered in terms of effectiveness (Havighurst, 1970; MacMillan & Forness, 1973; Zigler, 1971).

It has been suggested elsewhere that reinforcement hierarchies undergo systematic changes during normal development, so that those for older children are different from those for younger children, and also that they are susceptible to environmental influences, so that groups of children with unusual life histories may show atypical reinforcement hierarchies (Havighurst, 1970; Zigler, 1971). In normal children reared under relatively normal conditions effectance motivation probably remains a strong motive in the hierarchy, and the feelings of competency engendered by solving a problem without assistance from others may be a greater source of reinforcement than a tangible reward. (Even the behavior of chimpanzees and dolphins may show such evident intrinsic motivation, as the McIntyre and Rumbaugh cases cited in chapter 1 suggest.) Studies of children raised in institutions have shown that if a child is deprived of social reinforcement, the motive to gain approval from adults often becomes preeminent (Harter & Zigler, 1974; Zigler, 1971). Institutionalized children may therefore react differently to an imitation task than do noninstitutionalized children of comparable developmental level (Yando & Zigler, 1971; Zigler & Yando, 1972). Future research might profitably be directed towards exploring the nature of normal developmental changes in the hierarchy of motives for imitating as well as further examining the forms of environmental events that can alter the typical developmental pattern.

On the Interplay Between the Two Factors

The relationship between cognition and motivation is obviously a topic of such wide scope that it could (and does) generate a vast amount of research. As applied to the study of imitation, almost any test of our two-factor theory will necessarily result in some information about the interaction of cognition and motivation in children of different ages. We would like to comment on one particular issue here, the likelihood that spontaneous imitation decreases with age.

Because of cognitive and motivational changes, there should be a substantial developmental decrease in global imitativeness. The more one develops cognitively, the less one should need to rely upon the behavior of others as guides to action in countless everyday situations. Nevertheless, this hypothesis did not receive support in the study we reported in chapters 5-7. We found decreasing imitativeness as indexed by the relationship between imitation and recall, but we did not find decreasing spontaneous imitation.

Our reasoning as just described and our everyday observations of children make us reluctant at this time to abandon the view that across tasks and circumstances young children generally imitate more than do older individuals. We suggest that naturalistic, observational studies rather than laboratory studies might provide more support for this view. Informal observational support for the reduction of imitation with age is so compelling that we must wonder, in fact, why so few systematic observational studies of imitation have ever been done. As we have argued in earlier chapters, certainly the growth of our knowledge concerning children's behavior would be facilitated if experimental investigations of imitation, with their accompanying artificiality, could be preceded by the natural observation of children's imitativeness in a variety of everyday settings. In earlier writings, one of us (Zigler, 1963a) has provided more extensive discussion on the scientific rationale and arguments in favor of such a sequential approach to the understanding of children's behavior. The usefulness of observational studies has also been advocated by a number of researchers who have employed naturalistic observation successfully with young children (Barker,

1963; Barker & Wright, 1949; Gump & Sutton-Smith, 1955; Hartup & Coates, 1970, 1972; Wright, 1960). It would appear that observational work of this kind and of the kind that has been conducted with infrahuman primates (Dolhinow & Bishop, 1970; Hamburg, 1968; Hayes & Hayes, 1952; Kohler, 1925; Reynolds, 1965; Rumbaugh, 1970; Van Lawick-Goodall, 1968; Yerkes & Yerkes, 1929) could profitably be used in investigating the young of our own species.

FINAL COMMENTS

The nature of imitation remains in many ways a mystery. Despite considerable investigation, we still know little about such fundamental issues as the actual amount of imitativeness that typically occurs at different ages, whether children imitate their parents more than they imitate strangers, and the degree to which adolescents employ counterimitation in order to assert their independence and weaken their attachment with their family. These and many issues remain to be explored.

In recent years there has been a considerable upsurge in the number of developmental studies of imitation. Our review of the literature based on the search begun by Hartup and Coates (1970) has shown considerable increase in the number of studies available for examination. Among other theorists there also appears to be an increasing recognition of the significance of developmental considerations. Given these promising indications in both theory and research, we have every reason to expect that we may soon look forward to a much more comprehensive understanding of the nature of human imitation.

Appendix A: Proportion of Modeled Acts Recalled and Imitated on Each Task

TABLE A
Proportion of Modeled Acts Recalled and Imitated on Each Task

Part I: Recall

| | | Relevant Acts | | | | Irrelevant Acts | | | |
| | | | | Task | | | | | |
Age	Instructions	1	2	3	4	1	2	3	4
4	Problem	.44	.25	.17	.29	.31	.21	.25	.18
	Ambiguous	.42	.38	.11	.17	.40	.24	.20	.20
	No Problem	.47	.52	.18	.25	.43	.28	.23	.13
7	Problem	.67	.71	.60	.44	.58	.36	.17	.30
	Ambiguous	.54	.44	.49	.62	.62	.38	.26	.36
	No Problem	.51	.58	.49	.47	.55	.33	.16	.29
10	Problem	.57	.69	.69	.75	.65	.38	.37	.46
	Ambiguous	.64	.54	.75	.72	.80	.46	.38	.48
	No Problem	.62	.60	.53	.61	.69	.44	.42	.46
13	Problem	.57	.60	.85	.88	.69	.52	.52	.56
	Ambiguous	.57	.50	.53	.71	.71	.36	.24	.43
	No Problem	.57	.58	.51	.60	.62	.38	.23	.41

Part II: Imitation

| | | Relevant Acts | | | | Irrelevant Acts | | | |
| | | | | Task | | | | | |
Age	Instructions	1	2	3	4	1	2	3	4
4	Problem	.43	.19	.14	.29	.37	.30	.28	.13
	Ambiguous	.46	.42	.14	.15	.32	.31	.19	.17
	No Problem	.44	.48	.12	.21	.26	.26	.18	.16
7	Problem	.50	.48	.57	.43	.25	.35	.08	.23
	Ambiguous	.29	.15	.17	.25	.17	.30	.12	.19
	No Problem	.26	.23	.25	.33	.17	.26	.11	.20
10	Problem	.50	.42	.47	.60	.25	.25	.11	.36
	Ambiguous	.40	.35	.43	.31	.34	.25	.08	.26
	No Problem	.47	.19	.22	.38	.18	.25	.10	.21
13	Problem	.43	.48	.58	.65	.28	.36	.23	.36
	Ambiguous	.26	.23	.28	.42	.17	.18	.03	.17
	No Problem	.39	.15	.29	.36	.18	.20	.04	.23

Appendix B: Results of a Factor Analysis of Responses to Interview Questions

Responses to the 13 interview questions were factor analyzed using a principal-components factor analysis followed by a varimax rotation. Responses to Questions 9a and 9b ("Why did you imitate" and "Why didn't you imitate") were included even if they were of low overall frequency if they were given by more than 10% of the children in any one age group. Three explanations for imitation met this criterion ("I thought the model was right," "I wanted to," and "I couldn't think of another way"); five explanations for nonimitation met this criterion ("It would be cheating to imitate," "I thought the model's way was wrong," "I didn't want to," "I forgot what the model did," and "I wanted to do it my own way"). Since only those children who had seen the model responded to all 13 interview questions, the factor analysis was performed on responses from the 144 experimental children alone.

TABLE B
Factor Loadings for Interview Responses

Response Number	Response	Factor 1	2	3	4
1	Enjoyed games	−.20	.08	−.08	−.70
2	Remembered instructions	.57	−.06	.21	.05
3	Remembered model's favorite game	−.27	−.04	−.16	.30
4	Remembered child's favorite game	.03	.09	−.03	.52
5a	Described own behavior, Task 1	.58	−.02	−.12	.04
5b	Described own behavior, Task 2	.79	−.01	−.06	−.10
5c	Described own behavior, Task 3	.76	.05	−.01	.03
5d	Described own behavior, Task 4	.72	−.02	−.09	.01
6a	Described modeled behavior, Task 1	.73	.10	−.07	−.04
6b	Described modeled behavior, Task 2	.75	−.03	−.05	.08
6c	Described modeled behavior, Task 3	.72	.14	.31	.05
6d	Described modeled behavior, Task 4	.85	−.03	.17	−.08
7a	Right way to play, Task 1	−.03	.55	−.07	−.08
7b	Right way to play, Task 2	−.04	.62	.00	−.04
7c	Right way to play, Task 3	.08	.37	.20	−.12
7d	Right way to play, Task 4	.04	.51	.33	−.10
8	Number of other ways to play	.53	−.29	−.27	−.15
9a-1	Thought model was right	−.24	.40	.35	−.08
9a-2	Wanted to imitate	.00	.21	−.75	−.04
9a-3	Couldn't think of other ways	.21	−.30	−.02	−.17
9b-1	Thought it would be cheating	.04	−.08	.14	.59
9b-2	Thought model was wrong	.12	.15	.27	.05
9b-3	Didn't want to imitate	.04	.08	−.73	−.06
9b-4	Forgot what model did	.07	.23	.22	−.27
9b-5	Wanted to play own way	.31	−.27	.04	.01
10	Liked the model	.05	.04	−.04	−.73
11	Thought experiment was related to school work	.24	.04	.06	.04
12	Thought teacher would be informed	.18	.54	−.07	.11
13	Feelings if others know	.02	.68	−.25	−.04

Four factors, accounting for 40.4% of the variance, were extracted and interpreted. Table B presents the loadings of the responses on each of these four factors.

Factor 1 accounted for 18.8% of the total variance. Items with high loadings on Factor 1 were those requiring the children to describe verbally what their own performance and that of the model's had been, to recall the instructions, and to suggest alternative ways to play the games. That Factor 1 was not simply a memory factor is indicated by the relatively high loading of the number of suggested alternate ways to play the games. Thus, Factor 1 seems to describe an overall verbal adequacy in responding to requests for factual information.

The second factor accounted for 8.8% of the variance. Items with relatively high loadings on Factor 2 were Question 7, concerning the right way to play the games (with positive factor loadings denoting a response that the model's way was correct), Question 9a-1 (the child imitated because the model was right), Question 12 (the child believed that the teacher might be informed) and Question 13 (the child would feel good if others knew about his performance). Factor 2 thus appears to reflect a belief that the model's way was the correct way to play and the child's concern about how others might view his performance.

Only two responses showed high loadings on Factor 3, a factor accounting for 6.9% of the total variance. These two responses (9a-2, "I wanted to imitate," and 9b-3, "I didn't want to imitate") were relatively common 4-year-olds' explanations for imitation and nonimitation, respectively. (While approximately 20% of the 4-year-olds gave these explanations, almost no older children did so.) Factor 3 thus appears to reflect a relatively simplistic verbal style factor for 4-year-olds.

Factor 4, accounting for 6% of the total variance, appeared to reflect a negative opinion of the experiment and of attempts to influence the child's behavior. Items with a high loading on Factor 4 were Question 1 (with children responding that they did not enjoy the games), Question 4 (the child's favorite game was different from that chosen by the model), Question 9b-1 (that it would be cheating to imitate) and Question 10 (with children responding that they did not like the model).

All but 2 of the 13 questions (the exceptions were Questions 3 and 11 and several of the subitems of Question 9) showed a moderately high loading on one of the four factors. In general, it would appear that the first and third of these four factors refer to a general quality of verbal responses, while the second and fourth factors reflect the children's positive or negative feelings, respectively, about imitation.

9
References

Abelson, W., & Zigler, E. Is an intervention program necessary in order to improve economically disadvantaged children's IQ scores? Unpublished manuscript, Yale University, 1975.

Achenbach, T., & Zigler, E. Cue-learning and problem-learning strategies in normal and retarded children. *Child Development,* 1968, *39,* 827-848.

Adler, H. E. Some factors of observational learning in cats. *Journal of Genetic Psychology,* 1955, *86,* 159-177.

Ainsworth, M. D. S., & Bell, S. M. Some contemporary patterns of mother-infant interaction in the feeding situation. In A. Ambrose (Ed.), *Stimulation in early infancy.* London: Academic Press, 1969.

Alker, H. A. Is personality situationally specific or intrapsychically consistent? *Journal of Personality,* 1972, *40,* 1-16.

Allen, M. K., & Liebert, R. M. Effects of live and symbolic deviant modeling cues on adoption of a previously learned standard. *Journal of Personality and Social Psychology,* 1969, *11,* 253-260.

Ambrose, J. A. The development of the smiling response in early infancy. In B. M. Foss (Ed.), *Determinants of infant behavior* (Vol. 1.) New York: John Wiley & Sons, 1961.

Anastasi, A. The nature of psychological 'traits.' *Psychological Review,* 1948, *55,* 127-138.

Anastasiow, N. J., & Hanes, M. L. Cognitive development and the acquisition of language in three subcultural groups. *Developmental Psychology,* 1974, *10,* 703-709.

Argyle, M., & Little, B. R. Do personality traits apply to social behavior? *Journal of Theory of Social Behavior,* 1972, *2,* 1-35.

Argyris, C. Dangers in applying results from experimental social psychology. *American Psychologist,* 1975, *30,* 469-485.

Aronfreed, J. The origin of self-criticism. *Psychological Review,* 1964, *71,* 193-218.

Aronfreed, J. The problem of imitation. In L. P. Lipsitt & H. W. Reese (Eds.), *Advances in child development and behavior* (Vol. 4). New York: Academic Press, 1969.

Aronfreed, J., Cutlick, R. A., & Fagan, S. A. Cognitive structure, punishment and nurturance in the experimental induction of self-criticism. *Child Development,* 1963, *34,* 281-294.

Asch, S. E. Opinions and social pressure. *Scientific American,* 1955, *193,* 31-35.

Bach, M. J., & Underwood, B. J. Developmental changes in memory attributes. *Journal of Educational Psychology,* 1970, *61,* 292-296.

Baer, D. M., Peterson, R. F., & Sherman, J. A. The development of imitation by reinforcing behavioral similarity to a model. *Journal of Experimental Analysis of Behavior*, 1967, *10*, 405-416.

Baer, D. M., & Sherman, J. Reinforcement control of generalized imitation in young children. *Journal of Experimental Child Psychology*, 1964, *1*, 37-49.

Baldwin, J. D., & Baldwin, J. I. The dynamics of interpersonal spacing in monkeys and man. *American Journal of Orthopsychiatry*, 1974, *44*, 790-806.

Baldwin, J. M. *Mental development in the child and the race: Methods and processes* (3rd rev. ed.). New York: Macmillan, 1906.

Balinsky, B. An analysis of the mental factors of various age groups from nine to sixty. *Genetic Psychology Monographs*, 1941, *23*, 191-234.

Balla, D. A., Butterfield, E. C., & Zigler, E. Effects of institutionalization on retarded children: A longitudinal, cross-institutional investigation. *American Journal of Mental Deficiency*, 1974, *78*, 530-549.

Balla, D., Styfco, S. J., & Zigler, E. Use of the opposition concept and outerdirectedness in intellectually-average, familial retarded, and organically retarded children. *American Journal of Mental Deficiency*, 1971, *75*, 663-680.

Bandura, A. Social learning through imitation. In M. R. Jones (Ed.), *Nebraska symposium on motivation* (Vol. 10). Lincoln, Neb.: University of Nebraska Press, 1962.

Bandura, A. Influence of models' reinforcement contingencies on the acquisition of imitative responses. *Journal of Personality and Social Psychology*, 1965, *1*, 589-595.

Bandura, A. *Principles of behavior modification.* New York: Holt, Rinehart & Winston, 1969. (a)

Bandura, A. Social learning of moral judgments. *Journal of Personality and Social Psychology*, 1969, *11*, 275-279. (b)

Bandura, A. Social-learning theory of identificatory processes. In D. A. Goslin (Ed.), *Handbook of socialization theory and research.* Chicago: Rand McNally, 1969. (c)

Bandura, A. (Ed.) *Psychological modeling: Conflicting theories.* Chicago: Aldine-Atherton, 1971. (a)

Bandura, A. Vicarious and self-reinforcement processes. In R. Glaser (Ed.), *The nature of reinforcement.* New York: Academic Press, 1971. (b)

Bandura, A. *Aggression: A social learning analysis.* Englewood Cliffs, N.J.: Prentice-Hall, 1973.

Bandura, A. *Social learning theory.* Englewood Cliffs, N.J.: Prentice-Hall, 1977.

Bandura, A., & Barab, P. Conditions governing nonreinforced imitation. *Developmental Psychology*, 1971, *5*, 244-255.

Bandura, A., Grusec, J. E., & Menlove, F. L. Some social determinants of self-monitoring reinforcement systems. *Journal of Personality and Social Psychology*, 1967, *5*, 449-455.

Bandura, A., & Harris, M. B. Modification of syntactic style. *Journal of Experimental Child Psychology*, 1966, *4*, 341-352.

Bandura, A., & Huston, A. C. Identification as a process of incidental learning. *Journal of Abnormal and Social Psychology*, 1961, *63*, 311-318.

Bandura, A. & Jeffrey, R. W. Role of symbolic coding and rehearsal processes in observational learning. *Journal of Personality and Social Psychology*, 1973, *26*, 122-130.

Bandura, A., & McDonald, F. J. Influence of social reinforcement and the behavior of models in shaping children's moral judgments. *Journal of Abnormal and Social Psychology*, 1963, *67*, 274-281.

Bandura, A., & Perloff, B. Relative efficacy of self-monitored and externally imposed reinforcement systems. *Journal of Personality and Social Psychology*, 1967, *7*, 111-116.

Bandura, A., Ross, D., & Ross, S. A comparative test of the status envy, social power, and the secondary reinforcement theories of identificatory learning. *Journal of Abnormal and Social Psychology*, 1963, *67*, 527-534. (a)

Bandura, A., Ross, D., & Ross, S. Imitation of film-mediated aggressive models. *Journal of Abnormal and Social Psychology*, 1963, *66*, 3-11. (b)

Baratz, J. C. A bi-dialectal task for determining language proficiency in economically disadvantaged Negro children. *Child Development*, 1969, *40*, 889-901.

Barker, R. G. *The stream of behavior: Explorations of its structure and content*. New York: Appleton-Century-Crofts, 1963.

Barker, R. G., & Wright, H. F. Psychological ecology and the problem of psycho-social development. *Child Development*, 1949, *20*, 131-143.

Barnwell, A., & Sechrest, L. Vicarious reinforcement of children at two age levels. *Journal of Educational Psychology*, 1965, *56*, 100-106.

Bates, J. E. Effects of a child's imitation versus nonimitation on adults' verbal and nonverbal positivity. *Journal of Personality and Social Psychology*, 1975, *31*, 840-851.

Bayley, N. Consistency and variability in the growth of intelligence from birth to eighteen years. *Journal of Genetic Psychology*, 1949, *75*, 165-196.

Bem, D. J. Constructing cross-situational consistencies in behavior: Some thoughts on Alker's critique of Mischel. *Journal of Personality*, 1972, *40*, 17-26.

Berlyne, D. E. *Conflict, arousal and curiosity*. New York: McGraw-Hill, 1960.

Berlyne, D. E. Laughter, humor, and play. In G. Lindzey & E. Aronson (Eds.), *The handbook of social psychology* (Vol. 3) (2nd ed.). Reading Mass.: Addison-Wesley, 1969.

Bloom, B. S. *Stability and change in human characteristics*. New York: John Wiley & Sons, 1964.

Bloom, L., Hood, L., & Lightbown, P. Imitation in language development: If, when, and why. *Cognitive Psychology*, 1974, *6*, 380-420.

Bohannon, J. N., III. The relationship between syntax discrimination and sentence imitation in children. *Child Development*, 1975, *46*, 444-451.

Bohannon, J. N., III. Normal and scrambled grammar in discrimination, imitation, and comprehension. *Child Development*, 1976, *47*, 669-681.

Botvin, G. J., & Murray, F. B. The efficacy of peer modeling and social conflict in the acquisition of conservation. *Child Development*, 1975, *46*, 796-799.

Bower, T. G. R. Repetitive processes in child development. *Scientific American*, 1976, *235*, 38-47.

Bowers, K. S. Situationism in psychology: An analysis and a critique. *Psychological Review*, 1973, *80*, 307-336.

Bowlby, J. *Attachment and loss*. (Vol. 1) *Attachment*. New York: Basic Books, 1969.

Brackbill, Y. Extinction of the smiling response in infants as a function of reinforcement schedule. *Child Development*, 1958, *29*, 115-124.

Brainerd, C. J. Training and transfer of transitivity, conservation, and class inclusion of length. *Child Development*, 1974, *45*, 324-334.

Brehm, J. W. *A theory of psychological reactance*. New York: Academic Press, 1966.

Brehm, J. W. *Responses to loss of freedom: A theory of psychological reactance*. Morristown, N.J.: General Learning Press, 1972.

Bridges, K. M. B. Emotional development in early infancy. *Child Development*, 1932, *3*, 324-341.

Brigham, T. A., & Sherman, J. A. An experimental analysis of verbal imitation in preschool children. *Journal of Applied Behavior Analysis*, 1968, *1*, 151-158.

Bronfenbrenner, U. Freudian theories of identification and their derivatives. *Child Development*, 1960, *31*, 15-40.

Brown, A. L. Judgments of recency for long sequences of pictures: The absence of a developmental trend. *Journal of Experimental Child Psychology*, 1973, *15*, 473-480.

Brown, A. L. Recognition, reconstruction, and recall of narrative sequences by preoperational children. *Child Development*, 1975, *46*, 156-166.

Brown, A. L., & Campione, J. C. Recognition memory for perceptually similar pictures in preschool children. *Journal of Experimental Psychology*, 1972, *95*, 55-62.

Brown, I., Jr. Role of referent concreteness in the acquisition of passive sentence comprehension through abstract modeling. *Journal of Experimental Child Psychology*, 1976, *22*, 185-199.

Brown, R., & Hanlon, C. Derivational complexity and order of acquisition in child speech. In J. R. Hayes (Ed.), *Cognition and the development of language*. New York: John Wiley & Sons, 1970.

Bruner, J. S. The course of cognitive growth. *American Psychologist*, 1964, *19*, 1-15.

Bruner, J. S. Nature and uses of immaturity. *American Psychologist*, 1972, *27*, 687-708.

Bruner, J. S. Organization of early skilled action. *Child Development*, 1973, *44*, 1-11.

Bruner, J. S., Olver, R. R., & Greenfield, P. M. *Studies in cognitive growth*. New York: John Wiley & Sons, 1966.

Bryan, J. H., & Walbeck, N. H. Preaching and practicing generosity: Children's actions and reactions. *Child Development*, 1970, *41*, 329-353.

Burt, C. Quantitative genetics in psychology. *British Journal of Mathematical and Statistical Psychology*, 1971, *24*, 1-21.

Butler, R. A. Exploratory and related behavior: A new trend in animal research. *Journal of Individual Psychology*, 1958, *14*, 111-120.

Carmichael, L. The onset and early development of behavior. In L. Carmichael (Ed.), *Manual of child psychology* (2nd ed.). New York: John Wiley & Sons, 1954.

Carroll, W. R., Rosenthal, T. L., & Brysh, C. G. Social transmission of grammatical parameters. *Journal of Educational Psychology*, 1972, *63*, 589-596.

Charbonneau, C., Robert, M., Bourassa, G., & Gladu-Bissonnette, S. Observational learning of quantity conservation and Piagetian generalization tasks. *Developmental Psychology*, 1976, *12*, 211-217.

Chartier, G. M., & Ainley, C. Effects of model warmth on imitation learning in adult chronic psychotics. *Journal of Abnormal Psychology*, 1974, *83*, 680-682.

Coates, B., & Hartup, W. W. Age and verbalization in observational learning. *Developmental Psychology*, 1969, *1*, 556-562.

Collins, W. A. Learning of media content: A developmental study. *Child Development*, 1970, *41*, 1133-1142.

Collins, W. A., Berndt, T. J., & Hess, V. L. Observational learning of motives and consequences for television aggression: A developmental study. *Child Development*, 1974, *45*, 799-802.

Conrad, R. The chronology of the development of covert speech in children. *Developmental Psychology*, 1971, *5*, 398-405.

Conrad, R. The developmental role of vocalizing in short-term memory. *Journal of Verbal Learning and Verbal Behavior*, 1972, *11*, 521-533.

Corsini, D. A. Developmental changes in the effect of nonverbal cues on retention. *Developmental Psychology*, 1969, *1*, 425-435. (a)

Corsini, D. A. The effect of nonverbal cues on the retention of kindergarten children. *Child Development*, 1969, *40*, 599-607. (b)

Corsini, D. A. Kindergarten children's use of spatial-positional, verbal and nonverbal cues for memory. *Journal of Educational Psychology*, 1972, *63*, 353-357.

Corsini, D. A., Jacobus, K. A., & Leonard, S. D. Recognition memory of preschool children for pictures and words. *Psychonomic Science*, 1969, *16*, 192-193.

Cowan, P. A., Langer, J., Heavenrich, J., & Nathanson, M. Social learning and Piaget's cognitive theory of moral development. *Journal of Personality and Social Psychology*, 1969, *11*, 261-274.

Cramer, P. Evidence for a developmental shift in the basis for memory organization. *Journal of Experimental Child Psychology*, 1973, *16*, 12-22.

Cramer, P. Changes from visual to verbal memory organization as a function of age. *Journal of Experimental Child Psychology*, 1976, *22*, 50-57.

Crane, N. L., & Ross, L. E. A developmental study of attention to cue redundancy introduced following discrimination learning. *Journal of Experimental Child Psychology*, 1967, *5*, 1-15.

Crowley, P. M. Effect of training upon objectivity of moral judgment in grade-school children. *Journal of Personality and Social Psychology*, 1968, *8*, 228-232.

Daehler, M. W. Retention of sequences of responses by very young children as a function of instructional condition. *Developmental Psychology*, 1976, *12*, 473-474.

Décarie, T. G. *Intelligence and affectivity in early childhood: An experimental study of Jean Piaget's object concept and object relations.* New York: International Universities Press, 1965.

de Charms, R. *Personal causation: The internal affective determinants of behavior,* New York: Academic Press, 1968.

Denney, D. R. Modeling and eliciting effects upon conceptual strategies. *Child Development*, 1972, *43*, 810-823.

Denney, D. R. Recognition, formulation, and integration in the development of interrogative strategies among normal and retarded children. *Child Development*, 1974, *45*, 1068-1076.

Denney, D. R. The effects of exemplary and cognitive models and self-rehearsal on children's interrogative strategies. *Journal of Experimental Child Psychology*, 1975, *19*, 476-488.

DeVore, I. (Ed.). *Primate behavior: Field studies of monkeys and apes.* New York: Holt, Rinehart & Winston, 1965.

DiSimoni, F. G. Perceptual and perceptual-motor characteristics of phonemic development. *Child Development*, 1975, *46*, 243-246.

Dolhinow, P. J., & Bishop, N. The development of motor skills and social relationships among primates through play. In J. P. Hill (Ed.), *Minnesota symposium on child psychology* (Vol. 4). Minneapolis: The University of Minnesota Press, 1970.

Drucker, J. F., & Hagen, J. W. Developmental trends in the processing of task-relevant and task-irrelevant information. *Child Development*, 1969, *40*, 371-382.

Durrell, D. E., & Weisberg, P. Imitative play behavior of children: The importance of model distinctiveness and prior imitative training. *Journal of Experimental Child Psychology*, 1973, *16*, 23-31.

Eckerman, C. O., Whatley, J. L., & Kutz, S. L. Growth of social play with peers during the second year of life. *Developmental Psychology*, 1975, *11*, 42-49.

Eibl-Eibesfeldt, I. Ethological perspectives on primate studies. In P. Jay (Ed.), *Primates: Studies in adaptation and variability.* New York: Holt, Rinehart & Winston, 1968.

Elliott, R., & Vasta, R. The modeling of sharing: Effects associated with vicarious reinforcement, symbolization, age, and generalization. *Journal of Experimental Child Psychology*, 1970, *10*, 8-15.

Emmerich, W. Parental identification in young children. *Genetic Psychology Monographs*, 1959, *60*, 257-308.

Entwisle, D. R., & Frasure, N. E. A contradiction resolved: Children's processing of syntactic cues. *Developmental Psychology*, 1974, *10*, 852-857.

Ervin, S. Imitation and structural change in children's language. In E. H. Lenneberg (Ed.), *New directions in the study of language.* Cambridge, Mass.: MIT Press, 1964.

Falconer, D. S. *Introduction to quantitative genetics.* Edinburgh: Oliver & Boyd, 1960.

Fein, G. G. The effect of chronological age and model reward on imitative behavior. *Developmental Psychology*, 1973, *9*, 283-289.

Flanders, J. P. A review of research on imitative behavior. *Psychological Bulletin*, 1968, *69*, 316-337.

Flavell, J. H. Developmental studies of mediated memory. In H. W. Reese & L. P. Lipsitt (Eds.), *Advances in child development and behavior* (Vol. 5). New York: Academic Press, 1970.

Flavell, J. H., Friedrichs, A. G., & Hoyt, J. D. Developmental changes in memorization processes. *Cognitive Psychology*, 1970, *1*, 324-340.

Fouts, G. T. Imitation in children: The effect of being imitated. *Catalog of Selected Documents in Psychology*, 1972, *2*, 105.

Fouts, G. T. The effects of being imitated and awareness on the behavior of introverted and extroverted youth. *Child Development*, 1975, *46*, 296-300.

Fouts, G. T., & Liikanen, P. The effects of age and development level on imitation in children. *Child Development*, 1975, *46*, 555-558.

Fouts, G. T., Waldner, D. N., & Watson, M. W. Effects of being imitated and counterimitated on the behavior of preschool children. *Child Development*, 1976, *47*, 172-177.

Foss, B. M. Mimicry in Mynas (*Gracula religiosa*): A test of Mowrer's theory. *British Journal of Psychology*, 1964, *55*, 85-88.

Fraser, C., Bellugi, U., & Brown, R. Control of grammar in imitation, comprehension, and production. *Journal of Verbal Learning and Verbal Behavior*, 1963, *2*, 121-135.

Frasure, N. E., & Entwisle, D. R. Semantic and syntactic development in children. *Developmental Psychology*, 1973, *9*, 236-245.

Freedman, D. G. Smiling in blind infants and the issue of innate versus acquired. *Journal of Child Psychology and Psychiatry and Allied Disciplines*, 1964, *5*, 171-184.

Freud, A. *The ego and the mechanisms of defence.* New York: International Universities Press, 1946.

Freud, A. *Normality and pathology in childhood: Assessments of development.* New York: International Universities Press, 1965.

Freud, S. Three essays on the theory of sexuality. In J. Strachey (Ed. & trans.), in collaboration with A. Freud, *The standard edition of the complete psychological works of Sigmund Freud* (Vol. 7). London: The Hogarth Press and the Institute of Psycho-Analysis, 1953. (Originally published, 1905.)

Freud, S. Group psychology and the analysis of the ego. In J. Strachey (Ed. & trans.), in collaboration with A. Freud, *The standard edition of the complete psychological works of Sigmund Freud* (Vol. 18). London: The Hogarth Press and the Institute of Psycho-Analysis, 1955. (Originally published, 1921.)

Freud, S. Mourning and melancholia. In J. Strachey (Ed. & trans.), in collaboration with A. Freud, *The standard edition of the complete psychological works of Sigmund Freud* (Vol. 14). London: The Hogarth Press and the Institute of Psycho-Analysis, 1957.(Originally published, 1917.) (a)

Freud, S. On narcissism: An introduction. In J. Strachey (Ed. & trans.), in collaboration with A. Freud, *The standard edition of the complete psychological works of Sigmund Freud* (Vol. 14). London: The Hogarth Press and the Institute of Psycho-Analysis, 1957. (Originally published, 1914.) (b)

Freud, S. The dissolution of the Oedipus complex. In J. Strachey (Ed. & trans.), in collaboration with A. Freud, *The standard edition of the complete psychological works of Sigmund Freud* (Vol. 19). London: The Hogarth Press and the Institute of Psycho-Analysis, 1961. (Originally published, 1924.) (a)

Freud, S. The ego and the id. In J. Strachey (Ed. & trans.), in collaboration with A. Freud, *The standard edition of the complete psychological works of Sigmund Freud* (Vol. 19). London: The Hogarth Press and the Institute of Psycho-Analysis, 1961. (Originally published, 1923.) (b)

Freud, S. New introductory lectures on psycho-analysis. In J. Strachey (Ed. & trans.), in collaboration with A. Freud, *The standard edition of the complete psychological works of Sigmund Freud* (Vol. 22). London: The Hogarth Press and the Institute of Psycho-Analysis, 1964. (Originally published, 1933.)

Friedman, P., & Bowers, N. D. Student imitation of a rewarding teacher's verbal style as a function of sex and grade level. *Journal of Educational Psychology,* 1971, *62.* 487-491.

Garcia, E., Baer, D. M., & Firestone, I. The development of generalized imitation within topographically determined boundaries. *Journal of Applied Behavior Analysis,* 1971, *4,* 101-112.

Gardner, J., & Gardner, H. A note on selective imitation by a six-week-old infant. *Child Development,* 1970, *41,* 1209-1213.

Garner, W. R. *The processing of information and structure.* Potomac, Md.: Lawrence Erlbaum Associates, 1974.

Garrett, H. E. Differentiable mental traits. *Psychological Record,* 1938, *2,* 259-298.

Garrett, H. E. A developmental theory of intelligence. *American Psychologist.* 1946, *1,* 372-378.

Gelman, R. Conservation acquisition: A problem of learning to attend to relevant attributes. *Journal of Experimental Child Psychology,* 1969, *7,* 167-187.

Gerst, M. D. Symbolic coding processes in observational learning. *Journal of Personality and Social Psychology,* 1971, *19,* 7-17.

Gewirtz, J. L. Conditional responding as a paradigm for observational, imitative learning and vicarious reinforcement. In H. W. Reese (Ed.), *Advances in child development and behavior* (Vol. 6). New York: Academic Press, 1971. (a)

Gewirtz, J. L. The roles of overt responding and extrinsic reinforcement. In R. Glaser (Ed.), *The nature of reinforcement.* New York: Academic Press, 1971. (b)

Gewirtz, J. L., & Stingle, K. G. Learning of generalized imitation as the basis for identification. *Psychological Review,* 1968, *75,* 374-397.

Gibson, E. J. *Principles of perceptual learning and development.* New York: Appleton-Century-Crofts, 1969.

Gibson, J.J. *The perception of the visual world.* Boston: Houghton Mifflin, 1950.

Gibson, J. J., & Gibson, E. J. Perceptual learning: Differentiation or enrichment? *Psychological Review,* 1955, *62,* 32-41.

Glassco, J., Milgram, N. A., & Youniss, J. Stability of training effects on intentionality of moral judgment in children. *Journal of Personality and Social Psychology,* 1970, *14,* 360-365.

Goodall, J. Chimpanzees of the Gombe Stream Reserve. In I. DeVore (Ed.), *Primate behavior: Field studies of monkeys and apes.* New York: Holt, Rinehart & Winston, 1965.

Gottesman, I. I. Genetic aspects of intelligent behavior. In N. R. Ellis (Ed.), *Handbook of mental deficiency: Psychological theory and research.* New York: McGraw-Hill, 1963.

Gottlieb, G. Conceptions of prenatal behavior. In L. R. Aronson, E. Tobach, D. S. Lehrman, & J. S. Rosenblatt (Eds.), *Development and evolution of behavior.* San Francisco: W. H. Freeman, 1970.

Grusec, J. E. Demand characteristics of the modeling experiment: Altruism as a function of age and aggression. *Journal of Personality and Social Psychology,* 1972, *22,* 139-148.

Grusec, J. E. Effects of co-observer evaluations on imitation: A developmental study. *Developmental Psychology,* 1973, *8,* 141.

Grusec, J. E., & Brinker, D. B., Jr. Reinforcement for imitation as a social learning determinant with implications for sex-role development. *Journal of Personality and Social Psychology,* 1972, *21,* 149-158.

Grusec, J. E., & Mischel, W. Model's characteristics as determinants of social learning. *Journal of Personality and Social Psychology,* 1966, *4,* 211-215.

Guillaume, D. *Imitation in children* (E. P. Halperin, trans.), Chicago: University of Chicago Press, 1971. (Originally published, 1926.)

Gump, P. V., & Sutton-Smith, B. Activity-setting and social interaction: A field study. *American Journal of Orthopsychiatry,* 1955, *25,* 755-760.

Guthrie, E. R. *The psychology of learning* (Rev. ed.). New York: Harper & Row, 1952.

Guthrie, E. R. Association by contiguity. In S. Koch (Ed.), *Psychology: A study of a science. Study 1. Conceptual and systematic. Vol. 2. General systematic formulations, learning, and special processes.* New York: McGraw-Hill, 1959.

Gutzmann, H. A. *Des Kindes Sprache und Sprachfehler.* Leipzig: Weber, 1894.

Hagen, J. W. The effect of distraction on selective attention. *Child Development,* 1967, *38,* 685-694.

Hagen, J. W. Strategies for remembering. In S. Farnham-Diggory (Ed.), *Information processing in children.* New York: Academic Press, 1972.

Hagen, J. W., & Sabo, R. A. A developmental study of selective attention. *Merrill-Palmer Quarterly,* 1967, *13,* 159-172.

Hale, G. A., Miller, L. K., & Stevenson, H. W. Incidental learning of film content: A development study. *Child Development,* 1968, *39,* 69-78.

Hale, G. A., & Piper, R. A. Developmental trends in children's incidental learning: Some critical stimulus differences. *Developmental Psychology,* 1973, *8,* 327-335.

Hall, K. R. L. Observational learning in monkeys and apes. *British Journal of Psychology,* 1963, *54,* 201-226.

Hall, K. R. L. Social learning in monkeys. In P. C. Jay (Ed.), *Primates: Studies in adaptation and variability.* New York: Holt, Rinehart & Winston, 1968.

Hall, W. S., & Freedle, R. O. A developmental investigation of standard and nonstandard English among black and white children. *Human Development,* 1973, *16,* 440-464.

Hallahan, D. P., Kauffman, J. M., & Ball, D. W. Developmental trends in recall of central and incidental auditory material. *Journal of Experimental Child Psychology,* 1974, *17,* 409-421.

Hamburg, D. Evolution of emotional responses: Evidence from recent research on nonhuman primates. *Science and Psychoanalysis,* 1968, *12,* 39-54.

Hamilton, M. L. Imitative behavior and expressive ability in facial expression of emotion. *Developmental Psychology,* 1973, *8,* 138.

Harlow, H. F. Mice, monkeys, men, and motives. *Psychological Review,* 1953, *60,* 23-32.

Harlow, H. F. Basic social capacity of primates. In J. N. Spuhler (Ed.), *The evolution of man's capacity for culture.* Detroit: Wayne State University Press, 1959.

Harlow, H. F. The maternal affectional system. In B. M. Foss (Ed.), *Determinants of infant behavior* (Vol. 2). New York: John Wiley & Sons, 1963.

Harlow, H. F., & Zimmerman, R. R. Affectional responses in the infant monkey. *Science,* 1959, *130,* 421-432.

Harris, M., & Hassemer, W. Some factors affecting the complexity of children's sentences: The effects of modeling, age, sex, and bilingualism. *Journal of Experimental Child Psychology,* 1972, *13,* 447-455.

Harter, S. Pleasure derived by children from cognitive challenge and mastery. *Child Development,* 1974, *45,* 661-669.

Harter, S. Developmental differences in the manifestation of mastery motivation on problem-solving tasks. *Child Development,* 1975, *46,* 370-378. (a)

Harter, S. Mastery motivation and need for approval in older children and their relationship to social desirability response tendencies. *Developmental Psychology,* 1975, *11,* 186-196. (b)

Harter, S., Shultz, T., & Blum, B. Smiling in children as a function of their sense of mastery. *Journal of Experimental Child Psychology,* 1971, *12,* 396-404.

Harter, S., & Zigler, E. The assessment of effectance motivation in normal and retarded children. *Developmental Psychology,* 1974, *10,* 169-180.

Hartmann, H. *Ego psychology and the problem of adaptation* (D. Rapaport, trans.). New York: International Universities Press, 1958.

Hartmann, H., Kris, E., & Loewenstein, R. Notes on the theory of aggression. *Psychoanalytic Studies of the Child*, 1949, *3/4*, 9-36.

Hartup, W. W., & Coates, B. Imitation of a peer as a function of reinforcement from the peer group and rewardingness of the model. *Child Development*, 1967, *38*, 1003-1016.

Hartup, W. W., & Coates, B. The role of imitation in childhood socialization. In R. A. Hoppe, G. A. Milton, & E. C. Simmel (Eds.), *Early experiences and the processes of socialization*. New York: Academic Press, 1970.

Hartup, W. W., & Coates, B. Imitation: Arguments for a developmental approach. In R. D. Parke (Ed.), *Recent trends in social learning theory*. New York: Academic Press, 1972.

Haugen, G. M., & McIntire, R. W. Comparisons of vocal imitation, tactile stimulation, and food as reinforcers for infant vocalizations. *Developmental Psychology*, 1972, *6*, 201-209.

Havighurst, R. J. Minority subcultures and the law of effect. *American Psychologist*, 1970, *25*, 313-322.

Hayes, K. J., & Hayes, C. Imitation in a home-raised chimpanzee. *Journal of Comparative and Physiological Psychology*, 1952, *45*, 450-459.

Herbert, M. J., & Harsh, C. M. Observational learning by cats. *Journal of Comparative Psychology*, 1944, *37*, 81-95.

Hetherington, E. M. A developmental study of the effects of sex of the dominant parent on sex-role performance, identification, and imitation in children. *Journal of Personality and Social Psychology*, 1965, *2*, 188-194.

Hetherington, E. M., & Banta, T. J. Incidental and intentional learning in normal and mentally retarded children. *Journal of Comparative and Physiological Psychology*, 1962, *55*, 402-404.

Hetherington, E. M., & Frankie, G. Effects of parental dominance, warmth, and conflict on imitation in children. *Journal of Personality and Social Psychology*, 1967, *6*, 119-125.

Hill, K. T., & Zigler, E. The action-thought dimension and performance in an action versus though conflict situation. *Journal of Personality*, 1964, *32*, 666-681.

Honzik, M. P., Macfarlane, J. W. & Allen, L. The stability of mental test performance between two and eighteen years. *Journal of Experimental Education*, 1948, *17*, 309-324.

Hoving, K. L., Hamm, N., & Galvin, P. Social influence as a function of stimulus ambiguity at three age levels. *Developmental Psychology*, 1969, *1*, 631-636.

Hoving, K. L., Konick, D. S., & Wallace, J. Memory storage and retrieval within and across modalities in children. *Journal of Experimental Child Psycholoyg*, 1975, *19*, 440-447.

Hunt, J. McV. Intrinsic motivation and its role in psychological development. In D. Levine (Ed.), *Nebraska symposium on motivation* (Vol. XIII). Lincoln, Neb.: University of Nebraska Press, 1965.

Hunt, J. McV. Intrinsic motivation and psychological development. In H. M. Schroder & P. Suedfeld (Eds.), *Personality theory and information processing*. New York: Ronald, 1971.

Inhelder, B., & Piaget, J. *The growth of logical thinking from childhood to adolescence: An essay on the construction of formal operational structures*. (A. Parsons & S. Milgram, trans.). New York: Basic Books, 1958.

Inhelder, B., & Piaget, J. *The early growth of logic in the child: Classification and seriation*. (E. A. Lunzer & D. Papert, trans.). New York: Harper & Row, 1964.

Inhelder, B., & Sinclair, H. Learning cognitive structures. In P. Mussen, J. Langer, & M. Covington (Eds.), *Trends and issues in developmental psychology*. New York: Holt, Rinehart & Winston, 1969.

Jeffrey, D. B., Hartmann, D. P., & Gelfand, D. M. A comparison of the effects of contingent reinforcement, nurturance, and nonreinforcement on imitative learning. *Child Development*, 1972, *43*, 1053-1059.

Jensen, A. R. Estimation of the limits of heritability of traits by comparison of monozygotic and dizygotic twins. *Proceedings of the National Academy of Sciences*, 1967, *58*, 149-156.

John, E. R., Chesler, P., Bartlett, F., & Victor, I. Observation learning in cats. *Science*, 1968, *159*, 1489-1491.

Jones, H. R. The use of visual and verbal memory processes by three-year-old children. *Journal of Experimental Child Psychology*, 1973, *15*, 340-351.

Jones, L. V. A factor analysis of the Stanford-Binet at four age levels. *Psychometrika*, 1949, *14*, 299-331.

Jones, L. V. Primary abilities in the Stanford-Binet, age 13. *Journal of Genetic Psychology*, 1954, *84*, 125-147.

Joslin, D., Coates, B., & McKown, A. Age of child and rewardingness of adult model in observational learning. *Child Study Journal*, 1973, *3*, 115-124.

Kagan, J. The concept of identification. *Psychological Review*, 1958, *65*, 296-305.

Kamii, C., & Derman, L. Comments on Engelmann's paper. The Engelmann approach to teaching logical thinking: Findings from the administration of some Piagetian tasks. In D. R. Green, M. P. Ford, & G. B. Flamer (Eds.), *Measurement and Piaget*. New York: McGraw-Hill, 1971.

Katz, P., Zigler, E., & Zalk, S. Children's self-image disparity: The effects of age, maladjustment, and action-thought orientation. *Developmental Psychology*, 1975, *11*, 546–550.

Kaye, E. *The family guide to children's television: What to watch, what to miss, what to change, and how to do it*. New York: Pantheon Books, 1974.

Keasey, C. B. Experimentally induced changes in moral opinions and reasoning. *Journal of Personality and Social Psychology*, 1973, *26*, 30-38.

Kendler, H. H., & Kendler, T. S. Effect of verbalization on reversal shifts in children. *Science*, 1961, *134*, 1619-1620.

Kessen, W. Comparative personality development. In E. F. Borgatta & W. W. Lambert (Eds.), *Handbook of personality theory and research*. Chicago: Rand McNally, 1968.

King, D. L. A review and interpretation of some aspects of the infant-mother relationship in mammals and birds. *Psychological Bulletin*, 1966, *65*, 143-155.

Kohlberg, L. Moral development and identification. In H. W. Stevenson (Ed.), *Child psychology: The 62nd yearbook of the National Society for the Study of Education, Part I*. Chicago: University of Chicago Press, 1963.

Kohlberg, L. Development of moral character and moral ideology. In M. L. Hoffman & L. W. Hoffman (Eds.), *Review of child development research* (Vol. 1). New York: Russell Sage Foundation, 1964.

Kohlberg, L. Stage and sequence: The cognitive-developmental approach to socialization. In D. A. Goslin (Ed.), *Handbook of socialization theory and research*. Chicago: Rand McNally, 1969.

Kohlberg. L., & Zigler, E. The impact of cognitive maturity of the development of sex-role attitudes in the years four to eight. *Genetic Psychology Monographs*, 1967, *75*, 89-165.

Köhler, W. *The mentality of apes*. New York: Harcourt, Brace, 1925.

Kuhn, D. Mechanisms of change in the development of cognitive structures. *Child Development*, 1972, *43*, 833-844.

Kuhn, D. Imitation theory and research from a cognitive perspective. *Human Development*, 1973, *16*, 157-180.

Kuhn, D., & Angelev, J. An experimental study of the development of formal operational thought. *Child Development*, 1976, *47*, 697-706.

Kurtines, W., & Greif, E. B. The development of moral thought: Review and evaluation of Kohlberg's approach. *Psychological Bulletin*, 1974, *81*, 453-470.

Lamal, P. A. Imitation learning of information-processing. *Journal of Experimental Child Psychology*, 1971, *12*, 223-227.

Langer, J. *Theories of development.* New York: Holt, Rinehart & Winston, 1969.

Laughlin, P. R., Moss, I. L., & Miller, S. M. Information-processing in children as a function of adult model, stimulus display, school grade, and sex. *Journal of Educational Psychology*, 1969, *60*, 188-193.

LeFurgy, W. G., & Woloshin, G. W. Immediate and long-term effects of experimentally induced social influence in the modification of adolescents' moral judgments. *Journal of Personality and Social Psychology*, 1969, *12*, 104-110.

Leifer, A. D., Collins, W. A., Gross, B. M., Taylor, P. H., Andrews, L., & Blackmer, E. Developmental aspects of variables relevant to observational learning. *Child Development*, 1971, *42*, 1509-1516.

Lenneberg, E. H. *Biological foundations of language.* New York: John Wiley & Sons, 1967.

Leonard, L. B. The role of nonlinguistic stimuli and semantic relations in children's acquisition of grammatical utterances. *Journal of Experimental Child Psychology*, 1975, *19*, 346-357.

Levy, E. A., McClinton, B. S., Rabinowitz, F. M., & Wolkin, J. R. Effects of vicarious consequences on imitation and recall: Some developmental findings. *Journal of Experimental Child Psychology*, 1974, *17*, 115-132.

Lewin, K. *A dynamic theory of personality.* New York: McGraw-Hill, 1935.

Lewis, M. M. *Infant speech: A study of the beginnings of language.* London: K. Paul, Trench, Trubner & Co., 1936.

Liebert, R. M., & Fernandez, L. E. Imitation as a function of vicarious and direct reward. *Developmental Psychology*, 1970, *2*, 230-232.

Liebert, R. M., Hanratty, M., & Hill, J. H. Effects of rule structure and training method on the adoption of a self-imposed standard. *Child Development*, 1969, *40*, 93-101.

Liebert, R. M., Odom, R., Hill, J. H., & Huff, R. Effects of age and rule familiarity on the production of modeled language constructions. *Developmental Psychology*, 1969, *1*, 108-112.

Liebert, R. M., & Poulos, R. T. Vicarious consequences as a source of information: A reply to Peed and Forehand. *Journal of Experimental Child Psychology*, 1973, *16*, 534-541.

Liebert, R. M., & Swenson, S. Abstraction, inference and the process of imitative learning. *Developmental Psychology*, 1971, *5*, 500-504. (a)

Liebert, R. M., & Swenson, S. Association and abstraction as mechanisms of imitative learning. *Developmental Psychology*, 1971, *4*, 289-294. (b)

Lindzey, G. Psychoanalytic theory: Paths of change. *International Journal of Psychoanalysis*, 1968, *49*, 656-661.

Loewenstein, R. M., Newman, L. M., Schur, M., & Solnit, A. J. (Eds.), *Psychoanalysis—A general psychology: Essays in honor of Heinz Hartmann.* New York: International Universities Press, 1966.

Looft, W. R. Egocentrism and social interaction across the life span. *Psychological Bulletin*, 1972, *78*, 73-92.

Lovaas, O. I., Berberich, J. P., Perloff, B. F., & Schaeffer, B. Acquisition of imitative speech in schizophrenic children. *Science*, 1966, *151*, 705-707.

Lovaas, O. I., Freitas, L., Nelson, K., & Whalen, C. The establishment of imitation and its use for the development of complex behavior in schizophrenic children. *Behavior Research and Therapy*, 1967, *5*, 171-181.

Love, J. M., & Parker-Robinson, C. Children's imitation of grammatical and ungrammatical sentences. *Child Development,* 1972, *43,* 309-319.

Lovell, K., & Dixon, E. M. The growth of the control of grammar in imitation, comprehension, and production. *Journal of Child Psychology and Psychiatry and Allied Disciplines,* 1967, *8,* 31-39.

Luria, A. R. The role of language in the formation of temporary connections. In B. Simon (Ed.), *Psychology in the Soviet Union.* Stanford, Calif.: Stanford University Press, 1957.

Luria, A. R. *The role of speech in the regulation of normal and abnormal behavior.* New York: Liveright, 1961.

Maccoby, E. E. Role taking in childhood and its consequences for social learning. *Child Development,* 1959, *30,* 239-252.

Maccoby, E. E., & Hagen, J. W. Effects of distraction upon central versus incidental recall: Developmental trends. *Journal of Experimental Child Psychology,* 1965, *2,* 280-289.

MacMillan, D. L., & Forness, S. R. Behavior modification: Savior or savant? In R. K. Eyman, C. E. Meyers, & G. Tarjan (Eds.), Sociobehavioral studies in mental retardation. *Monographs of the American Association on Mental Deficiency,* 1973 (No. 1).

Mackworth, N. H., & Bruner, J. S. How adults and children search and recognize pictures. *Human Development,* 1970, *13,* 149-177.

Marks, L. E. On colored-hearing synesthesia: Cross-modal translations of sensory dimensions. *Psychological Bulletin,* 1975, *82,* 303-331.

Marks, L. E., & Miller, G. A. The role of semantic and syntactic constraints in the memorization of English sentences. *Journal of Verbal Learning and Verbal Behavior,* 1964, *3,* 1-5.

Maslow, A. H. The expressive component of behavior. *Psychological Review,* 1949, *56,* 261-272.

Masters, J. C., Gordon, F. R., & Clark, L. V. Effects of self-dispensed and externally dispensed model consequences on acquisition, spontaneous and oppositional imitation, and long-term retention. *Journal of Personality and Social Psychology,* 1976, *33,* 421-430.

Matheny, A. P., Jr. Twins: Concordance for Piagetian-equivalent items derived from the Bayley mental test. *Developmental Psychology,* 1975, *11,* 224-227.

Matsuda, S. Effects of mother-child relationships on the imitative behaviors of young children. *Japanese Journal of Psychology,* 1973, *44,* 79-84.

May, J. G., Jr. A developmental study of imitation. Doctoral dissertation, University of Indiana, 1965. (*Dissertation Abstracts,* 1966, *26,* 6852-6853.)

McCall, R. B. Imitation in infancy. Paper presented at the 1975 Biennial Meeting of the Society for Research in Child Development, Denver, Colorado, April 1975.

McDavid, J. W. Imitative behavior in preschool children. *Psychological Monographs,* 1959, *73* (Whole No. 486).

McGraw, M. B. *Growth: A study of Johnny and Jimmy.* New York: Appleton-Century-Crofts, 1935.

McGraw, M. B. *The neuromuscular maturation of the human infant.* New York: Columbia University Press, 1943.

McIntyre, J. (Ed.), *Mind in the waters.* New York: Scribners/Sierra Club, 1975.

McLaughlin, L. J., & Brinley, J. F. Age and observational learning of a multiple-classification task. *Developmental Psychology,* 1973, *9,* 9-15.

McNeil, D. The development of language. In P. Mussen (Ed.), *Carmichael's manual of child psychology* (3rd ed.). New York: John Wiley & Sons, 1970.

Menyuk, P. A preliminary evaluation of grammatical capacity in children. *Journal of Verbal Learning and Verbal Behavior,* 1963, *2,* 429-439. (a)

Menyuk, P. Syntactic structures in the language of children. *Child Development,* 1963, *34,* 407-422. (b)

Menyuk, P. Syntactic rules used by children from preschool through first grade. *Child Development,* 1964, *35,* 533-546.

Menyuk, P. Children's learning and reproduction of grammatical and nongrammatical phonological sequences. *Child Development,* 1968, *39,* 849-859.

Menyuk, P. *Sentences children use.* Cambridge, Mass.: MIT Press, 1969.

Metz, J. R. Conditioning generalized imitation in autistic children. *Journal of Experimental Child Psychology,* 1965, *2,* 389-399.

Miller, N. E., & Dollard, J. *Social learning and imitation.* New Haven, Conn.: Yale University Press, 1941.

Miller, R. S., & Morris, W. N. The effects of being imitated on children's responses in a marble-dropping task. *Child Development,* 1974, *45,* 1103-1107.

Mischel, W. On the empirical dilemmas of psychodynamic theory: Issues and alternatives. *Journal of Abnormal Psychology,* 1973, *82,* 335-344. (a)

Mischel, W. Toward a cognitive social learning reconceptualization of personality. *Psychological Review,* 1973, *80,* 252-283. (b)

Mischel, W., & Grusec, J. Determinants of the rehearsal and transmission of neutral and aversive behaviors. *Journal of Personality and Social Psychology,* 1966, *3,* 197-205.

Montgomery, K. C. The role of the exploratory drive in learning. *Journal of Comparative and Physiological Psychology,* 1954, *47,* 60-64.

Morris, W. N., & Miller, R. S. Effects of being imitated on preference for art media. *Catalog of Selected Documents in Psychology,* 1973, *3,* 122.

Mowrer, O. H. *Learning theory and personality dynamics.* New York: Ronald Press, 1950.

Mowrer, O. H. *Learning theory and the symbolic processes.* New York: John Wiley & Sons, 1960.

Murray, F. B. Acquisition of conservation through social interaction. *Developmental Psychology,* 1972, *6,* 1-6.

Murray, J. P. Social learning and cognitive development: Modelling effects on children's understanding of conservation. *British Journal of Psychology,* 1974, *65,* 151-160.

Mussen, P. Some antecedents and consequents of masculine sex-typing in adolescent boys. *Psychological Monographs,* 1961, *75* (Whole No. 506).

Mussen, P., & Distler, L. Masculinity, identification, and father-son relationships. *Journal of Abnormal and Social Psychology,* 1959, *59,* 350-356.

Mussen, P., & Parker, A. L. Mother nurturance and girls' incidental imitative learning. *Journal of Personality and Social Psychology,* 1965, *2,* 94-97.

Mussen, P., & Rutherford, E. Parent-child relations and parental personality in relation to young children's sex-role preferences. *Child Development,* 1963, *34,* 589-607.

Myers, A. K., & Miller, N. E. Failure to find a learned drive based on hunger: Evidence for learning motivated by "exploration." *Journal of Comparative and Physiological Psychology,* 1954, *47,* 428-436.

Nelson, K. Structure and strategy in learning to talk. *Monographs of the Society for Research in Child Development,* 1973, *38,* (1 & 2).

Nelson, K. Concept, word, and sentence: Interrelations in acquisition and development. *Psychological Review,* 1974, *81,* 267-285.

Nurss, J. R., & Day, D. E. Imitation, comprehension, and production of grammatical structures. *Journal of Verbal Learning and Verbal Behavior,* 1971, *10,* 68-74.

Odom, R. D., Liebert, R. M., & Hill, J. H. The effects of modeling cues, reward, and attentional set on the production of grammatical and ungrammatical syntactic construction. *Journal of Experimental Child Psychology,* 1968, *6,* 131-140.

Oliver, P. R., & Hoppe, R. A. Factors effecting nonreinforced imitation: The model as a source of information or social control. *Journal of Experimental Child Psychology,* 1974, *17,* 383-398.

Opie, I., & Opie, P. *The lore and language of school children.* Oxford: Clarendon, 1959.

Paraskevopoulos, J., & Hunt, J. McV. Object construction and imitation under differing conditions of rearing. *The Journal of Genetic Psychology,* 1971, *119,* 301-321.

Parsons, T. Family structure and the socialization of the child. In T. Parsons & R. F. Bales, *Family, socialization and interaction process.* Glencoe, Ill.: Free Press, 1955.

Parton, D. A. Imitation of an animated puppet as a function of modeling, praise, and directions. *Journal of Experimental Child Psychology,* 1970, *9,* 320-329.

Parton, D. A. Learning to imitate in infancy. *Child Development,* 1976, *47,* 14-31.

Parton, D. A., & Geshuri, Y. Learning of aggression as a function of the presence of a human model, response intensity, and target of the response. *Journal of Experimental Child Psychology,* 1971, *11,* 491-504.

Paskal, V. The value of imitative behavior. *Developmental Psychology,* 1969, *1,* 463-469.

Patterson, G. R., Littman, I., & Brown, T. R. Negative set and social learning. *Journal of Personality and Social Psychology,* 1968, *8,* 109-116.

Payne, D. E., & Mussen, P. H. Parent-child relations and father identification among adolescent boys. *Journal of Abnormal and Social Psychology,* 1956, *52,* 358-362.

Peed, S., & Forehand, R. Effects of different amounts and types of vicarious consequences upon imitative performance. *Journal of Experimental Child Psychology,* 1973, *16,* 508-520.

Perlmutter, M., & Myers, N. A. Recognition memory development in two- to four-year-olds. *Developmental Psychology,* 1974, *10,* 447-450.

Perlmutter, M., & Myers, N. A. Young children's coding and storage of visual and verbal material. *Child Development,* 1975, *46,* 215-219.

Perry, D. G., Bussey, K., & Perry, L. C. Factors influencing the imitation of resistance to deviation. *Developmental Psychology,* 1975, *11,* 724-731.

Peterson, R. F., Merwin, M. R., & Moyer, T. J. Generalized imitation: The effects of experimenter absence, differential reinforcement, and stimulus complexity. *Journal of Experimental Child Psychology,* 1971, *12,* 114-128.

Peterson, R. F., & Whitehurst, G. J. A variable influencing the performance of generalized imitative behaviors. *Journal of Applied Behavior Analysis,* 1971, *4,* 1-9.

Phillips, L., & Zigler, E. Social competence: The action-thought parameter and vicariousness in normal and pathological behaviors. *Journal of Abnormal and Social Psychology,* 1961, *63,* 137-146.

Piaget, J. *The psychology of intelligence* (M. Piercy & D. E. Berlyne, trans.). London: Routledge & Kegan Paul, 1950.

Piaget, J. *The moral judgment of the child.* New York: Collier, 1962. (a)

Piaget, J. *Play, dreams, and imitation in childhood.* New York: Norton, 1962. (b)

Piaget, J. *The child's conception of number.* New York: Norton, 1965. (a)

Piaget, J. Forward to T. G. Décarie, *Intelligence and affectivity in early childhood.* New York: International Universities Press, 1965. (b)

Piaget, J. Piaget's theory. In P. H. Mussen (Ed.), *Carmichael's manual of child psychology* (Vol. 1) (3rd ed.). New York: John Wiley & Sons, 1970.

Portuges, S. H., & Feshbach, N. D. The influence of sex and socioethnic factors upon imitation of teachers by elementary school children. *Child Development.* 1972, *3,* 981-989.

Reichle, J. E., Longhurst, T. M., & Stepanich, L. Verbal interaction in mother-child dyads. *Developmental Psychology,* 1976, *12,* 273-277.

Rest, J. R. The hierarchical nature of moral judgment: A study of patterns of comprehension and preference of moral stages. *Journal of Personality,* 1973, *41,* 86-109.

Reynolds, V. Behavioral comparisons between the chimpanzee and the mountain gorilla in the wild. *American Anthropologist,* 1965, *67,* 691-706.

Rheingold, H. L., & Eckerman, C. O. Fear of the stranger: A critical examination. In H. W. Reese (Ed.), *Advances in child development and behavior* (Vol. 8). New York: Academic Press, 1973.

Rheingold, H. L., Gewirtz, J. L., & Ross, H. W. Social conditioning of vocalizations in the infant. *Journal of Comparative and Physiological Psychology,* 1959, *52,* 68-73.

Rice, M. E. The development of responsiveness to vicarious reinforcement. *Developmental Psychology*, 1976, *12*, 540-545.

Roberts, M. C., Santogrossi, D. A., & Thelen, M. H. The effects of prior task experience in the modeling situation. *Journal of Experimental Child Psychology*, 1976, *21*, 524-531.

Roberts, W. A. An analysis of multitrial free recall learning with input-order held constant. *Journal of Psychology*, 1968, *68*, 227-242.

Rosenbaum, M. E. The effect of verbalization of correct responses by performers and observers on retention. *Child Development*, 1967, *38*, 615-622.

Rosenbaum, M. E., & Arenson, S. J. Observational learning: Some theory, some variables, some findings. In E. C. Simmel, R. A. Hoppe, & G. A. Milton (Eds.), *Social facilitation and imitative behavior*. Boston: Allyn & Bacon, 1968.

Rosenblith, J. F. Learning by imitation in kindergarten children. *Child Development*, 1959, *30*, 69-80.

Rosenblith, J. F. Imitative color choices in kindergarten children. *Child Development*, 1961, *32*, 211-23.

Rosenhan, D., & White, G. Observation and rehearsal of pro-social behavior. *Journal of Personality and Social Psychology*, 1967, *5*, 424-431.

Rosenthal, T. L., & Carroll, W. R. Factors in vicarious modification of complex grammatical parameters. *Journal of Educational Psychology*, 1972, *63*, 174-178.

Rosenthal, T. L., & White, G. M. Initial probability, rehearsal and constraint in associative class selection. *Journal of Experimental Child Psychology*, 1972, *13*, 261-274.

Rosenthal, T. L., & Whitebook, J. S. Incentives versus instruction in transmitting grammatical parameters with experimenter as model. *Behavior Research and Therapy*, 1970, *8*, 189-196.

Rosenthal, T. L., & Zimmerman, B. J. Modeling by exemplification and instruction in training conservation. *Developmental Psychology*, 1972, *6*, 392-401.

Ross, D. M. Relationship between dependency, intentional learning, and incidental learning in preschool children. *Journal of Personality and Social Psychology*, 1966, *4*, 374-381.

Rothbaum, F. M. Developmental differences in imitation of parents and strangers on objective and subjective judgments. Unpublished doctoral dissertation, Yale University, 1976.

Rothman, G. R. The influence of moral reasoning on behavioral choices. *Child Development*, 1976, *47*, 397-406.

Rumbaugh, D. M. Learning skills of anthropoids. In L. A. Rosenblum (Ed.), *Primate behavior: Developments in field and laboratory research* (Vol. 1). New York: Academic Press, 1970.

Rushton, J. P. Generosity in children: Immediate and long-term effects of modeling, preaching, and moral judgment. *Journal of Personality and Social Psychology*, 1975, *31*, 459-466.

Ryan, D., & Kobasigawa, A. Effects of exposure to models and concept identification in kindergarten and second-grade children. *Child Development*, 1971, *42*, 951-955.

Samuels, M. Scheme influences on long-term event recall in children. *Child Development*, 1976, *47*, 824-830.

Sanders, B., Zigler, E., & Butterfield, E. C. Outer-directedness in the discrimination learning of normal and mentally retarded children. *Journal of Abnormal Psychology*, 1968, *73*, 368-375.

Sanford, N. The dynamics of identification. *Psychological Review*, 1955, *62*, 106-117.

Santostefano, S., & Baker, A. H. The contribution of developmental psychology. In B. B. Wolman (Ed.), *Manual of child psychopathology*. New York: McGraw-Hill, 1972.

Sarason, S. B., & Gladwin, T. Psychological and cultural problems in mental subnormality: A review of research. *Genetic Psychology Monographs*, 1958, *57*, 3-290.

Sarnoff, I. *Testing Freudian concepts: An experimental social approach*. New York: Springer Publishing, 1971.

Schank, R. The role of memory in language processing. In C. Cofer & R. Atkinson (Eds.), *The nature of human memory.* San Francisco: W. H. Freeman, 1976.

Schleifer, M., & Douglas, V. I. Effects of training on the moral judgment of young children. *Journal of Personality and Social Psychology,* 1973, *28,* 62-68.

Scholes, R. J. The role of grammaticality in the imitation of word strings by children and adults. *Journal of Verbal Learning and Verbal Behavior,* 1969, *8,* 225-228.

Scott, J. P. Social facilitation and allelomimetic behavior. In E. C. Simmel, R. A. Hoppe, & G. A. Milton (Eds.), *Social facilitation and imitative behavior.* Boston: Allyn & Bacon, 1968.

Sears, R. R. Identification as a form of behavioral development. In D. B. Harris (Ed.), *The concept of development.* Minneapolis: University of Minnesota Press, 1957.

Sears, R. R., Maccoby, E. E., & Levin, H. *Patterns of child rearing.* Evanston, Ill.: Row, Peterson, 1957.

Sears, R. R., Rau, L., & Alpert, R. *Identification and child rearing.* Stanford, Calif.: Stanford University Press, 1965.

Seitz, S., & Stewart, C. Imitations and expansions: Some developmental aspects of mother-child communications. *Developmental Psychology,* 1975, *11,* 763-768.

Seitz, V. Integrated versus segregated school attendance and immediate recall for standard and nonstandard English. *Developmental Psychology,* 1975, *11,* 217-223.

Sgan, M. L. Social reinforcement, socioeconomic status, and susceptibility to experimenter influence. *Journal of Personality and Social Psychology,* 1967, *5,* 202-210.

Shallenberger, P., & Zigler, E. Rigidity, negative reaction tendencies, and cosatiation effects in normal and feebleminded children. *Journal of Abnormal and Social Psychology,* 1961, *63,* 20-26.

Sheffield, F. D. Theoretical considerations in the learning of complex sequential tasks from demonstration and practice. In A. A. Lumsdaine (Ed.), *Student response in programmed instruction.* Washington, D.C.: National Academy of Sciences/National Research Council, 1961.

Shultz, T. R., & Zigler, E. Emotional concomitants of visual mastery in infants: The effects of stimulus movement on smiling and vocalizing. *Journal of Experimental Child Psychology,* 1970, *10,* 390-402.

Siegel, A. W. Variables affecting incidental learning in children. *Child Development,* 1968, *39,* 957-968.

Siegel, A. W., & Stevenson, H. W. Incidental learning: A developmental study. *Child Development,* 1966, *37,* 811-817.

Siegel, P. S. Incentive motivation in the mental retardate. In N. R. Ellis (Ed.), *International review of research in mental retardation* (Vol. 3). New York: Academic Press, 1968.

Siegler, R. S., Liebert, D. E., & Liebert, R. M. Inhelder and Piaget's pendulum problem: Teaching preadolescents to act as scientists. *Developmental Psychology,* 1973, *9,* 97-101.

Silverman, I. W., & Geiringer, E. Dyadic interaction and conservation induction: A test of Piaget's equilibration model. *Child Development,* 1973, *44,* 815-821.

Silverman, I. W., & Stone, J. M. Modifying cognitive functioning through participation in a problem-solving group. *Journal of Educational Psychology,* 1972, *63,* 603-608.

Skinner, B. F. *Science and human behavior.* New York: Macmillan, 1953.

Skinner, B. F. *Verbal behavior.* New York: Appleton-Century-Crofts, 1957.

Slobin, D. I. Imitation and grammatical development in children. In N. S. Endler, L. R. Boulter, & H. Osser (Eds.), *Contemporary issues in developmental psychology.* New York: Holt, Rinehart & Winston, 1968.

Slobin, D. I. Cognitive prerequisites for the development of grammar. In C. A. Ferguson & D. I. Slobin (Eds.), *Studies of child language development.* New York: Holt, Rinehart & Winston, 1973.

Slobin, D. I., & Welsh, C. Elicited imitation as a research tool in developmental psycholinguistics. In C. A. Ferguson & D. I. Slobin (Eds.), *Studies of child language development.* New York: Holt, Rinehart & Winston, 1973.

Staats, A. W. *Learning, language, and cognition: Theory, research and method for the study of human behavior and its development.* New York: Holt, Rinehart & Winston, 1968.

Stein, A. H., & Wright, J. Imitative learning under conditions of nurturance and nurturance withdrawal. *Child Development,* 1964, *35,* 927-938.

Steinman, W. M. Generalized imitation and the discrimination hypothesis. *Journal of Experimental Child Psychology,* 1970, *10,* 79-99. (a)

Steinman, W. M. The social control of generalized imitation. *Journal of Applied Behavior Analysis,* 1970, *3,* 159-167. (b)

Stephenson, G. Cultural acquisition of a specific learned response among rhesus monkeys. In D. Starck, R. Schneider, & H. J. Kuhn (Eds.), *Progress in primatology.* Stuttgart, Germany: Gustav Fisher Verlag, 1967.

Sternlieb, J. L., & Youniss, J. Moral judgments one year after intentional or consequence modeling. *Journal of Personality and Social Psychology,* 1975, *31,* 895-897.

Stevenson, H. W. *Children's learning.* New York: Appleton-Century-Crofts, 1972.

Stevenson, H. W., & Zigler, E. Discrimination learning and rigidity in normal and feebleminded individuals. *Journal of Personality,* 1957, *25,* 699-711.

Stewart, D. M., & Hamilton, M. L. Imitation as a learning strategy in the acquisition of vocabulary. *Journal of Experimental Child Psychology,* 1976, *21,* 380-392.

Stone, L. J., & Church, J. *Childhood and adolescence: A psychology of the growing person* (2nd ed.). New York: Random House, 1968.

Sullivan, E. V. Acquisition of conservation of substance through film modeling techniques. In D. W. Brison & E. V. Sullivan (Eds.), *Recent research on the acquisition of conservation of substance.* Toronto: Ontario Institute for Studies in Education, 1967.

Sullivan, E. V. Transition problems in conservation research. *Journal of Genetic Psychology,* 1969, *115,* 41-54.

Taine, H. A., Observations sur l'acquisition du langage par les enfants. 1876. Cited in D. Guillaume *Imitation in children.* Chicago: University of Chicago Press, 1971.

Tayler, C. K., & Saayman, G. S. Imitative behaviour by Indian Ocean bottlenose dolphins (*Tursiops aduncus*) in captivity. *Behaviour,* 1973, *44,* 286-298.

Thelen, M. H., Dollinger, S. J., & Roberts, M. C. On being imitated: Its effects on attraction and reciprocal imitation. *Journal of Personality and Social Psychology,* 1975, *31,* 467-472.

Thelen, M, H., & Kirkland, K. D. On status and being imitated: Effects on reciprocal imitation and attraction. *Journal of Personality and Social Psychology,* 1976, *33,* 691-697.

Thelen, M. H., & Rennie, D. L. The effect of vicarious reinforcement on imitation: A review of the literature. In B. A. Maher (Ed.), *Progress in experimental personality research* (Vol. 6). New York: Academic Press, 1972.

Thorpe, W. H. *Learning and instinct in animals.* Cambridge, Mass.: Harvard University Press, 1956.

Tolman, E. C. Cognitive maps in rats and men. *Psychological Review,* 1948, *55,* 189-208.

Tolman, E. C. There is more than one kind of learning. *Psychological Review,* 1949, *56,* 144-155.

Tracy, J. J., & Cross, H. J. Antecedents of shift in moral judgment. *Journal of Personality and Social Psychology,* 1973, *26,* 238-244.

Turiel, E. An experimental test of the sequentiality of developmental stages in the child's moral judgments. *Journal of Personality and Social Psychology,* 1966, *3,* 611-618.

Turiel, E., & Rothman, G. R. The influence of reasoning on behavioral choices at different stages of moral development. *Child Development,* 1972, *43,* 741-756.

Turner, E. A., & Rommetveit, R. The acquisition of sentence voice and reversibility. *Child Development*, 1967, *38*, 649-660.

Turnure, J. Children's reactions to distractors in a learning situation. *Developmental Psychology*, 1970, *2*, 115-122.

Turnure, J., & Zigler, E. Outerdirectedness in the problem solving of normal and retarded children. *Journal of Abnormal and Social Psychology*, 1964, *69*, 427-436.

Underwood, B. J. Attributes of memory. *Psychological Review*, 1969, *76*, 559-573.

Uzgiris, I. C. Patterns of vocal and gestural imitation in infants. In F. J. Mönks, W. W. Hartup, & J. deWit (Eds.), *Determinants of behavioral development*. New York: Academic Press, 1972.

Uzgiris, I. C., & Hunt, J. McV. *Toward ordinal scales of psychological development in infancy*. Urbana, Ill.: University of Illinois Press, 1975.

Valentine, C. W. The psychology of imitation with special reference to early childhood. *British Journal of Psychology*, 1930, *21*, 105-132.

Van Lawick-Goodall, J. The behavior of free living chimpanzees in the Gombe Stream Reserve. *Animal Behavior Monographs*, 1968, *1*, 165-301.

Vasta, R. Feedback and fidelity: Effects of contingent consequences on accuracy of imitation. *Journal of Experimental Child Psychology*, 1976, *21*, 98-108.

Veroff, J. Social comparison and the development of achievement motivation. In C. P. Smith (Ed.), *Achievement-related motives in children*. New York: Russell Sage Foundation, 1969.

Vurpillot, E. The development of scanning strategies and their relation to visual differentiation. *Journal of Experimental Child Psychology*, 1968, *6*, 632-650.

Wachtel, P. L. Psychodynamics, behavior theory, and the implacable experimenter: An inquiry into the consistency of personality. *Journal of Abnormal Psychology*, 1973, *82*, 324-334.

Waddington, C. H. *The strategy of the genes: A discussion of some aspects of theoretical biology*. London: Allen & Unwin, 1957.

Waghorn, L., & Sullivan, E. V. The exploration of transition rules in conservation of quantity (substance) using film mediated modeling. *Acta Psychologica*, 1970, *32*, 65-80.

Walters, R. H. Some conditions facilitating the occurrence of imitative behavior. In E. C. Simmel, R. A. Hoppe, & G. A. Milton (Eds.), *Social facilitation and imitative behavior*. Boston: Allyn & Bacon, 1968.

Walters, R. H., & Brown, M. A test of the high magnitude theory of aggression. *Journal of Experimental Child Psychology*, 1964, *1*, 376-387.

Wapner, S., & Cirillo, L. Imitation of a model's hand movements: Age changes in transposition of left-right relations. *Child Development*, 1968, *39*, 887-894.

Ward, W. D. Process of sex-role development. *Developmental Psychology*, 1969, *1*, 163-168.

Waxler, C., & Yarrow, M. R. Factors influencing imitative learning in preschool children. *Journal of Experimental Child Psychology*, 1970, *9*, 115-130.

Waxler, C., & Yarrow, M. R. An observational study of maternal models. *Developmental Psychology*, 1975, *11*, 485-494.

Wechkin, S. Social relationships and social facilitation of object manipulation in *Macaca mulatta*. *Journal of Comparative and Physiological Psychology*, 1970, *73*, 456-460.

Weener, P. Language structure and free recall of verbal messages by children. *Developmental Psychology*, 1971, *5*, 237-243.

Weir, M. W. Developmental changes in problem-solving strategies. *Psychological Review*, 1964, *71*, 473-490.

Weir, R. H. *Language in the crib*. The Hague: Mouton, 1962.

Werner, H. *Comparative psychology of mental development*. New York: Harper, 1940.

Werner, H. The concept of rigidity: A critical evaluation. *Psychological Review*, 1946, *53*, 43-53.

Wheeler, L. Toward a theory of behavioral contagion. *Psychological Review*, 1966, *73*, 179-192.

White, G. M., & Burnam, M. A. Socially cued altruism: Effects of modeling, instructions, and age on public and private donations. *Child Development*, 1975, *46*, 559-563.

White, R. W. Motivation reconsidered: The concept of competence. *Psychological Review*, 1959, *66*, 297-333.

White, R. W. Competence and the psychosexual stages of development. In M. R. Jones (Ed.), *Nebraska Symposium on Motivation*. Lincoln: University of Nebraska Press, 1960.

White, S. H. Evidence for a hierarchical arrangement of learning processes. In L. P. Lipsitt & C. C. Spiker (Eds.), *Advances in child development and behavior* (Vol. 2). New York: Academic Press, 1965.

Whitehurst, G. J., Ironsmith, M., & Goldfein, M. Selective imitation of the passive construction through modeling. *Journal of Experimental Child Psychology*, 1974, *17*, 288-302.

Whitehurst, G. J., & Novack, G. Modeling, imitation training, and the acquisition of sentence phrases. *Journal of Experimental Child Psychology*, 1973, *16*, 332-345.

Whitehurst, G. J., & Vasta, R. Is language acquired through imitation? *Journal of Psycholinguistic Research*, 1975, *4*, 37-59.

Williams, M. L., & Willoughby, R. H. Observational learning: The effects of age, task difficulty, and observers' motoric rehearsal. *Journal of Experimental Child Psychology*, 1971, *12*, 146-156.

Wilton, K. M., & Boersma, F. J. *Eye movements, surprise reactions and cognitive development* (New ed.). Rotterdam, Netherlands: Rotterdam University Press, 1974.

Winer, B. J. *Statistical principles in experimental design* (2nd ed.). New York: McGraw-Hill, 1971.

Witkin, H. A., Dyk, R. B., Faterson, H. F., Goodenough, D. R., & Karp, S. A. *Psychological differentiation: Studies of development*. New York: John Wiley & Sons, 1962.

Witkin, H. A., Lewis, H. B., Hertzman, M., Maghover, K., Meissner, P. B., & Wapner, S. *Personality through perception: An experimental and clinical study*. New York: Harper & Brothers, 1954.

Wolf, T. M. A developmental investigation of televised modeled verbalizations on resistance to deviation. *Developmental Psychology*, 1972, *6*, 537.

Wright, H. F. Observational child study. In P. H. Mussen (Ed.), *Handbook of research methods in child development*. New York: John Wiley & Sons, 1960.

Yando, R., & Zigler, E. Outerdirectedness in the problem-solving of institutionalized and noninstitutionalized normal and retarded children. *Developmental Psychology*, 1971, *4*, 277-288.

Yarrow, M. R., & Scott, P. M. Imitation of nurturant and nonnurturant models. *Journal of Personality and Social Psychology*, 1972, *23*, 259-270.

Yerkes, R. M. The mind of the gorilla. *Genetic Psychology Monographs*, 1927, *2*, 1-193.

Yerkes, R. M. Suggestibility in the chimpanzee. *Journal of Social Psychology*, 1934, *5*, 271-282.

Yerkes, R. M., & Yerkes, A. W. *The great apes: A study of anthropoid life*. New Haven, Conn.: Yale University Press, 1929.

Yussen, S. R. Determinants of visual attention and recall in observational learning by preschoolers and second graders. *Developmental Psychology*, 1974, *10*, 93-100.

Yussen, S. R., & Levy, V. M., Jr. Effects of warm and neutral models on the attention of observational learners. *Journal of Experimental Child Psychology*, 1975, *20*, 66-72.

Yussen, S. R., & Santrock, J. W. Comparison of the retention of preschool and second-grade performers and observers under three verbalization conditions. *Child Development*, 1974, *45*, 821-824.

Zajonc, R. B. Social facilitation. *Science,* 1965, *149,* 269-274.

Zigler, E. Metatheoretical issues in developmental psychology. In M. Marx (Ed.), *Psychological theory* (2nd ed.). New York: Macmillan, 1963. (a)

Zigler, E. Zigler stands firm. *Contemporary Psychology,* 1963, *8,* 459-461. (b)

Zigler, E. Developmental versus difference theories of mental retardation and the problem of motivation. *American Journal of Mental Deficiency,* 1969, *73,* 536-556.

Zigler, E. The retarded child as a whole person. In H. E. Adams & W. K. Boardman, III (Eds.), *Advances in experimental clinical psychology* (Vol. 1). New York: Pergamon, 1971.

Zigler, E. Looking back 20 years. Autobiographical statement. In J. M. Kaufman & J. S. Payne (Eds.), *Mental retardation: Introduction and personal perspectives.* Columbus, Ohio: Charles E. Merrill, 1975.

Zigler, E., & Child, I. L. *Socialization and personality development.* Reading, Mass.: Addison-Wesley, 1973.

Zigler, E., & Harter, S. Socialization of the mentally retarded. In D. A. Goslin (Ed.), *Handbook of socialization theory and research.* Chicago: Rand McNally, 1969.

Zigler, E., & Kanzer, P. The effectiveness of two classes of verbal reinforcers on the performance of middle- and lower-class children. *Journal of Personality,* 1962, *30,* 157-163.

Zigler, E., Levine, J., & Gould, L. Cognitive processes in the development of children's appreciation of humor. *Child Development,* 1966, *37,* 507-518. (a)

Zigler, E., Levine, J., & Gould, L. The humor response of normal, institutionalized retarded and noninstitutionalized retarded children. *American Journal of Mental Deficiency,* 1966, *71,* 472-480. (b)

Zigler, E., Levine, J., & Gould, L. Cognitive challenge as a factor in children's humor appreciation. *Journal of Personality and Social Psychology,* 1967, *6,* 332-336.

Zigler, E., & Yando, R. Outerdirectedness and imitative behavior of institutionalized and noninstitutionalized younger and older children. *Child Development,* 1972, *43,* 413-425.

Zimmerman, B. J. Modification of young children's grouping strategies: The effects of modeling, verbalization, incentives, and age. *Child Development,* 1974, *45,* 1032-1041.

Zimmerman, B. J., & Lanaro, P. Acquiring and retaining conservation of length through modeling and reversibility cues. *Merrill-Palmer Quarterly of Behavior and Development,* 1974, *20,* 145-161.

Zimmerman, B. J., & Pike, E. O. Effects of modeling and reinforcement on the acquisition and generalization of question-asking behavior. *Child Development,* 1972, *43,* 892-907.

Zimmerman, B. J., & Rosenthal, T. L. Conserving and retaining equalities and inequalities through observation and correction. *Developmental Psychology,* 1974, *10,* 260-268. (a)

Zimmerman, B. J., & Rosenthal, T. L. Observational learning of rule-governed behavior by children. *Psychological Bulletin,* 1974, *81,* 29-42. (b)

Author Index

Numbers in *italics* refer to pages on which the complete references are listed.

Subject Index

Concrete operations, 8, 31
Conformity, 21
Conservation, 56–59
Contiguity learning, 60
Converging operations, 149
Cultural anthropology, 21
Curiosity, 8, 43

D

Defensive identification, *see* Identification,
    with aggressor
Delayed imitation, *see* Imitation, delayed
Demand characteristics, 88–89, 134–136
Differentiation, *see also* Motives for imita-
    tion, differentiation of
    of cognition and motives, 159–160, 168
    of cognitive abilities, 15, 142, 159, 162
    of motives, 14–19, 159–160
Disinhibition, 32

E

Educability, and imitation, 8, 29
Effectance motivation, *see also* Theories of
    imitation, effectance
    and imitation, 43–44, 66, 143, 167
Ego functions, 42
Ego psychology, 42
Egocentrism, 14–15, 30
Eidetic imagery, 60
Elicited imitation, *see* Recall, prompted
Ethology, 27
Evolution, 8
Expressive imitation, *see* Task-irrelevant
    imitation

F

Field independence, 140
Formal operations, 8, 31

G

Generalized imitation, 38–39, 142, 167
Gestural imitation, 9, 89–90, 162–163
Grammar, and imitation, 50–51, 53–54

I

Iconic coding, *see* Coding, iconic
Identification, *see also* Theories of imitation,
    psychoanalytic
    with aggressor, 24
    anaclitic, 23–24, 165

Identification *(contd)*
    criticisms of, 24–25, 62–63
    developmental nature of, 23–24
    and imitation, 4, 22–24, 62–65
Imitation
    accuracy of, 4, 7, 10–12, 30, 158, 161–
        162
    age-related changes in, 1–3, 6–8, 10–12,
        16, 26–31, 44–46, 69–70, 72–
        89, 92–93, 95–97, 111–113,
        120–121, 136–138, 141–145,
        148, 168–169, 170–171
    of attitudes, 4
    avoidance of, 17, 45, 64, 141–142,
        151–152, 165
    counter- 17, 165–166
    definition of, 4–5
    delayed, 4, 5–6, 10, 29, 50, 161–162
    as discrimination learning, 37–38
    evolutionary significance of, 4, 5, 8–10,
        156
    of familiar events, 11, 27–28, 32–33,
        143–145, 154, 161
    genetic basis of, 9, 156
    immediate, 5–6
    individual differences in, 9, 52, 67, 148,
        167–168
    of novel events, 10–11, 16–17, 25,
        28–29, 32, 143–145
    partial, 4, 29–30
    presymbolic, 7, 27–29
    reciprocal, 18, 67, 165–166
    of religious beliefs, 4
    representative, 29
    sporadic, 27–28
    systematic, 28
    in twins, 9–10
Imitation-by-training, 13, 27
Imitation tasks
    effects of, 46, 48–49, 62, 73–74, 90–
        93, 111, 120–125, 135, 138, 139,
        141, 145–148, 150, 153–154,
        164
    modeling sequence for, 101, 103–105
    scoring of, 105–109
    types of, 46, 68–70, 74, 89–90, 96–97,
        98–103
Imitative learning, permanence of, 55, 58–
    59
Imitative skill, *see* Imitation, accuracy of
Incentives, *see* Motives for imitation
Incidental learning, 69–70, 140
Infancy, imitation in, 6, 27–28, 49–50, 59,